The Lord's Supper in Anabaptism

Studies in
Anabaptist and Mennonite History
No. 33

The Lord's Supper in Anabaptism

*A Study in the Christology of Balthasar Hubmaier,
Pilgram Marpeck, and Dirk Philips*

John D. Rempel

Studies in Anabaptist and Mennonite History

Edited by Cornelius J. Dyck, Leonard Gross, Leland Harder, Albert N. Keim, Walter Klaassen, John S. Oyer, H. Wayne Pipkin, Editor-in-Chief Theron F. Schlabach, and John H. Yoder.

Published by Herald Press, Scottdale, Pennsylvania, and Waterloo, Ontario, in cooperation with Mennonite Historical Society, Goshen, Indiana. The Society is primarily responsible for the content of the studies, and Herald Press for their publication.

———
°*Out of print but available in microfilm or photocopies.*

The Lord's Supper in Anabaptism

A Study in the Christology of Balthasar Hubmaier, Pilgram Marpeck, and Dirk Philips

John D. Rempel

Foreword by Hans-Jürgen Goertz

HERALD PRESS
Waterloo, Ontario
Scottdale, Pennsylvania

Canadian Cataloguing-in-Publication Data
Rempel, John D.
    The Lord's Supper in Anabaptism : a study in the Christology of
Balthasar Hubmaier, Pilgram Marpeck, and Dirk Philips

(Studies in Anabaptist and Mennonite history ; no. 33)
Includes bibliographical references and index.
ISBN 0-8361-3112-6

1. Hubmaier, Balthasar, d. 1528. 2. Marpeck, Pilgram, ca. 1495-1556. Philips,
Dirk, 1504-1568. 4. Anabaptists - Doctrines - History - 16th century. 5. Lord's
Supper - Anabaptists. 6. Mennonites - Theology. I. Title. II. Series.

BX4930.R45 1993   284'.3   C93-093850-X

The paper used in this publication is recycled and meets the minimum requirements of American National Standard for Information Sciences—Permanence
of Paper for Printed Library Materials, ANSI Z39.48-1984.

All Bible quotations are used by permission, all rights reserved, and unless
otherwise indicated are from the *New Revised Standard Version Bible*, copy-
right 1989, by the Division of Christian Education of the National Council of
the Churches of Christ in the USA.

Credits: Jacket engraving, *Lord's Supper* (1523), is by Albrecht Dürer. Engraving of Dr. Balthasar Hubmaier is by Christoffel van Sichem (ca. 1606), presumably without historical basis. The 1974 portrait of Pilgram Marpeck, by Ivan D.
Moon, is an interpretation of his character. The portrait of Dirk Philips is from
an unknown source.

Zum Andenken an meinen Vater
(Henry Peter Rempel, 1907-1977)
und zum Dank an meine Mutter
(Katharina Ewert Rempel)

Contents

Foreword

Much has been written about the Anabaptist concept of the church. Strangely, however, little has been said about the most important symbol of their fellowship: the Lord's Supper, which they celebrated in a unique manner. The family of believers sat around a table, read the Holy Scriptures, broke the bread, distributed it, and drank wine from an earthen crock. That was a scene of everyday activity—no altar, no monstrance, no golden vessels, and particularly, no priests to repeat constantly the sacrifice of Christ offered on the cross of Calvary. All was transparent, simple, and solemn. There was no hidden magic, as Thomas Müntzer once wrote. This was the manner in which the Anabaptists remembered the death of Jesus Christ. The Lord's Supper was for them a meal of remembrance.

Over the Last Supper, to which Jesus had invited his disciples, lay the premonition of his imminent passion. During their celebration of the Lord's Supper, fear and trembling came over the Anabaptists. They did not announce place or time in advance, knowing what awaited them if their forbidden meetings should become manifest—persecution, torture, and martyrdom. An atmosphere of foreboding, which early Christianity knew so well, surrounded the celebration of the Supper, whether in Switzerland, the Tirol, or a Frisian village.

The Lord's Supper was deeply rooted in Anabaptist piety. Congregation, Christian discipleship, and martyrdom were central. It was not an ancillary ritual but the essential manifestation of their corporate worship. In the 1527 Schleitheim Articles we read: "Whoever does not share the calling of the one God to one faith, to one baptism, to one spirit, to one body together with all the children of God, may not be made one loaf together with them, as must be true if one wishes truly to break bread according to the command of Christ" (art. 3, tr. by John H. Yoder, *The Schleitheim Confession*). The *conformitas* to the body of Christ, which expresses itself in the Lord's Supper, is the foundation for the *nonconformitas* to the world. The one who sits at the table of the

Lord cannot at the same time sit at the table of the devil, which is found outside the church. In the eucharistic unity, one sees the difference and the distinctiveness of the Anabaptists.

When seen in this light, it is incomprehensible that the observance of the Lord's Supper among Anabaptists has not been investigated either by Mennonite or non-Mennonite historians and theologians. Indeed, Mennonite Anabaptist studies, which have contributed so much to put the history and theology of the Anabaptists in their proper light in this century, have somehow developed a certain reluctance with respect to the sacraments. Thus the two studies on baptism in Anabaptist thought (*Anabaptist Baptism*, 1966, by Rollin S. Armour; and *Täuferisches Taufverständnis*, 1976, by Christof Windhorst) have been done not by Mennonites but by a Baptist and Lutheran, respectively. Moreover, what they wrote on the Lord's Supper, rather incidentally and in brief passages, lacks distinction and depth. Thus it is all the more praiseworthy that John Rempel, a Canadian Mennonite, has tackled this topic and is now offering to a wider audience his revised dissertation, presented to the Toronto School of Theology. With this book he is certainly closing a significant gap—temporarily, of course, since all academic work is temporary.

I remember going over the outline of this dissertation in May 1986, while on a flight from Zürich to Toronto, and then discussing it with the author in the friendly atmosphere of Conrad Grebel College, Waterloo. Through that experience I learned much, and now I am pleasantly surprised to see how the author has improved the text. I am glad we were able to find a way to include his research in *Studies in Anabaptist and Mennonite History.* It takes us one step further.

John Rempel brings to his task three presuppositions that make for a successful investigation of the Anabaptist concept of the Lord's Supper. First, he has his roots in the tradition of Mennonite piety. He knows not only the theological but also (which is more important) the emotional significance of the Lord's Supper in the life of the church. Second, he knows the rules of academic historical research and so is not bound by confessional apologetics. Nothing is glossed over even when it appears to be historically embarrassing. Third, he is open for that sacramental spirituality which other traditions have developed. Hence, he is well equipped to identify with his own tradition regarding the Lord's Supper. At the same time, he shows no hesitation in subjecting his own tradition to critical examination, to open up the fullness of Christian spirituality which Anabaptists sought to grasp and which in the course of the centuries was lost among the Mennonites.

Rempel follows the polygenetic view of Anabaptism. From each branch of Anabaptism, he chooses one trustworthy representative who has concerned himself with the problems of the Lord's Supper in an intense manner: The Swiss Balthasar Hubmaier, Pilgram Marpeck from South Germany, and Dirk Philips of Anabaptism in the Netherlands. Thus Rempel succeeds in grasping something of the vastness and diversity of Anabaptism, and he confirms this in an impressive manner—something already evident for other topics, such as the role of the government, the principle of nonresistance, the concept of the community of goods, and the view of baptism. With these as for the Lord's Supper, the number of theological differences among Anabaptists is greater than what they have in common.

From the standpoint of systematic theology, this selection is justified. From a historical standpoint, however, one might have hoped for a careful, historical-genetic approach. This would have helped to explain how the doctrine of the Lord's Supper emerged out of the thicket of controversy at the time of the Reformation, and how it was shaped and formed in the concrete life-situations of early Anabaptists. With this historical perspective, it would soon have become obvious that none of the three representatives, whom Rempel has chosen, really represents the current movement of which they were a part.

The Swiss Anabaptists were theologically not as astute as Hubmaier, who had deeply pondered the question of the Lord's Supper. Moreover, the South German Anabaptists could not have accepted the doctrine of the Lord's Supper as Marpeck developed this with great discrimination, often setting forth contrary opinions. Besides, Marpeck reached only a relatively small circle of Anabaptists in this region. In the same way, it must be said, Dirk Philips is hardly representative of Anabaptists in the Netherlands. He was only one elder among several, and not the most original one at that.

The reason Rempel latches onto these historical personages is obvious: no one has written more about the Lord's Supper than these three Anabaptists—a trained theologian (Hubmaier), a self-taught theologian (Marpeck), and a runaway monk (Philips). Methodologically, the approach taken in this volume on the Lord's Supper, that of following the available texts, is commendable. We discover what three Anabaptists thought about the Lord's Supper, how they took what they found in Christian tradition, and how they then transferred it in their own way to an Anabaptist understanding of the Supper.

Two results of this study are particularly significant. First, Rempel is able to demonstrate that these Anabaptists argued dogmatically rather than biblically and exegetically. Nothing strikes the eye so much in this regard as the formative influence of their Christology on the subject. It would be wrong simply to reiterate that the Anabaptists had recovered the biblical concept of the Lord's Supper in their churches. Second, the view that the Anabaptists had a purely symbolic understanding of the Lord's Supper, as represented by Ulrich Zwingli, has now been corrected. Instead, Rempel demonstrates that the Anabaptists tried to understand the sacrament not simply as a symbol of human response to salvation in Jesus Christ, but especially as an event in which God even to this day works for the salvation of humankind.

This conclusion has impressed me. Many years ago I tried to do something similar with the concept of baptism in Anabaptism. I pointed out that for early Anabaptists, believers baptism was often more than a human act of confession (*Die Mennoniten,* 1971; and *Die Täufer,* 1980 and 1988). The response to that effort was not as strong among Mennonites as I had anticipated, so I did not pursue it further. Now Rempel comes to a similar understanding of the Lord's Supper. Perhaps it would still be worthwhile to begin a broad discussion in which we no longer simply think of the Lord's Supper as one scene in which we mutually affirm the transformation of our hearts through God's redemptive act in Jesus Christ. We also always emerge again from celebrating the Lord's Supper as transformed individuals.

Rempel's research could help us recognize the loss of the true meaning of the Lord's Supper that has gradually come to prevail in Mennonite churches. It could help to set us, in harmony with our Anabaptist forebears and in conversation with our ecumenical brothers, on the track once again to overcome that loss. This does not mean that we simply adopt their thinking—how could this even be possible, in the light of their disparate and contradictory thoughts? Instead, we can attempt to retrieve once again the fullness of sacramental experience.

Rempel's purpose in this study is not to draw for our churches an idealized picture of our Anabaptist past—which in any case cannot be achieved by imitation. This has often been attempted, but always without success. As an ideal, the past never remains constantly present. Rempel shows that in the effort to discover a sacramental spirituality, everything opens up for our churches in communication with God, to which all those who are weary and heavy laden are invited (Matt. 11:28).

—*Hans-Jürgen Goertz*
Hamburg, Germany
Spring 1992

Editor's Preface

This volume is a timely addition to the Studies in Anabaptist and Mennonite History series. Its publication is cause for celebration and was encouraged by many. Rempel has transformed his work from its original incarnation as a doctoral dissertation to the more digestible version here presented.

The appearance of this volume represents a landmark, the first in-depth historical and theological inquiry into the Anabaptist understanding of the Lord's Supper. It is surprising that we had to wait this long for such a study to appear. Rempel's book is a welcome arrival.

It is an engaging piece of theological writing. It is clearly written, and not overly technical. It is theologically nuanced, in dialogue with broader Reformation and Medieval theological issues, and conversant with the primary sources. Moreover, it seeks to involve the past with the present. It is methodologically conscious, critical, and constructive. It is not a hagiographical treatment of an Anabaptist theme.

This volume is significant not only for its rigorous and critical historical investigation, but also for its potential to stimulate contemporary theological conversations among Mennonites on the nature and place of the sacraments in spirituality, theology, and ministry.

I must thank John Rempel for his heartfelt willingness to create the time and space, in the midst of pastoral duties, to make the necessary revisions for the publication of this work. I also take special pleasure in thanking Hans-Jürgen Goertz for the important and useful foreword he has prepared, to which I refer the readers of this volume. It provides a necessary context in which to place Rempel's work. It is my hope that this volume will contribute significantly to revitalizing a long-neglected area in Anabaptist-Mennonite theology and practice.

—*Howard John Loewen*
Academic Dean and Professor of Theology
Mennonite Brethren Biblical Seminary
Fresno, California

Author's Preface

This book began as a dissertation, written to meet the requirements of the doctoral program of the School of Theology at the University of Toronto. It has gone through a series of revisions for purposes of publication. This process has given my original research the advantage of being read and criticized by additional scholars in the field of Anabaptism.

So much of my life, its time and its intensity, has been caught up in this dissertation that it seems appropriate, first of all, to thank all those who gave me knowledge, inspiration, and companionship during its preparation. These gifts often came in ways not immediately related to my work; nevertheless, they helped me persevere in my research and believe in its worth. Included among them are people whose specific contribution to my dissertation deserves specific mention.

For his patience and insight, for his capacity to alert me to unfruitful hypotheses and unexplored possibilities alike, I want to thank my adviser, Iain Nicol. His probing criticism of every section of my work challenged my thinking and at the same time left me with the confidence that he saw something worthwhile in my attempt to do theology.

For their critical and substantive engagement with my thought and writing, I am grateful to Hans-Jürgen Goertz, Calvin Pater, Werner Packull, John Howard Yoder, Christof Windhorst, James Stayer, Sjouke Voolstra, Neal Blough, Attila Mikloshazy, Walter Klaassen, and William Keeney.

For their helpful observations and suggestions, I am indebted to Heinold Fast, Peter Erb, C. J. Dyck, Ervin Wiens, to colleagues of the Conrad Grebel College faculty and the Anabaptist research circle, which meets each year.

For the sustained hospitality they offered me, especially in the form of a peaceful place in which to reflect and write, I want to thank Ervin and Linda Wiens, Peter and Rita Brown, and Ron and Lynn Tiessen. For his intellectual companionship during the last two years of my research, I am grateful to Larry Willms.

For encouragement and affirmation in my dissertation subject and in the work it took during years of full-time duties at Conrad Grebel College, my thanks go to Ralph Lebold and Rod Sawatsky.

For their skill and generosity of spirit, I want to thank Joan Weber and, in the final stage of my work, Rosemary Smith. They were of great help with typing, reproduction, and computer use, and Rosemary also prepared the bibliography. For his long-suffering willingness to solve otherwise insoluble computer problems, I am indebted to Nelson Scheifele. The library staff at Conrad Grebel College, Knox College, and the Mennonite Historical Library in Hamburg, Germany, were always thoughtful and solicitous.

Howard John Loewen was appointed by the SAMH editorial board as the editor of this volume. His detailed study of the manuscript and probing response to its content went well beyond the call of duty. SAMH Editor-in-Chief Theron Schlabach saw to it that the manuscript went through the necessary stages of scrutiny as quickly as possible. He and Neal Weaver unraveled computer problems of unnerving complexity. S. David Garber, Herald Press book editor, suggested many editorial changes which have greatly enhanced the clarity of the text. My gratitude goes out to them.

This book is dedicated to my mother and father. The course of my life has been set by their passion for the survival of memory—theirs as well as that of generations before them—and for passing it on to another generation.

It is my heart's and mind's desire to make this book, in all its incompleteness, an act of *eucharistia*, thanksgiving to God for the fact that, in Marpeck's words, "Christ became a natural man for natural men." I thank him for sustaining my faith in that truth during the difficulties and discoveries which set the course of my work.

—*John D. Rempel*
New York City
Ascension Day 1991

Hubmaier, Marpeck, and Dirk: The Theological Context of Their Views

	Background Influences	*Relationship with Contemporaries*
Hubmaier —initiator —dissenter —thesis maker	—academic theologian —liturgical reformer (especially of communion) —extensive association and common development with Zwingli —extreme reaction to sacramentalism and commitment to combat the corporeal presence of Christ in the Lord's Supper —pioneered in Anabaptist positions	—anti-Catholic, but viewed church as "monastic" community and Lord's Supper as martyr's meal —distant from Lutheranism as insufficiently reformed (with Lord's Supper still a corporeal reality) —pro-Zwinglian: memorial, church as body of Christ, similar liturgy—but rejected Z.'s view of church and his exegesis of institutional narrative —identified with and built on ecclesiology and sacramentology of Swiss Brethren, but went further in formal theology —implicit anti-spiritualism, but not threatened with it as a movement
Marpeck —mediator —protector —negotiator —synthesizer	—engineer by profession —radical reformers' influence in Austria —Mystical/South German, Dutch, and Swiss Anabaptist influence in Strasbourg; Münsterite Rothmann shaped his view of ceremonies —commonalities with Bucer and Capito —decisive influence on theology and ceremonies vis-à-vis Schwenckfeld, whose extreme spiritualism endangered Anabaptism from the left as much as Catholicism from the right	—anti-Catholic, but retained incarnationist sacraments —distant from Lutheranism, but borrowed its critique of spiritualism —influenced by diverse Anabaptist community in Strassburg (including mystical-spiritualist strands in Bünderlin, Hoffmann, and others) —compatability of eucharistic doctrine with Bucer and Capito —corrective theology, shaped greatly by controversy, to establish Anabaptism as a distinct and radical form of orthodoxy against a heterodox spiritualism —circle of kindred Anabaptist church leaders included his collaborator, Scharnschlager —found "third way" between sacramentalism and spiritualism via Rothmann

Dirk
—defender
—codifier
—apologist
with
antitheses

—born into priest's family
—shaped by sacramentari-
anism, an alternative to
Catholicism by his time
—anti-Catholic/sacramental
—anti-Münsterite (too close
to Rothmann, e.g., to use
him as did Marpeck)
—late in life, anti-spiritualist,
especially vs. Franck

—anti-Catholic, but emphasized eating
Christ's flesh as a mystical reality
—distant from Lutheranism
—hostile to Reformed theologians like
á Lasco in part because similarities and
differences were evenly matched
(agreed on sacraments as outward
signs of inward reality)
—unspoken assumptions absorbed from
Hoffmann, especially concerning Spirit
and flesh, but hostile to anarchism in a
beleaguered setting where authority
was needed
—hostile to Münsterites and unable to use
mediating theological attempts like that
of Rothmann
—kindred spirituality to that of Spiritualists like Franck until he realized that
they had no place for his ecclesiology

A Profile of Hubmaier's, Marpeck's, and Dirk's Theology of the Supper

	Christology	Lord's Supper, Ceremonies	Church
Common Views —create theology and liturgy of Lord's Supper alternative to both sacramentalism and spiritualism	—ascension of Jesus —impossibility of his corporeal presence on earth —"stretched" Trinitarianism —attraction to Fourth Gospel —innovative exegesis —tendency to conflate Christ in his divinity with the Spirit	—no automatic efficacy; no reality without presence of faith and love —outward actions imitating Christ and manifesting the Gospel —indefinite number of symbols, but baptism and communion as anchor ones	—body of Christ is existential community of believers —communion is event taking place when church gathers with bread and wine —prolongs Jesus' humanity
Hubmaier —stresses being rather than receiving the body of Christ	—incarnation is historically bound mode of revelation; ascension removes Christ from history —Spirit is mode of God's presence in church; by it, church continues to incarnate Christlike life	—baptism acts out faith; communion acts out love —communion: body and blood in remembrance, pledge of love; human and outward act in response to preceding divine and inward act —neighbor love is part of Supper —Anabaptist communion liturgy —Christ present as demand	—moral community —capable of walking in new life, laying down life —keeper of keys in Christ's absence

Marpeck	—incarnation is ongoing form of God's presence in church ('humanity of Christ'); continues "natural" life of Jesus in church, and by extension, in ceremonies	—ceremony is not an object but an event	—prolongation of Christ's incarnation in history
—stresses being and receiving the body of Christ		—when faith responds to the Spirit, the elements become witnesses to the reality (union with Christ) given in this dynamic	—primal sacrament
	—Father works inwardly through Spirit, outwardly through Son	—manifestation of the church, which is the manifestation of Christ's humanity	

Dirk	—unfallen and heavenly human nature of Christ, who did not share our fallen flesh because it cannot bear Spirit	—outward signs of inward realities	—more an institution than an organism
—stresses receiving more than being the body of Christ		—paradigmatic experiences of union with Christ in Supper	—communal dimension of Supper less emphasized than individual experience of Christ
	—incarnation is historically bound mode of revelation, but heavenly Christ is active in church and received by believers	—seven ceremonies with baptism and Supper as sacraments	
		—significance of minister as presider	

Document Abbreviations

Dirk

AML	Van dat Auontmael des Heeren Jesu Christi, onse Belidinghe
Doope	Van der Doope
ENC	Enchiridion
FRANCK	Een verantwoordinghe ende Refutation op twee Sendtbrieven Sebastian Franck
GEM	Van de Gemeynte Godts
KENN	Van de rechte kennisse
MNG	Van der Menschwerdinghe
Third Epistle	De derde vermaninghe

Hubmaier

Achtzehn	Achtzehn Schlussreden
Einfältiger	Ein Einfältiger Unterricht
Gespräch	Ein Gespräch auf Zwinglis Taufbüchlein
Messe	Etliche Schlussreden vom Unterricht der Messe
Nachtmahl	Eine Form des Nachtmahls Christi

Marpeck

CV	Clare Verantwortung
KU	Klarer Unterricht
VMN	Vermanung
VWG	Verantwortung (Verantwurtung über Caspern Schwenckfelds Judicium)
VWG I	First 111 pages of Verantwortung
VWG II	Last 389 pages of Verantwortung

Rothmann

BEK	Bekenntnis von beiden Sakramenten

Schwenckfeld

JDM	Über das Neu Büchlin der Tauffbrüder, or Judicium

1
Introduction

The Nature of the Enquiry

At the heart of Christianity stands a relationship between Creator and creation. In the incarnation the Creator became a Savior. Ever since Jesus' earthly life, Christian devotion and theology have claimed to know God through the person Jesus. The New Testament makes the paradoxical assertions that God has come in the flesh and that spirit is the means by which humanity and God relate to each other. Throughout its history, the church has sought to hold fast to both of these claims. In its formative years, Christianity asserted the spiritual nature of religion, that God cannot be reduced to or identified with any external reality, thus standing against the opposite tendency of popular paganism.

But by the end of the second century, a new threat confronted the church. It came from Gnosticism, with its contempt for the material world and its denial of any possible relationship between the realms of matter and spirit. In response, the church asserted the dogma of the incarnation, the claim that spirit is known in history through matter. Josef Jungmann describes how this ancient struggle came to expression in the celebration of the Lord's Supper.

> Whereas formerly mention was hardly ever made of the material gifts of bread and wine, but only of the thanksgiving which was pronounced over them, now it is precisely this material side which is stressed.[1]

The Eucharist is the pinnacle of the communion of the church and the Christian, yet its transcendent reality is effected by the rudimentary elements of earthly existence, bread and wine. I have attempted to keep this fundamental paradox in the foreground of my thesis. Its structure reflects developments in the character of the Eucharist toward communion with a spirit, unbounded in any way yet mediated by the earthbound elements of natural existence. This paradoxical reality was possible because in Jesus, God had taken flesh. The Lord's Supper was the prolongation through time of this mystery of the incarnation.

To illustrate how these doctrines were developed in the sixteenth century, this volume explores what three Anabaptist theologians believed concerning the Lord's Supper and the relationship between the Supper and the Christology of each of the three writers. Such an undertaking is fraught with difficulties peculiar to the subject. One of them is that, from the beginning, the movement was diverse.[2] The propagators of Anabaptism ranged from unlearned women and men with little interest or talent for systematic thought to those with considerable intellectual skill as apologists for the movement.

A second difficulty is the anthropological focus of the Radical Reformation. Anabaptism was preoccupied with the human response to the Gospel. This concern carried over to its thinking about the Eucharist. In the thought of Catholicism and the Magisterial Reformation, the definitive characteristic of a sacrament was God's initiative, but for Anabaptism it was the human response of faith and love. The nature of the human action with the sacrament, rather than the nature of the sacrament itself, stands at the center of Anabaptist interest. This means that the theology of the Lord's Supper had a direct relationship not only to Christology but also to *ecclesiology and ethics.*

A final difficulty that confronts this study is the corrective nature of Anabaptist theology. Anabaptists placed themselves distant from the theology and practice of the late medieval church and of much of the Reformation. Their theologies, as their doctrines of the Lord's Supper, developed through the controversies which distanced the Anabaptist movement from both (1) sacramentalism (the automatic mediation of grace through priestly power and the elements themselves) and (2) spiritualism (a divorce between the inwardness of religious reality and the outwardness of the material world).

Emerging Eucharistic Thought
at the End of the Middle Ages

Because of the complexity and specificity of the topic of Eucharist and Christology in Anabaptism, the examination of the subject must be limited primarily to the perspective of the authors themselves and to their judgments about the world against which they defined themselves. For example, they misrepresent pre-Tridentine Catholic eucharistic doctrine as uniformly vulgar, mechanical materialism.[3] Any attempt to situate Anabaptist views of the Lord's Supper within the overall development of Christian tradition on the subject would have to take into account the misunderstandings on which certain of its claims were based. This study, however, describes Anabaptist eucharistic thought in its own terms and must leave the larger task for future research.

While Anabaptists regarded themselves as standing in opposition to major developments within both the Catholic and the other Reformation churches, their relation to one of these developments was, in fact, exemplary. It is the trend toward subjectivism.

Joseph Lortz describes the transition from Middle Ages to modernity, which climaxed in the Reformation, in the following way:

> Seen as a religious and ecclesiastical event the Reformation is the denial of the visible Church, rooted and grounded in the objective teaching authority and in the sacramental priesthood; and it is the acceptance of a religion of conscience erected upon the judgment of the individual with regard to the biblical word. This is to say: along these two lines of its development, the Reformation replaced the basic medieval attitudes of objectivism, traditionalism, and clericalism by those of subjectivism, spiritualism, and laicism.[4]

The categories of subjectivism, spiritualism, and laicism will be accepted as a guide to establishing a frame of reference for our study. At the same time, these categories will be qualified to the extent that they do not adequately describe the Anabaptism of our subjects.

Alike in the university theology and the lay spirituality of the age, a growing place was given to the personal and subjective in religion.[5] Killian McDonnell writes of the *devotio moderna,* the most studied movement of lay spirituality in that era, that its "personal, individualistic pursuit was realized dogmatically within the church but psychologically outside it."[6] When this lay spirituality, particularly in its eucharistic thought and devotion, broke out of the Roman dogmatic mold, it lacked a theology to describe its experience. This is emphatically true of sacramentarianism, the stream of new Dutch spirituality which was a formative influence in early Anabaptism.

The tendency toward subjectivism was furthered by two developments which altered the theology and practice of the Lord's Supper. One of them is the infrequency of communion and the receiving of only one part of the sacrament (bread). For a millennium prior to the Reformation, receiving communion had been in decline in the Western church.[7] One of the reasons for this was the dread of unworthy reception of the body and blood of the Lord. Though the mass was celebrated every week, Christ was adored from a distance and was not received sacramentally. The new spirituality endowed an ancient belief with a novel status. Since the age of the fathers, the church had contended that even when Christ was not received in bread and wine, he could be spiritually encountered in the soul of each believer. The novelty in the writings of certain precursors of sacramentarianism is that they elevated a spiritual communion with Christ above a sacramental one.[8]

Increasingly, such persons took subjective factors as the sufficient basis for the reception of grace. This emphasis placed classical sacramental definitions within a new interpretive context. Protestants perceived a tendency in Catholicism to objectify sacramental reality such that sacraments were thought to automatically convey the grace they signified. Oberman's definition reflects this perception: *ex opere operato* means "on grounds of the performance of the rite and designates the ability of an exterior rite to bring about what it signifies." *Ex opere operantis* affirms the efficacy of a rite as determined by the interior disposition of the administrant or the recipient.[9] The conventional application of the latter definition was to claim grace over and above that given *ex opere operato*. Gradually it became loosened from its objective precondition. This tendency was accentuated in the Reformation and received its most radical expression in Anabaptist conceptions of baptism and the Lord's Supper.[10]

In his characterization of church life on the eve of the Reformation, Lortz contrasts its spiritualism with the traditionalism of the old church. By traditionalism he means the life of the visible church in its constitution, teaching, view of the sacraments, and ordained priesthood. The point to Lortz's contrast is that the internal and subjective, whose deepening in the late Middle Ages he lauds, was now pitted against the external and objective. This subjective piety diverted the believer "from the objectivity of the liturgical-sacramental organism of the risen Lord and from the mediation of the special priesthood."[11]

This tendency to associate spiritual reality with subjective response had been present throughout church history, sometimes, as was the case with Bérenger de Tours, to counteract a materialist realism. It was compounded by a philosophical shift which made use of certain recent interpretations of Augustine's early writings.[12] This late medieval theology and piety contended that the external world was unable to comprehend the internal one. Christof Windhorst makes a lucid application of this dualistic picture of the world to the question of sacraments:

The basic concept at issue is that spiritual things cannot adequately be recognized through corporeal signs. Between spiritual things (*res*) and significatory signs (*signa*), there stands an ontological barrier. As a consequence, *signa*, as opposed to *res*, are deficient, inadequate realities.[13]

This tendency to erect an ontological barrier between the sensible and spiritual worlds deprived matter of a capacity to mediate spirit. This assumption came to Anabaptism most fully through sacramentarianism, the peculiar Dutch form of lay spirituality.[14] It was to have a formative influence on all radical reformers, being the most accessible way of refuting Catholic authority in general and its sacramental teaching in particular. But its influence in Anabaptism was limited by that movement's ecclesiology.

The third background factor to a consideration of Anabaptist eucharistic theology is anticlericalism. Late medieval opposition to the pastoral power of the clergy and their sometimes indulgent lifestyle led gradually and sometimes inadvertently to a repudiation of their exclusive mediation of salvation.[15] Without the sacramental power of the priesthood, medieval definitions of sacramental efficacy were dislodged and with them the authority of the church as a sacramental and hierarchical guardian of grace. The laicization of the Eucharist meant that its reality depended more and more on the disposition of its recipients. Subjectivism, spiritualism, and laicization all reinforced each other in this process by which the Holy Supper was removed from the structures on which its character and power had heretofore depended. In Anabaptist treatments of the Supper, the repudiation of priestly mediation is presupposed. But they do not develop far in the direction of individualism and subjectivism. Anabaptists retained the authority of the community—though admittedly broken into factions from the beginning of the movement onward—as the agent of communion and the place of appointed presiders.

Eucharist and Christology in the Reformation

Dispute over the Lord's Supper was a telling embodiment of the spiritual, theological, and political conflict of the Reformation. It was much more than an isolated issue of dogmatic debate.[16] The vastness of this subject forbids its consideration except in strict relation to the topic under examination.

Martin Luther's (1483-1546) sacramental writings established for the Reformation the overthrow of the Lord's Supper as a sacrifice and as an *ex opere operato* communion with the body and blood of Christ.[17] However, in the end Luther's Christology determined his eucharistic doctrine and made his work an indispensable reference point for Anabaptist theologizing on the subject.[18] Against the more spiritualistic interpretations of the sacrament, Luther argued that the Lord was present in both his natures. He asserted this claim by the "peculiar and original tenet" of the "communication of idioms."[19] This implied a mutual transference of qualities such that divine attributes may be predicated of the human nature of Christ. By means of this predication, Christ in his human nature was able to be both at the right hand of the Father and in the sacrament.

All other innovations in eucharistic doctrine in the first generation of the Reformation may be classified according to their acceptance or rejection of this view. The consequential philosophical tenet at stake in Luther's claim was summarized in the dictum that *finitum est capax infiniti* (the finite is not capable of the infinite). This axiom was of extreme significance directly for Christology and also for the nature of a sacrament: finite elements of bread and wine were asserted to be capable of mediating the infinite reality of God.

The first generation non-Lutheran stream of the continental Reformation had the course of its sacramental theology and its christological confession set by the writings of Andreas Karlstadt (1480-1541) and Ulrich Zwingli (1484-1531). Walter Koehler, the dean of early twentieth-century studies of the initial Reformation eucharistic developments, summarizes the tenets these men popularized as follows: faith as the means of sacramental efficacy, a real but mystical presence, the ethically binding nature of the Supper, and the role of remembrance.[20] These beliefs are not novel; they appear widely in patristic and scholastic writing on the Eucharist. As a cluster of claims about the Lord's Supper, they are innovative, however, because they exclude other traditional themes and elevate the status of these four tenets in a definitive way.

Karlstadt significantly influenced the subjects of this study in three areas. One of them was his appropriation of Augustine's sacramental theory. From Augustine he took a theological formulation and used it to express a view of reality. Windhorst's notion of the *ontologische Schranke* (ontological barrier) between sign and the thing signified comes to full articulation in Karlstadt. He reduced the reality of a sign to that of an outer, material entity.[21] The *res* (thing) alone had spiritual reality; it alone was a means of grace. Calvin Pater concludes that Karlstadt erases the traditional *res* and *signum* (sign) relationship; outer entities are material signs of grace only where they are received by a faith which precedes them.[22] In this precisely formulated position, spiritualism left its mark on Anabaptist sacramental thought.[23]

Karlstadt's second and decisive influence on Anabaptism was the Christology he wedded to his sacramental views. He distinguished the divine and human natures of Christ so clearly that they functioned separately. Christ in his humanity was in heaven at the right hand of God and could not, therefore, be present in bread and wine.

His third influence on Anabaptism was his exegesis of the words of institution. Karlstadt held that when Jesus said, "This is my body," he had been referring to his own self sitting at the table and not to the elements.[24] This reading of the demonstrative pronoun plays a part in the evolution of Anabaptist exegesis of the accounts of the Last Supper.

Luther had extreme antipathy toward his erstwhile teacher and colleague Karlstadt. Anabaptists had fears concerning his revolutionary and spiritualistic tendencies. Therefore, most Reformation historians have left Karlstadt to languish in obscurity. His direct and indirect influence on Anabaptism is gradually being acknowledged. Karlstadt's Christmas Mass of 1521, with its revolutionary liturgical innovations, became the prototype for all later worship reform in the non-Lutheran continental Reformation. His insistence that all communicants take the bread and cup into their own hands might be the inspiration behind Conrad Grebel's (ca. 1498-1526) insistence on this practice. At the Second Disputation in Zurich in 1523, Grebel debated against Zwingli's traditional form of distribution.[25] Pater has documented the direct dependence of the Zurich Anabaptists on Karlstadt's theology of the sacraments.[26]

Karlstadt never became the leader of an ongoing movement. Hence, theological breakthroughs which he first propounded became known only through people who built on them or who thought them through on their own, subsequent to Karlstadt. It exceeds the frame of reference for this study to try to define the relationship between Zwingli's thought and Karlstadt's. It suffices here to point to the presence of several eucharistic concepts in the writings of both theologians which proved to be decisive, especially for Swiss and Dutch–North German Anabaptism.

Both of them interpreted John 6 with reference to an inward, nonsacramental feeding on Christ.[27] Of broader significance for much of Anabaptism were the theological premises from which radical eucharistic doctrine emerged. Karlstadt opposed the use of images in worship as idolatry; in their place he put the proclamation of the Word of God and the faith of the believer. Zwingli sharpened and popularized this contrast. His most far-reaching influence in the Reformation stems from his understanding of the nature of faith. What he believed is revealed in C. W. Dugmore's comparison between Zwingli and Luther on that subject.

> Because of his starting point, Luther saw faith as the opposite of justification by works and directed his reformation against the latter, but from his different perspective Zwingli opposed faith primarily to idolatry and directed his Reformation against trust in anything creaturely rather than in the Word of God. This in itself sets the eucharistic debate in an illuminating context.[28]

In addition, two christological assumptions common to Karlstadt and Zwingli were carried over to Anabaptism. First, they emphasized the ascension almost as a proof of the fact that Christ could not be present in the sacrament.[29] Second, they understood the term "communion of the body of Christ" as the transformation of the congregation into the body of the Lord.[30]

One of the notions peculiar to Zwingli's development of a theology of the Lord's Supper had an enduring influence on Swiss, South German, and Dutch–North German Anabaptist eucharistic thought. It is his tropistic interpretation of the words of institution for Holy Communion.[31]

None of the Anabaptist positions under examination is either a simple agreement with, an extension of, or a repudiation of the theologies of the mainstream of the Reformation. Factors unique to Anabaptism, among them its own appropriation of medieval theological themes and its peculiar ecclesiology, led to novel developments in its christological and eucharistic claims.

Eucharist and Christology in Anabaptism

Recent Anabaptist historiography has changed the prevailing assumptions about the origin and character of Anabaptism. Earlier historians like H. S. Bender[32] and theologians like J. A. Oosterbaan understood Anabaptism as a secondary movement of the Reformation,[33] "a correction of a correction, a negation of a negation, . . . the completion and conclusion of the whole Reformation." Researchers since the early 1970s have depicted Anabaptism as a phenomenon made up of diverse origins and movements. At the same time, this newer research has identified Anabaptism as a primary movement of reformation with characteristics not essentially the extension of the Magisterial Reformation, whether by means of correction or negation.[34]

These two changes in scholarly perception are of immense significance for an examination of the Lord's Supper and Christology in Anabaptism. The diverse geographic and intellectual origins of the movements which constituted Anabaptism make it untenable to advance many generalizations about the phenomenon as a whole.[35] It is no longer plausible to assert, as many do, that all Anabaptist eucharistic teaching is derived from Zwingli and that its exclusive original setting is the Zurich reformation.[36] There is growing agreement among scholars that Anabaptism, while not independent of other streams of reformation, is a primary movement in its own right. This means that Anabaptist views concerning the Lord's Supper cannot be adequately grasped as essentially positive or negative deductions from some point within the polarity occupied by Luther on one side and Karlstadt and Zwingli on the other. Anabaptist borrowings came as much from the margins of the Reformation as from its centers.[37] At the same time, as the three subjects of this study illustrate, there were original solutions at work in Anabaptist eucharistic theories to the controversies of the day.

In both the Magisterial and the Radical wings of the Reformation, the Lord's Supper was integral to the identity and development of the contending parties.[38] That this is so for Anabaptism may be seen by examining within it the interdependent relationship of the Eucharist, baptism, and ecclesiology. The baptismal theology and practice of Anabaptism distinguished it from both the Magisterial Reformation and from other radical movements. Baptism made the ecclesiological assumptions of Anabaptism unmistakable and became the model for relating sacraments to personal faith and to participation in the church. John Howard Yoder derives the relationship between baptism and the church from the notion of the body of Christ. The same can be said for the relationship between the Lord's Supper and the church.[39]

> If you search for the breaking point at which the Anabaptists separated themselves from the Reformation, their first concern was with the church, its visibility and its capacity to act. If you ask why the church should be visible and able to act, the answer is this: What's at issue is the life of Christ in his members. Ultimately, the two issues are inseparable precisely because discipleship is not a Franciscan ethic of imitation for the individual but the work of the body of Christ.[40]

The church as the body of Christ on earth was inevitably also a eucharistic image! Both conceptually and practically, the Eucharist, as the Anabaptists understood it, manifested what the Anabaptists in this study believed about baptism and the church. They made the church as a community the agent of the breaking of bread. There is still a presider who symbolizes the community's order and authority. But it is the congregation which does the action. The Spirit is present in their action, transforming them so that they are reconstituted as the body of Christ. The life of the congregation, concentrated in its faith and love, consecrates the elements. For that reason, little attention is given, positively or negatively, to the function of the minister in the Supper. It is solely derivative and representative.

In his analysis of this development among the Swiss Brethren, J. F. G. Göters describes their administration of the Lord's Supper as a movement from the self-communion of a priest without a congregation to the self-communion of a congregation without a priest.[41] The Eucharist is the act of the congregation, and its covenanted life is the immediate warrant for its celebration.[42] Communion is the self-expression of the life of covenanted love given by the Spirit. This explains, at least in part, the secondary attention accorded to the words of institution, as manifest both in the biblical and liturgical commentaries in our sources. Their interest is not so much in an exegesis of these words as in an explanation for the dynamic of the communal event. Almost no mention is made of a liturgical role for the institutional narrative.

The place of Christology in Anabaptist theology as a whole, as well as in the Lord's Supper, is more difficult to assess. The Anabaptist emphasis on the practice of Christianity meant that the radical movements carried out little dogmatic speculation for its own sake. Where questions of belief were raised by the existential situation of controversy, a theological defense was readily undertaken. The earthly life of Jesus was presented as the church's ethical norm and the sole authority for its observance of the ceremonies or sacraments he had ordained. But it was primarily with regard to the Lord's Supper that Anabaptist christological reflection was expanded beyond the earthly Jesus to include the present relationship of Christ to the church. This claim involved more than historical considerations; it demanded the formulation of beliefs concerning the two natures of Christ and his relationship with the Holy Spirit.

In general, we may say that Anabaptism tended toward the christological assumptions developed by Karlstadt and Zwingli. The outstanding trait of this view was the sharp distinction between the two natures of Christ. This formulation of the relationship between the two natures of Christ has a long history. The original reason for it was to

safeguard the claim that God had fully taken human nature into his being.[43] Its focus was Christ's incarnation. In the Reformation this formulation was given a novel, inverted development. Here its focus was on
the two natures of Christ after his ascension. The appeal of this
localizing (one might almost say *relegating*) of the human nature of
Christ to heaven came from the spiritualistic and subjectivistic tendencies which flowed into the Reformation.

Such a dualistic Christology came into prominence because of its
usefulness in defending the spiritual nature of Christ's present relationship to the church. Since in his humanity, Christ is located in heav-
en, his humanity cannot be part of his ongoing work on earth. At this
point the Holy Spirit rather than the human nature of Christ is the medium of the divine presence: God's immediacy to the world is now not
through flesh but through Spirit.

This cluster of claims provided the bulwark of Karlstadt's and
Zwingli's eucharistic doctrines. Many Anabaptists accepted both the
christological principle at stake and the eucharistic deductions taken
from it. Because Christ had ascended, went the argument, he could not
be physically or essentially in the bread and wine of the Supper.[44]

The Reformation debate about the Eucharist was primarily christological and only secondarily exegetical. This study of the documents
will proceed with that fact in mind. It was by means of their christological positions, implicit or explicit, that all of those engaged in disputes
about the Eucharist validated their stances. Within each camp, Lutheran and non-Lutheran, there was disagreement on the nature of the
Lord's Supper, but these altercations emerged from differences in how
a similarly conceived view of Christ expressed itself eucharistically.[45]

Because of its dominant christological picture, which portrayed
Christ's present work on earth as unmediated by his humanity, the
Anabaptist Lord's Supper had a bias toward the spiritualization of reality. This bias was in conflict with that of its ecclesiology, a conflict evident in all the subjects of this study. But on the basis of its ecclesiology,
Anabaptism developed another christological picture, not directly
drawn from the classical alternatives. Anabaptists portrayed Christ as
present in the church in his humanity. This presence was a prolongation of his incarnation. In a certain sense the church was the human
body of Christ; in the church's external life, Christ was known by Christians who gave their body and blood for their neighbor as Christ had
given his for them.[46] The ceremonies participated in the revealing of
Christ by means of his outwardness, i.e., the human nature he had tak-
en upon himself in the incarnation.[47] The encounter between these two

christologies, more than anything else, shapes the eucharistic doctrines presented here as case studies.[48]

We now turn to a brief description of the dialectical development in the relationship between ecclesiology and Eucharist in connection with the incarnationist Christology introduced earlier in the discussion. To summarize what has been spelled out so far, the theologians in our study all repudiated the mediating principles of dogma, hierarchy, and priesthood. They rejected the objective structures which mediated salvation—*ex opere operato*. But they did not intend to substitute individuality and inwardness for what they rejected.[49] In its place they sought to put the community of believers. This exchange of one form of ecclesial authority for another is different only in degree and not in kind from the medieval model. That is to say, the authority by which the church was ruled—the Scripture and the Spirit together—was interpreted in Anabaptism by the community rather than by the hierarchy.

However, this description of the community as the subject of its own relationship to God, without mediating sacramental structures, would be incomplete without reference to the role of the faith of the individual. The common belief of our subjects on this matter is that the existential faith of the individual believer is indispensable to the community's relationship with God. This faith is not the cause of that relationship but it is the condition for such a relationship. Such faith exists only in connection with the faith of the church but, at the same time, the church and its ceremonies are revelations of grace only in the presence of such faith.[50] That, above all else, is the point of Anabaptist theologies of baptism. An understanding of the nature of faith in Anabaptism is of decisive importance to this study because faith is the *sine qua non* of human participation in the reality of the Lord's Supper. It is clear in the writings of all our subjects that the Spirit is the one who makes Christ present and that only by faith can Christ be received. Neither the church nor the sacraments are *ex opere operato* realities, i.e., ones which come into being independent of human response.

In this sense, Anabaptist eucharistic thought is incarnationist: Christ takes form in the faith and love of the church. It follows from these claims that the primary dualism at work in Anabaptism is not one between spirit and matter but between church and world. The church is the point of co-incidence between Spirit and matter. In other words, the church, "although existing in spirit, . . . is also visible."[51] The world is that realm where the Spirit's rule is rejected. Baptism and the Lord's Supper are the visible ceremonies by which the church is constituted.[52] By the power of the keys, this church binds and looses in Christ's stead.

These ecclesiological and sacramental claims, deduced from the teaching of the humanity of Christ in the church, lead to an outer church and visible sacraments.

Two christological tendencies asserted themselves in Anabaptist eucharistic thought, one dominated by the incarnation, the other by the ascension. What is the outcome of the encounter between these two different formulations of Christology? A detailed answer to this question is at the heart of this research and will be developed in relation to the different christological constructions in each of the theologians in our study. One general observation may be made, however, by way of introduction to the question. Where the person of Christ is divided, and one of his natures conceived of as the exclusive medium of his presence, a one-sided sacramentology results.[53]

On one hand, where Christ's divinity is made the exclusive mode of his presence, there the outward cannot be made one with the inward, and ceremonies have no participation in grace. Communion with Christ is individual and inward. On the other hand, where Christ's humanity is the exclusive mode of his presence (the church as the prolongation of his earthly ministry), the church itself becomes the *res* of which the ceremonies are the *signum*, and then grace has no participation in the ceremonies. By excluding either corporate moral oneness with Christ's humanity or individual, inward communion with Christ—both christological premises, when taken to an extreme, separate communion with Christ from the church as it takes on form in the breaking of bread. In the end, they both are spiritualistic in separating the gift of grace from anything outward. Where Christ is believed to be present in both his natures, there his humanity is at work in the external acts of the church, uniting them with his divinity, which is at work in the internal life of the church, in its collective faith.

Was there a single source in the New Testament on which the theologians in our study especially depended for their eucharistic and christological motifs? For all three of them, the Fourth Gospel is more decisive than the Pauline and Synoptic institutional narratives and christological claims. This is emphatically true where these thinkers attempt to come to terms with the most contentious problem in sixteenth-century eucharistic debate, the communion of the body and blood of Christ.[54] They use the Johannine materials in overlapping as well as contradictory ways. Their different exegetical and theological uses of John make the distinctiveness of each of their eucharistic doctrines the fruit of a debate over the correct interpretation of that Gospel.

The Subjects of This Study

The study will proceed by means of an examination of the eucharistic and christological writings of three Anabaptist theologians, Balthasar Hubmaier (1480?-1528), Pilgram Marpeck (1495?-1556), and Dirk Philips (1504-1568). Each of these men was chosen for two reasons. First, his body of writing includes not only occasional pastoral or confessional statements, as are found in many Anabaptists, but a sustained treatment of the Lord's Supper in relation to his theology as a whole. Second, each person represents the dominant biases and issues of a stream of Anabaptism in his generation. Each of them speaks for the community of thought and faith from which he emerged, yet each of them creates a theology and a eucharistic doctrine which distinguishes him as an individual.

Thus, although Hubmaier emerges from the world of Zwingli and the Swiss Brethren, his unique ecclesiastical experiments shaped his theology and practice of the Lord's Supper differently from the Swiss Brethren as a whole. Although Marpeck absorbed influences from radical dissenters in the South German realm, his theology had an originality to it which was never taken over by the communities of Anabaptists which endured in that region. Dirk's theology has a close kinship with the thought of Melchior Hoffmann and was developed through his collegiality with Menno Simons, the two towering figures in early Dutch–North German Anabaptism. Yet Dirk's eucharistic thought develops beyond that of either of his mentors.

Hubmaier was a restless and radical theologian who pursued his new interpretation of the gospel to its logical conclusion. He wrote on behalf of a beleaguered minority with an uncertain future. His Christ was the sufferer incarnate again in every act of selflessness, his Lord's Supper the pledge of selfless love. Marpeck was an eclectic and irenic thinker who created an intellectual apology for a movement tempted on all sides by rival understandings of the gospel. His Christ was both patient Savior and gracious Lord, his Lord's Supper the gift of corporate union with him. Dirk was a pastor who reluctantly undertook a defense of his community's faith; its stability and continuity were of utmost importance to him. His Christ was both the unfallen, mysteriously condescending man and the God who shared his divine nature with those he had chosen. His Lord's Supper was an act of awe at Christ's condescension and an act of oneness with his glory.

Individually and collectively these three men, all inseparably theologians and ministers, wrote with a breadth of understanding and sophistication on the subject of the Lord's Supper and Christology which has not been exceeded in subsequent generations. Even though their views have receded in the communal consciousness of Mennonites, their work remains foundational and exemplary for Mennonite theology and church life. It has kept alive aspects of eucharistic docrine which can add to the fullness of the Lord's Supper in the universal church.

Dr. Balthasar Hubmaier (1480?-1528)

2
Balthasar Hubmaier

Introduction

In Vienna on March 10, 1528, less than fifty years after his birth, Balthasar Hubmaier's immense journey was stopped by death. The Austrian crown had acted on the church's declaration that Hubmaier was a heretic for (among other reasons) his views on the Lord's Supper. Thus ended the life of a person whose sense of calling led him into a life of ministry in the church. In early adulthood he had entered the Roman Catholic priesthood. Though outwardly esteemed, he was theologically unsatisfied and spiritually restless. The ferment of his age led him to seek direction from Martin Luther and Ulrich Zwingli. In Hubmaier's judgment, these men failed consequentially to follow their own insights. This dissatisfaction with the course of reform led him to the Anabaptists, who claimed to restore the life of the church solely according to the Bible. Yet even in their company, he was alone. As a matriculated theologian, his mind was graced and burdened with a world of ideas which none of the reformational movements could quite contain.

The theology of Hubmaier, like the man, stands between the fronts of the Reformation. The purity of the church was of such importance to Hubmaier that church discipline and the ban were part of his essential definition of the church. Yet he was the one, of all the Anabaptists, who persisted after 1525 in the belief that it was possible to establish a believers church as a mass church. He made two attempts at this, the first in Waldshut, diocese of Constance, and the second in Nikolsburg, diocese of Olmütz. Torsten Bergsten, his biographer, describes the church which emerged under Hubmaier's tutelage as "a unique historical appearance of this type."[1] Bergsten claims that this outcome was the result of Hubmaier's goal to bring baptism and the Lord's Supper into conformity with Scripture.

Birgit Stolt, a linguist who worked with the editors of Hubmaier's writings, sees the tragedy of his life as that of someone "who stood between the various views but belonged to none of them."[2] She adds that this falling between the fronts finds expression also in Hubmaier's writing style. This most significant fact of Hubmaier's life makes him demanding to read but also accounts for his originality in synthesizing diverse elements from the theological ferment of his age. David Steinmetz describes the dual tendencies in Hubmaier's thought.

> Hubmaier faces in two directions. His view of baptism and of the voluntary church represents a break with the past and anticipation of new currents which gained in significance after his death. But his views of grace and free will represent a continuation into the sixteenth century of conservative theological motifs from the later Middle Ages over against the radical theological insights of Luther.[3]

A second decisive characteristic of Hubmaier bears mention at the outset. Hubmaier was a systematic thinker, but he did not stay with most of his themes long enough to develop them into full-fledged doctrines. Considering Hubmaier's writing on a favorite theme, word and Spirit, Christof Windhorst observes, "One cannot find evidence of a doctrine of word and Spirit in Hubmaier."[4] This characteristic is true of his scholarship as a whole. As needed, Hubmaier amassed historical, theological, biblical, and rational evidence for his arguments. His interest was not in a comprehensive system of thought. It had an apologetic purpose. This was to refute false forms of Christian thought and practice and to build up the life of his beleaguered church. The turbulence of his life and times bore directly on his approach. He was a practical theologian. In his Catholic days as cathedral preacher in Regensburg, he had been known for his ability to address the common people. His writing as an Anabaptist had the same intention.

The great passion of Hubmaier's work as an Anabaptist theologian was to correctly set forth the relationship between the divine initiative and the human response in salvation. In order to do this, he concentrated much of his writing on grace, faith, Spirit, human nature, and the church. Nowhere are these themes presented as vividly and frequently as in Hubmaier's writings on the sacraments. The breakthrough in which all else culminated was Hubmaier's notion that "sacraments" were acts of human response, means of obedience. They should not be confused, he taught, with the grace which makes faith possible. The spiritual and inward was divine activity; the material and outward was human. Both were indispensable to the Christian life. Hubmaier even made bold to say that without baptism and the Lord's

Supper, there is no church. What he meant by each of these claims is the subject matter for this investigation.

Hubmaier's Theological Background and Mentors

In chapter 1 an attempt was made to describe the theological setting in which the eucharistic debates of the sixteenth century took place. In the case of the other two subjects of this study, Pilgram Marpeck and Dirk Philips, little factual documentation concerning each individual may be offered beyond this general description. Happily, it is possible to say more about Balthasar Hubmaier. He was an academic theologian whose years of study and whose chief professor are known. Hubmaier studied at the University of Freiburg im Breisgau from 1505 to 1507 under Johannes Eck. He interrupted his studies in 1507 to become a teacher in Schaffhausen, near Waldshut. There he was later to lead the congregation and become involved with peasant revolts.

Hubmaier finished his studies and in 1509 became professor at Freiburg. In 1510 he took over the chair in biblical studies when it was vacated by Eck. Then in 1512 he followed his mentor Eck to the University of Ingolstadt. There he earned a doctorate in theology. At both universities the dominant schools of contemporary theology were represented. Eck was a nominalist. A tendency toward the *via moderna* is evident in Hubmaier's scholarly associations as well as in his writings. He had a close academic relationship with Eck and was the rector of the nominalist college in Freiburg.[5]

Steinmetz identifies biographical data, such as Hubmaier's years as a student of the nominalist theologian Johannes Eck, as well as tenets in Hubmaier's thought which link him to this school.[6] Foremost among them is his concept of free will and the covenantal bond between God and a person. Walter Moore identifies extensive common ground between Eck and Hubmaier. He also notes that their anthropology is quite different. Nothing of Hubmaier's tripartite views can be found in Eck.[7] Moore's point is well taken and should be accepted as a caution against trying to identify Hubmaier completely with any one theology or trying to locate all his notions in the writings of known theologians.

In 1516 Hubmaier accepted the invitation to become dean of the cathedral (*Domprediger*) in Regensburg. This role involved clashes with local authorities, which no doubt contributed to his departure for Waldshut in late 1521.[8] In his first years there as parish priest, he was known for his introduction of ceremonial to highlight the liturgy and especially the sacrament of the altar. At the same time, his correspondence betrays a reading knowledge of Oecolampadius, Luther, and Erasmus and contact with humanist theological circles in Freiburg and Basel.[9] By the time of Hubmaier's participation in the First Disputation on the Eucharist, held in Zurich in 1523, he had obviously crossed over to the evangelical movement. At this time he began to introduce fragments of liturgical innovation into the life of his congregation in Waldshut. How that part of the story unfolded is attended to later in the chapter.

In company with other evangelical reformers, Hubmaier insisted that the Roman Church had misunderstood the atonement. He saw this misunderstanding tied to the expression it had been given in the Lord's Supper and regarded it as the root of the church's sickness. In the fifth of his *Achtzehn Schlussreden* (18 Concluding Statements), written in 1524 in the spirit of the Zurich Disputation of the previous year, Hubmaier asserts that the mass is not a sacrifice and cannot be offered up for the living or the dead.[10] In his initial posture as a reformer, Hubmaier saw the mass as a repetition of Christ's sacrifice and therefore repudiated the mass as a precondition for the restoration of the church. He adopted a Christology which made impossible a traditional belief in the corporeal presence of Christ in the sacrament. Only thus did Hubmaier think he could be successful in doing battle against the mass as a sacrifice. That is to say, if Christ in his physical nature were in heaven, he could not be offered as a sacrifice again on an altar.

Hubmaier had a second preoccupation, the human response to grace and the freedom of the will. This conviction turned him as much against the magisterial reformers as against Catholicism. Zwingli's emphasis in his teaching on the sacraments and the church was on the divine will. The Catholic sacramental doctrine was another way of making the same claim: *ex opere operato,* effective by virtue of the action, without depending on the merits of minister or recipient.[11] By means of commonplace Catholic anthropology, Hubmaier opposed the Catholic sacraments. Hubmaier argued that because human nature was in possession of a free will, it was possible for people to repent and accept the grace offered them. From this anthropological basis, he asserted that the church could and must be a voluntary community of believers and that Lord's Supper was a pledge to live out the grace previously given.

We need to sketch out Hubmaier's understanding of human nature. In his tripartite anthropology, human flesh is completely fallen. The soul is imprisoned in the flesh, but the spirit is not totally the captive of fallen human nature. The saving power of Christ's work on the cross was such that human beings can regain the freedom of their will as it existed before the Fall. Through the Fall, the flesh lost its goodness and freedom irrevocably. Through it also, the soul was afflicted with a sickness unto death: it had lost its knowledge of good and evil. The imprisonment of the soul is only partially overcome in redemption. The spirit is inseparable from both flesh and soul, but unfallen. In redemption, the soul is united with the spirit; together they make the flesh their prisoner.[12]

Hubmaier built his theology on medieval anthropological motifs different from those held by the magisterial reformers. His beliefs about human nature stand in especially sharp contrast to those of Luther and Calvin. From the vantage point of his older anthropology, Hubmaier was convinced that belief in both the bondage of the will and predestination violates the biblical picture of the human will and undermines human responsibility before God. On this foundation, Hubmaier makes his most radical assertion: baptism and the Lord's Supper are human acts of commitment in response to grace. Rollin Armour summarizes the matter nicely by pointing out that for Hubmaier, freedom of the will is the corollary to the doctrine of believers baptism.[13]

Before we examine details of Hubmaier's views, we need to survey the components of his intellectual landscape and their role in the development of his ideas. The spiritualistic tendency of the late Middle Ages, in its parental Augustinian form as well as that of its sacramentarian offspring, has been identified in the introduction to this study. As our examination of Hubmaier proceeds, we shall see that two contesting influences vie with each other in his thought. His Christology shows a spiritualistic tendency which works itself out negatively in his sacramentology. On the other hand, his ecclesiology is incarnationist and results in a positive reconstruction of the concept of sacrament. The spiritualistic critique of existing sacramental thought and practice has chronological priority in Hubmaier. Without it, the development of his thought cannot be understood. The working out of this bias in his writing came through the impact of his contemporaries; they were foils for him, stepping-stones toward convictions which transcended all of them. I will demonstrate this as the development of Hubmaier's thought is documented.

At the same time that Hubmaier resisted the anthropological innovations of the Reformation, he was caught up in the spiritualistic tendencies which had existed unofficially for some time and were given confessional status by the non-Lutheran reformers. What Hubmaier believed about faith ruled out entirely the notion of *ex opere operato* sacramental reality. He assumed the existence of an ontological barrier between spirit and matter. By faith, the Christian now lived in the realm of spirit.

Hubmaier was not satisfied with the innovative reinterpretation of sacraments advanced in the writings of the Dutch sacramentarian Cornelius Hoen (1524?) and its radicalization in the eucharistic thought of Zwingli. Hoen held that by faith Christ was mystically present in the Supper.[14] Zwingli went further than Hoen but still allowed the elements a symbolic role in relation to communion with Christ.[15] Even Hubmaier's most radical colleague, Karlstadt, was not consistent enough for him. Pater summarizes the revolutionary conclusions of Karlstadt in the following words. "Karlstadt erases the traditional *res* [thing] and *signum* [sign] relationship. *Res* and *signum* have been severed."[16] But even Karlstadt allows the element a symbolic role in relation to the action of Christ in the sacrament.

In the following detailed examination of Hubmaier's texts, we shall see that he has left behind all such reinterpretation of sacramental language—where God is the actor and the communicant is a recipient of Christ in some relation to the element. He sees the *est-significat* (is-signifies) debate as the perpetuation of a frame of reference he has already rejected. For him, the Spirit rather than the Son is the divine presence in the church since Christ's ascension. It is his nature to work inwardly, without external manifestations. The outward actions of the church are its response of obedience to previously given grace. In Hubmaier's scheme the ceremony of Lord's Supper becomes a mutual act of love on the part of the community toward its members and the world. In itself the breaking of bread is not an event of grace and faith by the individual or the community toward God.

The radicality of Hubmaier's sacramental thought is not accounted for solely by his attachment to late medieval Augustinianism as it evolved in a sacramentarian and spiritualistic direction. His originality consisted, in part, in borrowing aspects of Luther's thought, especially his understanding of the word as the primal means of God's action and presence. That great reformer knew Augustine's words, "When the word is joined to the element, the sacrament is effected; the word becomes the visible sign." Luther made use of this dictum to critique the popular Catholic understanding and practice of sacraments in his day.[17] He also employed *word* and *faith* as Augustine had formulated them to put into question the *ex opere operato* function of sacraments. Windhorst concludes:

In the close, indispensable link between faith and sacrament, in which faith may always be seen to arise from the basis of the word, Hubmaier thinks along Lutheran lines.[18]

The sacramentarian and Lutheran sources of Hubmaier's ideas meshed with and interpenetrated each other. Sometimes, as an examination of his writings shows, this encounter was disjointed, but it was always more than a simple juxtaposition of principles from separate sources. The larger thrust of Hubmaier's eucharistic thought led him to creatively use both of the dominant schools of Reformation thought.

The Structure of Hubmaier's Theology of the Sacraments
Preliminary Definitions

Hubmaier's writing has an eclectic character. He borrowed successively from the dominant schools of Catholic and Reformation thought. Some strands of his theology, like the antitransubstantiationism which stands at the beginning of his eucharistic writing, are essentially a negation of positions he held to be inadequate. But his novel syntheses, like the application of his anthropology to the Lord's Supper, result in a positive theology which was more than the sum of its parts.

The building blocks for Hubmaier's sacramental edifice are his anthropology, ecclesiology, and Christology. Thus we will pay attention to these categories in the following examination of Hubmaier's writings. In order to supply a framework for the detailed investigation of Hubmaier's writings on the Lord's Supper, several typical descriptions of what he understood by *sacrament* and *Lord's Supper* will be quoted or summarized. The most concise statement of what he believed is taken from the concluding commentary of his baptismal liturgy.

> We have called the water of baptism, like the bread and wine of the altar, a *sacrament*, and keep the word for that. Yet not the water, bread, or wine but rather the baptismal commitment or the pledge of love is really and truly *sacrament* in the Latin—that is, a commitment by oath and a pledge given by the hand, which the baptized one gives to Christ.[19]

The oath replaces the baptismal water and the covenant replaces the eucharistic bread and wine as the object of the ceremony. This human action of oath-taking and covenant-making remains the primary definition of a sacrament. Elsewhere, Hubmaier specifies further that baptism and the Lord's Supper are signs, instituted by Christ to gather a church, to pledge oneself outwardly to live according to the word of

Christ in faith and brotherly love, and because of sin, to submit oneself to discipline and the ban.[20]

It is noteworthy that the memorial of the Supper is not a devotional contemplation of the crucifixion of Christ. It is an ethical summons to imitate Jesus' surpassing act of self-giving. Just as Jesus offered himself for me, I ought to offer myself for others. Behind this summons stands a view of the atonement in which the sinner is accordingly made to be able and willing to act as Jesus acted.[21]

> Thus as the body and blood of Christ became my body and blood on the cross, so likewise shall my body and blood become the body and blood of my neighbor, and in time of need theirs become my body and blood, or we cannot boast at all to be Christians. That is the will of Christ in the Supper.[22]

Hubmaier's most precisely formulated definition of the secondary meaning of the Eucharist is derived from his exegesis of the words of institution in Luke and Paul. This is the crucial formulation: the bread of the Supper is the body of Christ in remembrance.[23] The body of Christ kept in memory (*in der gehaltnen Gedechness*) stands over against the body of Christ substantially (*wesenlich*).[24] In Hubmaier's judgment, only the former usage can be derived from the accounts of the Last Supper.

The "body of Christ kept in memory" is a description of what happens in the breaking of bread. It is a contrasting concept to the "body of Christ substantially" and also to the body of Christ as the church. Hubmaier's thought develops to a second stage in which this latter definition becomes the decisive one. He progresses away from the term *body* as a reference to Christ's corporeal presence and toward the action and being of the church. This allows him to restructure the signification in the Lord's Supper. In it the *res,* the body, has become the church. It follows from this that the dominical ceremonies of baptism and the Lord's Supper are not means of grace but responses to grace. Their agent is not God but the church and, within the church, the believers in it. These signs are part of what constitutes the church because they embody the condition of its existence, that is, the response of faith and obedience. For Hubmaier, *sacraments* are human pledges and witnesses that the gospel has been believed and acted on. In that indirect sense only are they signs that God is present and at work.

The work of the Holy Spirit has a prominent place in Hubmaier's scheme. The Spirit's work is prior to and separate from all human ceremonies. The word is allotted a mediating function between the Spirit and the individual believer. God's presence comes in the Spirit, who is given by means of the word. The Spirit's work alone is life-giving. It assures the believer of eternal life. This action of the Spirit stands in contrast to our action with bread and wine, tokens of Christ's love, with which we remember that he died for us.[25] The divine word comes through the Spirit to promise the forgiveness of sins. The work of the Spirit is inward, within the person.[26] The Spirit uses the preached word to work inwardly.[27] The carnal side of human nature finds no peace outwardly before the preached word nor inwardly in the Spirit.[28] Here the word, without any relationship to the elements, functions sacramentally as the outward sign and means of an inward reality.

Developments in Hubmaier's Eucharistic Thought
Beginnings

We now proceed from the matter of definitions to examine the unfolding of Hubmaier's beliefs concerning the Lord's Supper. The initial piece of evidence relevant to our interest comes from the earliest phase of Hubmaier's unambiguous commitment to radical reformation. It is documented in the proceedings of the Second Disputation in Zurich in October 1523.[29] Its subjects were images and the mass. By this time Hubmaier had moved from Catholicism through the Lutheran-influenced phase to a period in which his own thinking paralleled that of the reformation in Zurich. In his lengthiest contribution to this disputation, Hubmaier enunciates his theology of the Lord's Supper. He begins by identifying his views with those of Jud and Zwingli.[30] Hubmaier proceeds to define sacrament as "an outward, visible sign and seal through which we are completely assured of the forgiveness of our sins."[31] From there, Hubmaier continues with points concerning the Eucharist, which he says follow from his definition:

1. The mass cannot be a sacrifice for anyone either living or dead; it is a sign instituted to anchor the faith of the one who believes.
2. Since the *body* and *blood* of Christ are tokens and seals of the words of Christ, nothing other than the word should be proclaimed in the mass. [Here, as elsewhere, traditional language is employed. The way it is used, however, is a clear departure from custom.]
3. Where there is no proclamation of the word, there is no mass.
4. The mass should be said in the vernacular.
5. Whenever the mass is held, the whole congregation should join the presider in receiving communion.[32]

While these claims express Hubmaier's earliest participation in eucharistic reform, they fall short of his mature theology on the matter. In 1523, the Zurich reformation was still reforming in continuity with Catholic tradition. For Hubmaier at this time, the sacrament of holy communion was still a visible sign which offers assurance of the forgiveness of sins. In his later writing, Hubmaier radicalized his views such that the sacrament was no longer a divinely instituted and effective sign of forgiveness but a human witness to it. This is not to understate the significance of the position articulated at the Second Disputation. It was the seedbed of the Zurich reformation. From it, the radical Reformed and Anabaptist trees were to grow.

It is worth looking at the liturgical profiles of Zwingli and Conrad Grebel (the future leader of the Swiss Brethren) which emerged in the course of that disputation. Both men left distinctive theological and liturgical marks on Hubmaier. Grebel's comments follow Hubmaier's five points and show his adamant biblicism and the ensuing preoccupation with external form. He opposes the use of unleavened bread by means of dominical example.[33] Zwingli urges Grebel not to try to prove too much, but the latter presses on to argue with equal severity that no scriptural precedent exists for the mixing of water with wine. The altercation is repeated when Grebel interrupts Zwingli's proposal of deacons to distribute the elements. He insists that all communicants take the elements for themselves.

Karlstadt's innovation in the Christmas mass of 1521 is the probable precedent for Grebel's argument; in any case, it suggests a greater affinity between Grebel and Karlstadt than between Grebel and Zwingli in their approach to liturgical reform. Ecclesiological assumptions stand in the background of this distinction: Karlstadt was already at this early date the advocate of an independent church, anticlerical and prolaity to the point where they could administer the sacraments.[34]

These instances clearly show that Zwingli had a less stringent biblicism than the radicals. His less literalistic attitude gave his spiritualism greater scope. Zwingli's later writings made it explicit that the external life of the church was not one with its internal reality.[35] For the Grebel circle and Hubmaier, the two were inseparable. Therefore, it mattered greatly, for example, whether the deacon gave the bread in communion or whether each communicant took it for oneself. The two practices expressed different understandings of the church.

The Zwinglian Influence

The christological presuppositions of Zwingli's reformation, especially as they expressed themselves eucharistically, set the direction of

Hubmaier's beliefs as well. Three related aspects of Zwingli's thought are of decisive significance for Hubmaier. All of them deal with faith and its object in light of Christ and his saving work. They are (1) faith and Jesus' sacrifice, (2) faith and the ascended Christ, and (3) faith as the opposite of idolatry. The first eucharistic principle in the as-yet-undivided reformation in Zurich was that the mass was not a sacrifice.[36] The once-for-all sacrifice of Jesus was not repeated in the mass; it could be appropriated only by faith in the historical fact of the Lord's death.[37] For Zwingli and his followers, in contrast to Luther, sacrifice and real presence in the traditional categories were inseparable. Gottfried Locher explains that

> Zwingli's protest against Luther's sacramental realism did not arise from rationalism but from his Christology, out of concern for the complete and exclusive validity of the atonement which he had made on the cross.[38]

Locher goes on to explain Zwingli's alternative to sacramentally mediated grace. The means of grace since the ascension of Christ is the Holy Spirit. The Spirit alone is the one who mediates the work of Christ to the believer. Nothing external can do that. Outward actions can have no role as causes in the realm of the Spirit.[39] Here is the result of this trinitarian postulate, in which the Spirit is the mode of the divine presence in the life of the church: the relationship between Christ and the breaking of bread is a historical one. The Supper sets forth his atoning death and recalls to the assembled believers that there alone salvation is to be found. What the sacrament signifies is not the presence of Christ in the world now, but his incarnation and sacrifice. Memory is the mode of contact between sign and thing signified.

The consequence Zwingli drew from this was that Christ's presence is causally separated from the elements of bread and wine entirely. At the same time, he did not gainsay the event character of the Eucharist; he separated what happens in the communion service from the elements. In his new order of the Supper, introduced at Easter 1525, the transformation which takes place is that of the congregation rather than of the elements. In the comments and prayers which replace the canon of the mass, the people are referred to three times as the "body of Christ." The term is avoided in reference to the bread.[40]

Note that the notions which defined the Lord's Supper for Zwingli and those in his sphere of influence were not original to them. The novelty associated with these concepts lay in the new status given to them. This is true, for example, of the concept of memorial as well as applying to the congregation the concept of transformation. The church as the mystical body of Christ was foundational for Augustine's eucharistic thought, though not as an alternative to his sacramental body.[41] It was also explicitly present in Luther. In his thought, the transformation of the people paralleled the change in the elements. But this aspect was only one of twenty-two characteristics which distinguished the breaking of bread.[42]

The Zurich reformation's radicality consisted of two inseparable parts. The traditional dimensions of the Eucharist were reduced to those which could be retained and even made more prominent after any metaphysical correlation between bread and wine and Christ's body and blood had been repudiated. Hubmaier's innovative reductionism, abetted by his ecclesiology, turned out to be greater than Zwingli's.

For example, in Zwingli's *On the Lord's Supper* of 1526, he crisply sets forth his position for the common people. The essential argument still revolves around the nature of a sacrament rather than the faith of the congregation gathered to celebrate it: "A sacrament is the sign of a holy thing."[43] The reference here is clearly to Augustine's schema of *res* and *signum*. Zwingli points out that sign and thing signified cannot be the same. Using such traditional arguments, Zwingli justifies his doctrine of the Lord's Supper. Because he has returned to the Scriptures and the fathers, Zwingli insists in his book *On the Lord's Supper* that he has been able to understand the eucharistic problem in a new way. The *anamnēsis* (remembrance) in the communion becomes the foundation of this novel understanding. What is meant by *sacrifice* is not signified by the elements but by the worshiping community. The sacrifice was the self-offering of the saints.[44]

The Hubmaier Synthesis

These notions were entirely compatible with Hubmaier's perception of the breaking of bread as a human response to the divine initiative. They provided him with a prototype for his even more radical departure from tradition. We shall see below, as Hubmaier's thought unfolds, that he completely broke with the conventional eucharistic schema as it had been formulated since the time of Augustine. Was Hubmaier's opposition to the mass so rigid on the matter of sacrifice that he was unable to reinterpret its traditional components? Was his biblicism so strong that he shied away from Zwingli's continued use of classical sacramental language? It can be assumed from our earlier examination of Hubmaier's anthropology that he was not naive or unpracticed in scholastic thought. Adherence to such thought would have been as politically helpful for him as it was for Zwingli because both of them wanted to reform the existing church.

Because of his radical antipathy to what he perceived to be the materialism of medieval eucharistic doctrine, only the most extreme break with that tradition was possible for Hubmaier. His opposition to the mass was such that he was unable to reuse its language. His biblicism alienated him from classical sacramental concepts, yet in this matter his stance was not categorically different from that of other reformers. What took Hubmaier decisively beyond the reformation at Zurich was his understanding of faith and of the church. Faith as a willed response of obedience and church as the voluntary pact of those who had come to faith—these provided him with an outward historical entity which enacted the sacraments.

Neither the sacrament *ex opere operato* nor the priest by virtue of his sacral office was the agent of the action. An ontological shift followed in which the visible church became the *res* referred to by the *signum.* That is to say, for Hubmaier the breaking of bread became preeminently a sign of the church and its covenant of obedience. Only in a lingering way, which was to be gradually displaced, did the Supper continue to be an immediate sign of Christ. With these assumptions, which had taken him to the boundary of conventional eucharistic thought, Hubmaier returned to Waldshut to carry out a radical reformation. His subsequent writings built on interpretations to which he had come through his participation in the Zurich reformation. The association continued both with Zwingli and with the established church, as well as with the disestablished visions for reform in Zurich.

In his first publication, the *Achtzehn Schlussreden* (*Achtzehn:* Eighteen Concluding Statements) from the spring of 1524, Hubmaier summarizes his ideas on church order. Much of what he said in Zurich half a year earlier is included. The mass is not a sacrifice but a memorial (conclusion 5). Proclamation of the word of God defines both the priest and the liturgy (conclusion 12). The mass should be said in the vernacular (conclusions 6, 10). At other points, the sacrificial and priestly character of the Eucharist is undone. The baptized and believing individual can judge the pastor on the basis of Scripture. Each Christian has direct access to Christ as mediator (conclusions 8-9).[45] The effect of these claims is to take from the priest and sacrament their mediatorial role.

Etliche Schlussreden vom Unterricht der Messe (*Messe:* Several Theses Concerning the Mass) from the year 1525 is the first step in

Hubmaier's peculiar development of the theology of the Lord's Supper beyond the common ground he shares with his mentors. By way of introduction to this proposal, Hubmaier sets forth what is involved in the breaking of bread. The Lord's Supper is (1) the memorial of Christ's suffering, (2) the proclamation of his death, and (3) an outer symbol to signify how he gave up his body and blood for us so that we may do so for our neighbor.[46] Near the end of *Messe*, this trilogy is repeated as a summary of what makes the Lord's Supper different from another meal.[47]

In their introduction to this treatise, Westin and Bergsten identify its content with Zwingli's thought, noting one exegetical addendum from Karlstadt.[48] This assessment underestimates the originality at work in Hubmaier's borrowing. The three claims he has taken over from Zwingli become the departure point for a synthesis of several sources. In the next paragraph of *Messe*, where "this is my body" is taken to refer to Jesus' corporeal presence at the Last Supper, Hubmaier's debt to Karlstadt is clear. This is the case also with Hubmaier's use of the image of many kernels and one loaf.[49]

In this text, Hubmaier lists tenets not organically related to each other. This suggests two things. First, the tenets come from several sources. Second, *Messe* is a preliminary document sketching out as-yet-undeveloped ideas. This is especially evident in the next reference to the Spirit. The life-giving power is the Spirit who comes with the word.[50] The Spirit, as present with the word, assures the believer of eternal life. Bread and wine point away from themselves to the Spirit, who comes with the word. In Hubmaier's later writings, including his major treatise on the Holy Supper, *Ein Einfältiger Unterricht (Einfältiger: A Simple Instruction)*, the Spirit has no temporal relationship to the event of the breaking of bread. The Spirit works without references to visible signs.

This absolute distinction between spirit and matter revolutionizes the sign character of the Supper. Its elements of bread and wine have an ethical rather than a metaphysical sign character in relation to Christ. As the second person of the Trinity, wholly divine and wholly human in one person, Christ has ascended to heaven. There are tangential references to Christ's presence in the church, but they are never developed nor are they introduced in conjunction with the Lord's Supper. Though Hubmaier nowhere denies the presence of Christ in his divine nature in the ongoing course of history, he makes no use of this dogma in constructing his theology of the Lord's Supper. Only in an ethical sense is Christ's life in his humanity prolonged in the life of the church. Thus, the memorial reference is of a piece with the emphasis on the church as his body in the world. Both of them are immanent and not transcendent realities. Bread and wine, it follows, are tokens (*Wortzaichen*) of Christ's love by which we remember his gift of love and our calling to love.[51] We are the bread and the body.[52]

The unmistakable implication of this progression of thought in *Messe* is that the life-giving work of the Spirit is separate from and prior to the sacrament.[53] This sequence and separation is made clearer in Hubmaier's baptismal theology.[54] Through the word, faith is given and eternal life assured. In the power of this established certainty, the church celebrates the Supper. Therefore, to detach the sign character of the Eucharist from Christ and attach it to the church is not, in Hubmaier's conception of things, to reduce it. Its proper function is that of an oath or pledge made visibly and collectively by a community which has received grace.

The evolution in Hubmaier's eucharistic thought is illustrated by his reworking of the notion of the communion of the body and blood of Christ within the text of *Messe*. When Hubmaier turns to the Pauline concept of the "communion of the body of Christ," he interprets as follows:

> For the bread which we break means and commemorates the communion of the body of Christ with us, that he is our own, for he gave his body for us through the drink of the communion of his blood which he poured out for the forgiveness of our sin.
>
> (Dann das brot, das wir brechen ist inn der bedeutung und inn der widergedechtnuss die gemainschaft des leybs Christi mit vns, das er vnser aygen sey, wann er ye den selben fur uns hab das geben durch das trank dz gemainschaffts seins bluts, das er zu verzeihung vnser sind vergossen hat.)[55]

Hubmaier is in the process of reinterpreting the foundational eucharistic concept, formulated here in the Pauline language of the "communion of the body and blood of Christ." In its meaning and in its *anamnetic* role, the bread is the communion of the body of Christ. The grammatical structure of these lines is obscure. The sense of the text is that we remember, through the drink of the communion of his blood, that this blood was shed for the forgiveness of our sins. The obvious antecedent for "the same" (*den selben*) is "the communion of the body of Christ" (*die gemainschaft des leybs Christi*). The text is claiming that through participation in the bread and cup, we commune with the body and blood of Christ.

When, however, the author moves beyond his cryptic formulation to an explanation, nothing is said about communion with Christ. In the next sentence, which begins a new paragraph, the communion is not with Christ, as expected, but with one another (*mit ainander*). In the remainder of *Messe*, nothing is said to reinforce the suggestion that Christ is received through the outer communion of bread and wine. The quotation under examination seems to be a remnant of the traditional view of the mass, temporarily existing side by side with elements which are soon to squeeze it out.

The permanent direction Hubmaier's eucharistic thought will take is charted by his redefinition of the whole eucharistic terminology. In the comment already referred to in *Messe*, Hubmaier asserts that we, the congregation, are the bread. From this he concludes that unworthiness at the Lord's table consists in not letting oneself, as a grain of wheat, be ground together with others. This idea is suggested in the final paragraph of the treatise where, in lucid and imaginative language, the essence of Hubmaier's thought on the Lord's Supper is restated.

> We conclude that the bread and wine of the Christ meal are outward word symbols of an inward Christian nature here on earth, in which a Christian obligates himself to another.[56]

In this summary, Hubmaier makes it clear that bread and wine are outer signs of an inner essence here on earth. This essence is the Christian covenant of love. The Lord's Supper is still a sacrament in the formal sense: it has an outward symbolic part and an inward reality. That reality is the church's covenant of love. But the role of a sacrament as a bridge between the human and the divine has been rejected. The will of Christ in Holy Communion is that

> as the body and blood of Christ became my body and blood on the cross, so likewise shall my body and blood become the body and blood of my neighbor.[57]

We thus conclude that *Messe* is a creative but still transitional document, the foundation of Hubmaier's mature teaching on the Eucharist. By the end of *Messe*, the die has been cast. All other notions will be cut on the hard iron of the Lord's Supper as a symbol of love between brothers and sisters. The Lord's Supper is supremely an ethical reality.

Lest one assume, however, that behind this emerging doctrine of the Holy Supper stands a theology of good works, it is necessary to recall that Hubmaier is unequivocal about the initiative of God's grace in saving humanity. That imitation of Christ's love which Hubmaier enjoins is possible only by grace and by the presence of the Spirit. In *Von der christlichen Taufe* (*Taufe:* On Christian Baptism), Hubmaier makes certain that his hearers understand this.[58] The prevenience of grace is vouchsafed by Hubmaier's understanding of the ubiquity of the Spirit. Everything salvific is the work of the Spirit; even the symbolic role of Hubmaier's ceremonies is meaningless unless it is clear that they point to the life-giving work of the Spirit which precedes them.[59] Hubmaier's pneumatology safeguards the work of grace in relation to an anthropology, ecclesiology, and Christology in which human response rather than divine initiative is emphasized.

In these aspects of his theology, Hubmaier pursues an extreme corrective to the course set by Luther, whose anthropology is well summarized in the dictum, *simul justus et peccator* (simultaneously righteous and sinner). Hubmaier posits the full restoration of free will. His understanding of the church presupposes that Christians can imitate Christ. Anthropocentrism is the almost inevitable outcome when one brings those positions together with a concept of the Trinity in which the second person is in heaven and his earthly role is confined to that of a historical figure. But Hubmaier's anthropology, ecclesiology, and Christology are all interpreted by his pneumatology; it is the hermeneutical key not only to the sacramental but to all aspects of his theology.

Hubmaier's Biblical Interpretation

Hubmaier's exegetical work at once informs and follows from the three presuppositions we have illustrated in the preceding sections of this chapter. First, since his ascension Christ himself is not, at least directly, the medium of God's presence in the church. Second, this role belongs to the Holy Spirit. The Spirit's only outward medium is the word. Neither the Spirit nor the word can be identified with outward ceremonies. Third, the Lord's Supper is the sign of the church as the body of Christ in the world. It is the response of brother, sister, and neighbor love to previously given grace. This cluster of convictions sets Hubmaier free from the need to reconcile his biblical investigation with traditional interpretations of any of his presuppositions. It allows him to continue the momentum of his innovative approach by transferring it from the general to the particular.

Hubmaier claims the Bible as the only norm for Christian faith and practice. In his treatment of baptism, his presuppositions and method become clear.[60] In *Ein Gespräch auf Zwinglis Taufbüchlin* (*Gespräch*: Dialogue with Zwingli's Baptism Book), Hubmaier charges that Zwingli's exegesis of a baptismal text rejects the "right, natural understanding" of the passage. Hubmaier goes on to accuse him of doing the same with the words of institution of the Lord's Supper. There is neither need nor reason in the text to substitute *significat* for *est.*[61] Hubmaier is apprehensive about the very instance of interpretation which was to be the turning point in Zwingli's mature theology of the Eucharist![62]

Here Hubmaier's astonishing rejection of an interpretation consonant with the evolution of his own position suggests two things. First, his biblicism is a deeply rooted disposition and not merely an expedient way of dealing with his opponent's use of Scripture to justify infant baptism. Second, Hubmaier finds Zwingli to be anachronistic in his decision to remain *within* the traditional eucharistic frame of reference.

All of this is not to say that Hubmaier's biblicism is simple and straightforward. This is apparent in his chief work on the Eucharist, *Einfältiger*, written some months later in 1526. In it Hubmaier proposes exegetical rules according to which one may arrive at the true meaning of a passage. Where there is a conflict between the literal reading of a text and his theological position, Hubmaier abandons the strict literalism he has previously asserted in his altercation with Zwingli.

We turn now to an analysis of *Einfältiger*, Hubmaier's most substantive exegetical work on the Lord's Supper. It begins with a summary of fifteen different medieval understandings of the Eucharist.[63] Hubmaier concludes that the confusion and disunity they have brought about does not hurt the Christian who tests everything by faith and turns to God alone for understanding. The confusion evident in the past is increased in the present by theologians who proffer tropistic interpretations of the sacred text. One claims that "this is my body" refers not to the bread but to Jesus himself (Karlstadt). Another forces Scripture to claim that "this signifies my body" (Zwingli). Others speak of a figurative body.[64] Hubmaier is worried by the arbitrary nature of tropistic exegesis: "For if this is the practice then no one would be certain as to where *est* [is] stands in the Scripture for *significat* [signifies] or for itself."[65] He proceeds to argue that there is equal precedent in Scripture to argue a literal antecedent for the words of institution. Linguistically, it is quite possible to support a literal rendering of *est* in the case under consideration.

Hubmaier is grateful for the conclusion reached by his contemporaries, that bread is bread and wine is wine. But he volunteers a more faithfully biblical way of arriving at that position. This way is based on three hermeneutical rules. The first one is to interpret an obscure passage in light of a plain one. Relating this principle to the controversy concerning the Eucharist, Hubmaier contends that the Lukan and Pauline versions of the institutional narrative are not as brief as the Matthean and Marcan ones and must be used to clarify the meaning of the latter. In the decisive expansion of the narrative in Luke and Paul, Jesus commands, "Do this in remembrance of me."[66] This means that the bread is the body of Christ in memory (*in der gedechtnuss*).

At this juncture, Hubmaier introduces his second hermeneutical rule: Preceding words should be understood in relation to those that follow them. Now his manner of exegesis changes from setting forth the "natural" meaning of words to analyzing them according to principles of logic. He admits that a literal reading of the passage in question leads to the conclusion that the broken bread is the body of Christ.[67] But a logical study of the text leads to quite another conclusion, as follows. We know from the story of Jesus' Last Supper that the bread he broke was not crucified for us. So the bread could only be his body in memory. Expanding the application of the second interpretive principle, Hubmaier argues that the eating of the bread is not a feeding on Christ's body because that body is at the right hand of the Father in heaven. What we now do is to eat in faith that the Lord's body was martyred for us.

The third rule of interpretation is that difficult passages may be understood by comparing them with similar forms of speech. When we look at a picture, we say, for example, That is Mrs. S. What we mean is, That is she in memory.[68]

Anticipating a challenge to his position, Hubmaier lists five criticisms and refutes them by means of his hermeneutical rules. The only novelty comes in response to the fifth criticism.[69] He asks, How do you make sense out of Jesus' assertion that he would not again drink of the fruit of the vine until he does so in the kingdom of God? This question prompts Hubmaier to turn to a different text with a different description of the breaking of bread. The story in Luke 24 tells of Jesus' encounter with his followers on the road to Emmaus. It concerns not the doomed Savior at a farewell meal with his disciples but a victorious Lord seeking to convince his friends that he is with them. The unique character of this eucharistic incident is not acknowledged by Hubmaier. He sees the meal at Emmaus strictly as a parallel to the Last Supper. This becomes clear from his comment on the announcement his disciples make, that Jesus is risen. It is portrayed by Hubmaier as a vindication of Paul's claim that as often as the church observes the feast, it proclaims the Lord's death.

The next stage in Hubmaier's exegetical progression consists of six texts with which he intends to show that "Christ does not come to us in his essence until he shall come in the hour of the last judgment."[70] The first account is Matthew's version of the words of institution. Five deductions relevant to liturgical practice are made from it. The first one is that the disciples ate together. It follows from this that no one can hold the Supper alone, whether one be sick or well. The purpose of this claim is undoubtedly to invalidate private masses, the reservation of the sacrament for the sick, and masses where a congregation does not commune and only the priest partakes.

Another deduction is that *blessing* (*benedeyen*) and *consecrating* (*consecrierung*) are not the same. To bless God is to thank or praise him. This, rather than a change in the elements, is the purpose of prayer at the breaking of bread. A third deduction from the text for purposes of worship comes from the dominical instruction to take bread, not to give it or offer it up. A fourth conclusion is that the bread is to be eaten—not elevated, divided into three, dipped into wine, or carried in procession or reservation. The last deduction from the Matthean record is that all table guests are to drink the cup.[71]

Next the author returns to the Marcan record of the words of institution. From it he points out that the disciples were instructed to drink the cup, after which Jesus made the comment, "This is my blood." How then, Hubmaier asks, could these words have the power to transform wine into blood if they were uttered after it had been consumed?[72]

From the Corinthian institutional narrative, Hubmaier makes a novel deduction concerning the phrase "in remembrance of me." Jesus said that so his followers would not focus on his visible, natural body. "The summation and final purpose" of the Lord's Supper is to be a remembrance (*widergedechtnuss*), a point of reflection (*denckzaichen*), and a reminder (*ermanung*) of Christ's suffering—and not a sacrifice.[73] This is to be done until he comes. It follows that he is not present.

> If he were present, then we would hold the Supper in vain and against the words of Christ and Paul. For where a person is essentially and bodily present, there a remembrance is not necessary.[74]

The last three biblical excerpts all come from the Acts of the Apostles. Their purpose is to show that Christ is in heaven. Later we will refer to these passages for their christological significance.

These fragments of textual analysis mark the end of Hubmaier's exegetical work in *Einfältiger*. Having summarized them, we now turn to an assessment of their individual and cumulative significance for Hubmaier's teaching on the Lord's Supper. One of his crucial hermeneutical decisions is to give priority to the longer institutional narratives in Luke and Paul. He contends that it is the totality of Jesus' words, interpreted by the longer ending, which yields their true meaning.

> From all these words follows the final conclusion that the bread offered, broken, taken, and eaten is the body of Christ in remembrance.[75]

From whence comes the formulation, "This is the body of Christ in remembrance"? It obviously does not come verbatim from any of the Scriptures under scrutiny. This interpretive epigram is not typical of Zwingli or Karlstadt, the two theologians referred to by Hubmaier who are closest to him. Likely this turn of phrase comes from Hubmaier himself because it so nicely solves two of the problems with which he is faced. It preserves the literal force of *est* (over against Zwingli's tropism) while at the same time making a corporeal presence impossible because the bread is the body only in remembrance. The action which takes place in communion is not the priestly consecrating of bread but the communal response of recollecting.

The difficulty with Hubmaier's exegetical work on the eucharistic passages is that his conclusions are not as strictly drawn from individual texts as he claims them to be. To be sure, exegesis and doctrine always coexist in a dialectical relationship. The exegetes use the fruit of their labor to give substance to what they believe. At the same time, their doctrinal commitments determine the vantage point from which the text is perceived. This fact becomes problematic in Hubmaier's case because he commits himself to deriving his theological claims only from the "right, natural meaning" of the text—in contrast to what he sees his detractors doing. But repeatedly, christological assumptions imported from beyond the passage in question, in tandem with exercises in logic, take him beyond what his text permits.

Christologically speaking, Hubmaier's point of departure is the ascension. His eucharistic ideas are plausible only if the Christ who broke the bread and whose body was broken has left the plane of history. Classical Christian theology confesses the ascension of Christ but, by means of its trinitarian doctrine, continues to claim that the Son is present in history. To keep the present discussion within the frame-

work of this chapter, we shall concern ourselves with Christology only
to the extent that it bears directly on Hubmaier's beliefs about the Supper. For Hubmaier, the ascension of Christ removes him from the plane
of history. The Eucharist as a memorial says all that can be said
christologically. Therefore, the *anamnēsis* becomes a limiting characteristic and a precondition for its second aspect, the Supper as pledge.
That will be explained below.

Two levels of logic come into play when Hubmaier applies his
second hermeneutical rule: preceding words may be understood in
light of those which follow them. By juxtaposing "bread" and "body,"
the institutional narrative logically implies that bread is the body of
Christ. But if we think logically, at a deeper level, about the meaning
rather than simply the progression of words in the text, we conclude
that the bread could not be identical with the body since the bread was
not crucified for us.[76]

Hubmaier's third interpretive principle, in which similar forms of
speech are placed beside each other, not only relies on logic but
employs it reductively. He applies his interpretive epigram, that the
bread is the body of Christ in remembrance, to a bust or a portrait. The
eucharistic bread is deemed comparable to a memento of an absent
person. But in an unexpected final turn of thought, Hubmaier's concluding comments in *Einfältiger* suddenly fix upon the mystery of the
breaking of bread! It cannot be grasped by human reason but only by
faith and obedience.[77] This is a most amazing claim because Hubmaier's
interpretive work has sought to account for every tick in the eucharistic
mechanism.

There are shortcomings in the case Hubmaier is putting forth. Its
propositions are not related to one another. They are placed on top of
one another, like stacking chairs of different designs, in the hope that
their cumulative impact will be convincing. The pile of propositions is,
like odd-sized stacking chairs, both unstable and difficult to disentan-
gle. This heaping up of propositions expresses a mind no longer at
home in the theological debate of the day, a mind on the boundary, im-
patient with other theologians' lingering preoccupation with the elements. Hubmaier is trying to break out of this captivity. He seems not to
have been plagued with the struggle other reformers endured in trying
to preserve the divine presence as the *res* to which the *signum* referred.[78]

In his formative writings, *Messe* for example, Hubmaier calls the
Lord's Supper a sign (*wortzaichen*).[79] But this nomenclature disappears
in later writings like *Einfältiger*, where he attempts to derive his

eucharistic language directly from the New Testament. We have seen that his conclusions are not purely derived from his exegetical work. At the same time, Hubmaier's engagement with the Bible moves him farther and farther from traditional sacramental language toward new terms and concepts.

Hubmaier's favorite turn of phrase, "the body of Christ in remembrance," exemplifies this tendency. The subject of the action is the church: the breaking of bread is a human means of recalling Christ and imitating him. The church as the subject of the sacrament is even more prominent in Hubmaier's second belief about the Holy Communion, the *Liebespflicht* (pledge of love). In this instance, the sign character of the Supper is stronger. The Supper is the primal sign that Christians are committed to live in love toward each other and the world.

The Eucharist as memorial is necessary in order to rule out the popular Catholic belief that each celebration of it is an effective reenacting of the sacrifice of Christ. More modest claims of the Supper as a sacrament in the Lutheran or Calvinist sense are ruled out by Hubmaier's understanding of memorial.[80] Hubmaier's use of the notion of a sacrament is primarily negative in function, making traditional sacramental claims impossible to uphold. With it in place as an insuperable defense against the views of those he considered mistaken, Hubmaier was able to occupy himself with a positive claim: the pledge of love as the heart of the Lord's Supper. In this aspect it was the sign not of a past but of a present reality.

The force of Hubmaier's revisionist momentum does not, however, lead him to *spiritualize* (internalize) the ceremonies of the New Testament. In his second foray into 1 Corinthians 11 in *Einfältiger*, this becomes unmistakable. To take the bread and cup unworthily is to be guilty of profaning the body and blood of Christ. Worthiness at the Lord's Supper, as Hubmaier understands it, consists of the following:

> But let the person examine himself, however, etc., as to whether he has real internal and intensive hunger and thirst for this bread and drink, as Christ also had when he said, "With fervor have I desired to eat the supper with you." And all this in faith, so that he wholly believes that his sins are remitted through the death of Christ. Likewise, in love, in which he obligates himself now, and with this breaking of the bread and drinking of the cup publicly before the church commits himself and promises that for the sake of his neighbor he is also willing to let his flesh and blood be broken and sacrificed, with which he has now become one bread and one drink. It is also in thanksgiving to God our heavenly Father and his only begotten Son.[81]

This passage is more in the nature of commentary on a biblical text rather than exegesis of it. Once Hubmaier is no longer fighting off rival eucharistic doctrines, he makes positive claims for the ceremony. One should hunger and thirst for this bread and wine as Christ did; one should desire it in the faith that one's sins have been remitted through Christ's death; one should pledge oneself publicly through the taking of the elements to give up self. Finally, one should give thanks.

Even though bread is not body, Hubmaier goes on to say in the next paragraph, we should have the same stake in the bread and wine as we do in the body and blood of Christ![82] His Supper must be distinguished from other meals. Whoever looks down upon or misuses the two dominical ceremonies, misuses Christ. There is awe and longing here, but it is not for meeting Christ in the event of the Lord's Supper. The breaking of bread is for those who believe that their sins are forgiven through Christ, who promise to give up their lives for others, and who are grateful for salvation. In this emphasis on the church becoming the body of Christ, there is a resonance with Augustine's notion of the mystical body.[83] The transformation, however, is not sacramental, that is, a divine pledge in which the word is added to the "element." This transformation is an ethical one, brought about by a sanctified human pledge.

By way of conclusion, the following may be said of Hubmaier's interpretation of biblical eucharistic texts. While his theology of baptism was sustainable only by means of a literal method of interpretation, his view of the Supper was not. He attempted to base his view on a literal reading, however, at the most astonishing point, where Zwingli proposed *est* in place of *significat.* This hermeneutical key was to be decisive for all reformational eucharistic doctrines to the left of Calvin. Zwingli's tropistic understanding of the words of institution was of no value to Hubmaier in penetrating their meaning in the original setting. Why this is so has been mentioned above. In brief, he found his own interpretive epigram, "the body of Christ in remembrance," to be a more faithful rendering of the biblical text.

Second, he saw the event of the breaking of bread as a pledge of love among believers. Hubmaier overturned the traditional *res* and *signum* of the sacrament. He held that the thing signified by the bread was the church.[84] This significatory role of the church is actualized in two ways. In the first instance, it is the church's faith which brings the body of Christ to remembrance. In the next case, it is the church's pledge of love which brings Christ to the neighbor. Because Hubmaier believed he had found the right interpretation of the words of institution, he did not need either Zwingli's or Karlstadt's tropism, the sacramentarian alternatives to Catholic and Lutheran biblical interpretation. This freed him to part company with Zwingli and Karlstadt at a point of revolutionary significance for the non-Lutheran Reformation.[85] The distinguishing trait of Hubmaier's eucharistic doctrine was that love displaced faith as the fundamental response called forth by and in the Supper. This completed the shift from divine to human action and did away with the need to interpret the eucharistic narratives, particularly the words of institution, in relation to a divine presence.

A final comment: the theology of the Lord's Supper before us is not as simple as it looks or as Hubmaier would have it be. His exercise in exegesis was not the initial investigation of a biblical text without prejudice or preconception. At times he laid out a passage which then finally functioned as a kind of dogmatic shorthand to summarize an already-established notion of what takes place in the Eucharist. What was sometimes implied by Hubmaier to be a straightforward literalism is actually premeditated and preconceived. This fact should caution the reader against a naive view of his biblical scholarship. He undertook a comprehensive study of the critical texts. Hubmaier's interpretive epigram, "the body of Christ in remembrance," made it clear that he was not satisfied to imitate other people's thinking, even those who were his allies. While his biblical study molded his judgment, his exegesis of the eucharistic texts also expressed an already-defined doctrine of the ceremonies of Christ and a Christology which stood behind it.

The Christology Behind the Lord's Supper

In his teaching on the Lord's Supper, Balthasar Hubmaier dissociated himself from all claims by which Christ was held in some fashion to be the present reference point for the communion elements.[86] He fashioned a Eucharist which had, instead, only a historical and an imitative relationship to Christ. The Lord was not present either to repeat his sacrifice or to mediate its fruits to believers. He was present only to the believer's act of memory. Further, the believers themselves became Christ's body as they pledged to imitate his love. As they did this, they made him present to the world. To put the matter into traditional sacramental language, the "real presence" in the Lord's Supper is that of the church. Our purpose in this chapter is to identify the Christology behind a Eucharist in which the believers' relationship with Christ is historical and imitative. The former notion Hubmaier developed by means of the memorial, the latter by means of an ecclesiology in which the church is the extension of the incarnation, collectively and individually.

Hubmaier's exaltation of the memorial to one of only two aspects of the Eucharist was made possible in the first instance by what he believed about the resurrection and ascension of Christ. Both of these dimensions of the Lord's exaltation have negative consequences for Hubmaier's eucharistic doctrine. With the departure of the incarnate Christ from the world, the second person of the Trinity is absent from history, absent from the Lord's Supper. Hubmaier qualified how Christ is absent: essentially and corporeally.[87] Yet he nowhere developed a profile of Christ's nonessential, noncorporeal presence in the world. In addition, Christ's resurrection and ascension have no immediate relationship to the Eucharist. To be sure, he spoke of them as part of the content of the church's faith in preaching, but their significance is never pursued for the Eucharist.

This is illustrated in the exegetical work Hubmaier does in *Einfältiger* on the eucharistic meal described in Luke 24. Even though Hubmaier acknowledges that the disciples recognized that Jesus was back with them when he broke the bread at Emmaus, he does not allow this fact to alter his association of the breaking of bread with the Last Supper. To do otherwise would put into question his insistence that the Supper is a memorial or testimony of a dead man.[88] The resurrection is something which happens after the institution of the Lord's Supper. It contributes nothing to the essence of the Supper. The Last Supper is the prototype for the Lord's Supper. Hubmaier binds his eucharistic doctrine to the Last Supper and to Jesus' death alone.

The appearance of the risen Lord does not change the testamental character of the meal. Hubmaier even describes it as a *letz* or farewell meal, the same term he earlier uses for the Last Supper.[89] That is to say, Jesus instituted the Lord's Supper not as the promise of his presence when his disciples broke bread in his name but as a commemoration of his absence. What Jesus instituted on the night of his betrayal did not take effect until the ninth hour on the day of his crucifixion, when he died.[90] Rather than being an unraveling of his fate in death, Jesus' resurrection, according to Hubmaier, takes him away from history rather than back into it. In *Taufe*, Hubmaier states this conclusion without qualification of any kind. When the Eucharist proclaims the Lord's death until he comes, it thereby proclaims "das er nit da ist."[91] If one understands, as Hubmaier does, that the ascension of Jesus involves his removal from history, then it makes sense to portray also his resurrection appearances as a farewell rather than a return.

Later in that same treatise, Hubmaier gathers together Scriptures which show that Christ does not essentially (*wesenlich*) come to us until the parousia. Short exegetical comments on three passages from the Acts of the Apostles illustrate his approach. The ascended Christ does not dwell in "temples built with human hands," be they monstrances or loaves of bread (Acts 7:48, KJV/NRSV).[92]

All of this gives the notion of memorial a unique intensity and centrality in Hubmaier's eucharistic thought.[93] The memorial character of the Supper of Christ is decisive not so much as the cornerstone of his teaching on the subject as it is a crowbar to pry the Lord's Supper free from the crushing weight of the medieval eucharistic edifice. As a weapon in Hubmaier's hands, the memorial broke the Supper loose from its relationship to the presence of Christ. Once that was accomplished, it became possible to make the church, in its pledge of imitative love, the thing signified by the elements. What required ritual embodiment in the community was not Christ's sacrifice but obedience to its grace and willingness to act it out in the present.

We now turn to the second christological principle according to which Hubmaier developed his eucharistic thought, that of the incarnation. Popular and scholarly thought alike in the medieval church believed that a sacrament was an analogue of the incarnation. Because God had revealed himself in flesh, it was believed that any material thing consecrated for that purpose could be the instrumental cause of the mediation of spirit. A sacrament was the primal meeting point between God and the world.

All the same, voices of dissent throughout the centuries had cautioned against making an analogue of the incarnation into a literal expression of it. Augustine was widely credited with the original formulation, discussed earlier, of dissent against a plainly physical view of the Eucharist.[94] Windhorst has identified the existence of an "ontological barrier" within reality as the cardinal presupposition of the late medieval Augustinian world and of the sacramentarian movements which issued from it. Belief that there was such a chasm through the middle of reality created an irresistible tendency toward spiritual religion. Those whose search led in that direction feared that a crudely materialist popular piety had become idolatrous, worshiping the sign rather than the thing signified. Windhorst presents that late medieval-Augustinian ontology as the soil in which Hubmaier's thought grew and flourished.[95]

This habit of thought shaped Hubmaier's use of the dogma of the incarnation and consequently his eucharistic doctrine. This is illustrat-

ed by his debate with one Heinrich Luthy at the Second Zurich Disputation. Luthy rehearses the conventional understanding of the incarnation in the argument he makes for graven images in churches: because
Christ became a human being, it is not wrong to create pictures of him.
He is drowned out by objections, among them Hubmaier's. For one
thing, Luthy's opponents contend, where the Spirit is present, all outward images fall away. For another thing, Christ is in heaven. For a
third, Moses and the prophets denounce images.[96] The sum of the re-
formist view is that Jesus taking on flesh is not a paradigm for the role of
the material world in the mediation of salvation. At the heart of Hubmaier's picture of creation is this view of the incarnation as a unique
moment of divine revelation, superseded by the coming of the Spirit.

Hubmaier drew the consequences for the incarnation from a formulation of the natures of Christ in which the human nature of Christ
ceased to have a role in the mediation of salvation after the ascension.
The incarnation as the historical act of God taking on flesh ceased to be
of significance for our relationship with him. At the same time, and
from within quite another christological frame of reference, Hubmaier
drew consequences from the incarnation for his understanding of the
church and the Lord's Supper.[97] The direct link between Jesus' incarnation and ministry on earth and the life of the church becomes clear
in Hubmaier's teaching on the power of the keys. In baptism, the
church uses the key of initiation; in the Lord's Supper, it applies the
key of excommunication. This is the power which Christ exercised
while he was on earth, Hubmaier explains.[98]

> It follows that the Christian church now has this authority to forgive and to
> retain sins here on earth until the second coming of the Lord, just as the
> same Christ also possessed when bodily upon earth.[99]

How critical the power of the keys is for Hubmaier's ecclesiology
and Christology is shown by an addition concerning it in his rendering
of the Apostles' Creed. He addresses baptismal candidates and adds to
the statement in the creed concerning the church:

> Christ assigned all his authority to the holy Christian church and hung the
> promised keys at her side, that she should use the same for the loosing and
> binding of sins according to his command in his bodily absence.[100]

Further on, Hubmaier summarizes his position. God the Father had all
power in heaven and on earth. When his Son took on flesh, the Father
passed this power on to him. When the Son was ready to ascend, he

passed this power on to the church.[101] In the church as a body and through the individuals who are its members, Christ's incarnation is extended through history.

Sometimes the language expounding this claim suggests that in its mediation of divine power, the historical event of Jesus' incarnation is an unbroken, existential reality stretched to include the present. At other times, the church's calling since the ascension of Christ is to imitate how he brought the Father to earth. In both descriptions it is clear that the vocation of the church is to prolong the incarnation in history. The present activity of God in the world is as Spirit. God's historic encounter with the world by means of incarnation is preserved in the life of the church, but God's immediate presence supersedes its incarnate form and comes to us as spirit.

The student of Hubmaier's work looks in vain for language which develops a positive claim about Christ's activity in the world in his divine nature. In his preface to *Von dem christlichen Bann* (*Bann:* On the Christian Ban) the role of the church as the keeper of the keys is most fully unfolded. There the author asserts without any elaboration that in his grace, Christ is present with the church though not in his body.[102] With few exceptions, Hubmaier's sacramental treatises lack even such unsubstantiated statements as the one just cited. Nowhere does he acknowledge the christological implications of the trinitarian theology to which he is at least formally bound.

There are two reasons for the disappearance of the ascended Christ from Hubmaier's work. The first one is that his reinterpretation of the Lord's Supper is successful only if Christ is removed from history to heaven. Any reference to the presence of the ascended Christ in relation to the breaking of bread would threaten the memorialist presupposition on which everything in his eucharistic doctrine depends. The conflict within his christological belief structure is not great because Hubmaier's dogmatic claims concern almost exclusively the historical Jesus, his ethics, and his sacrifice. His preexistence receives no attention. The heavenly Christ remains an abstraction who is never brought to bear on Hubmaier's theological system. Hubmaier has no Christology explicitly set in a trinitarian framework, in which the ongoing work of the heavenly Christ is as necessary to the salvation of the world as was his historical mission. Thus he also lacks both the necessity and the possibility of a eucharistic theology in continuity with the received tradition.

In Hubmaier's thought, the significance of the incarnation is both contracted and expanded. It is negative and limiting in that there is no room in it for the classical Christian claim that in the incarnation the created order is redeemed and made a means of divine self-disclosure. God was present to humanity in material form only for the duration of Jesus' earthly life.[103] The incarnation did not give enduring material form to the world of spirit; instead, the ascension removed spirit beyond the natural world.

In another sense, though, Hubmaier's thought on the subject expanded the role of incarnation beyond the sacramental manifestations traditionally derived from Nicaea and Chalcedon. In them, the prolongation of Christ's work in the obedience of the church is not elevated, as it is in Hubmaier, to the status of a defining principle of ecclesiology. We become Christ to others. Thereby we bring them into communion with Christ when we imitate his obedience and self-offering.[104]

In summary of Hubmaier's view, the incarnation has an entirely negative relation to the Eucharist as a means or sign of communion with Christ. By the same token, the incarnation has an entirely positive relation to the church as a community of the sanctified. By redefining the terms of reference, Hubmaier's Christology transcends the problem of formulating the presence of Christ in the Lord's Supper as it climaxed in the Reformation.

Hubmaier's redefinition had two parts. First, through the materiality of the church, that is, the community of believers as bearers of salvation in history, God is made present in the world. Having removed the incarnation from its relation to sacraments, Hubmaier proceeded to allow it full sway in his ecclesiology. This brought him to the second part of his redefinition. In it the Lord's Supper becomes the medium of the church as incarnation. The Eucharist is the church's pledge to God and sign to itself and the world that Christlike love is present and active. Christ's sacrifice for humanity becomes the transforming power of history when those who claim it imitate its sacrifice. The breaking of bread is a double confession of faith in Christ and obedience to him. This radically anthropocentric Lord's Supper is the surpassing symbol of Anabaptist ecclesiology when taken to its logical extreme.

Was Hubmaier's truncated Christology developed in order to put together a defensible theology of the Lord's Supper and subsequently integrated with his theology as a whole? Or was it the starting point of his theology from which a eucharistic doctrine was deduced? The answer to these questions lies in his teaching concerning the Holy Spirit.

Christology and Pneumatology

This section sets the work of the Son and the Spirit side by side for comparison, beginning with their roles in baptism and the Lord's Supper. In *Eine christliche Lehrtafel* (A Christian Catechism), written in 1526, the same year as *Einfältiger,* Hubmaier makes the case for baptism on confession of faith. His comparison of the two dominical ceremonies is illuminating. "The water concerns God, the Supper our neighbor; therein lie all the Law and the Prophets."[105] Baptism concerns God. It has inner and outer aspects. The inner aspect is baptism with the Spirit and fire. In it the sinner is brought back to life with the word through the Spirit.[106] The outer aspect is baptism with water. Baptism is the believer's confession of sin and salvation, the church's means of bringing one into the body of Christ, and a witness to the faith God has wrought in that one.[107]

God is the first cause of baptism in a way that he is not of the Lord's Supper.[108] The divine agency is often described with the trinitarian formula when the act of coming to faith or being baptized is at issue.[109] Hubmaier sometimes refers to God in the generic sense but most often talks of God at work in the world as Spirit. Only rarely are the Spirit and Christ mentioned in relation to each other. Once Hubmaier speaks of the "Spirit of Christ," and once he states that the Spirit gives life while Christ lives in the believer.[110] Any reference to the present work of the Son is a minor, almost discordant note in the score of a symphony composed with quite different themes in mind. The pattern of this score derives from a trinitarianism in which God is present in the world only as Spirit between the ascension and return of Jesus.

Usually Christ is the divine agent only where the reference to salvation is historical, for example, with John's baptism in relation to Jesus' earthly ministry. He must speak to us and our souls shall be healed.[111] When the author proceeds to explain how this historic offer becomes salvific, he talks of the believer's existential encounter with God through the Spirit. What the incarnate Son spoke before his ascension is made effective through time by the Spirit. The historical work of the Son and the present activity of the Spirit are both mediated through the church. But there is an essential difference in their natures. The Spirit is placed within a trinitarian framework in a way that is not spelled out for the Son: the Spirit is both immanent and transcendent. The Son, in his human nature, is immanent to the life of the church and to heaven. But his human nature is separated from his divine nature such that it has no transcendence and, hence, no participation in the present activity of God.

The work of the Spirit has two loci of activity. The Spirit is the agent of baptism and the power of the church. The parallel which Hubmaier establishes is between baptism and the church rather than between baptism and the Lord's Supper. The same power which mediates the forgiveness of sins in baptism does so as well in the life of the church. The church as community binds and looses, but the Eucharist is given no role in the mediation of grace. In Catholic ecclesiology the church also wields the power of the keys, but in its sacrament of reconciliation and in the Eucharist, sins are forgiven.

We see that Hubmaier's Christology necessitated a reconceptualization of the Lord's Supper more radical than his redefinition of baptism. Baptism retained its traditional pneumatological reference point. It is not a sacrament in the inherited sense, but it is inseparable from the work of the Spirit. Hubmaier found a way of relating the sacrament and Spirit in baptism without endangering his first principle, the temporal and theological priority of grace and faith to sacrament.

The breaking of bread, on the other hand, is more explicitly christological in nature. Any claim for divine action in the Eucharist would focus on the person of Christ and would need to specify the character of that presence. Hubmaier concluded that the only adequate way to correct the error of transubstantiation was to deny the real presence in the Lord's Supper altogether. Therefore, to relate the Spirit to the Supper raised insoluble questions for Hubmaier. If taking the bread, like asking for the waters of baptism, is done in response to the working of the Spirit, the Supper is placed in relationship to a divine act. Hubmaier's unfolding theology and his pastoral ministry convinced him that the "real presence" in the Lord's Supper is that of the church as the body of Christ. For that reason the Supper is a human act of faith and love, a pledge of self-sacrifice and obedience in imitation of Christ.

While classical sacramentology asserted a parallel between baptism and Eucharist as initial and ongoing means of grace, Hubmaier asserted a parallel between baptism and the church. Thus he removed the Eucharist from the danger of "false" interpretation. His ecclesiology, in which the church was the agent of grace, was not jeopardized by this move. It was a way of loosening the Lord's Supper entirely from its traditional moorings without sailing into the seas of ecclesiological spiritualism. To do this, Hubmaier withheld the Spirit from the Supper. This was a deliberate strategy. Whereas the absence of Christ from the plane of history occasions the coming of the Spirit to the church, Hubmaier put forward no such claim for the Eucharist, even though the language of absence and departure is applied to it in equal degree. In its power to bind and loose and in its pledge to love, the church—instead of the Lord's Supper—perpetuates the power of the incarnate Christ through history.

Hubmaier's Christology and pneumatology both limit and undergird each other in their relationship to the Eucharist. They limit in that his Christology is self-contained, with no integral role in his sacramental theology beyond Jesus' earthly ministry. His pneumatology is not a way to make Christ present in time and, specifically, in the breaking of bread. It is a way to keep him absent. The Holy Spirit replaces Christ in the world rather than mediating him across time and space. By the same token, Christology and pneumatology undergird each other. The Spirit continues the work of Christ in baptism and in the church. Thus, there can be a Lord's Supper with no "real presence" and yet a church in which God as Spirit is salvifically at work.

In conclusion, we return to the question posed at the close of the preceding chapter. Was Hubmaier's Christology developed to defend his theology of the Lord's Supper or was it the starting point from which his eucharistic doctrine was deduced? The evidence presented suggests that it was the former. Hubmaier was interested above all else in a eucharistic doctrine in which there was no immediate presence of Christ. He created it by working out a Christology in which Christ after his ascension was no longer the person of God's presence in history.

A Liturgy of the Lord's Supper

We turn now from the language of theology to that of worship. Our aim is to compare the law of prayer (*lex orandi:*) with the law of belief (*lex credendi:*) and to include in our picture new dimensions which the language of prayer might contribute to Hubmaier's beliefs about the Lord's Supper. Extending the comparison in the other direction, we then proceed to analyze whether and to what extent Hubmaier's rite for the breaking of bread expresses the theology which stands behind it.

Eine Form des Nachtmahls Christi (*Nachtmahl:* A Form for Christ's Supper), printed for the Anabaptist congregation in Nicolsburg in 1527, is the most impressive of the three orders of worship Hubmaier wrote in that setting because of its liturgical completeness. It stands between two other orders of service, one for baptism and one for the ban, and follows a typically evangelical pattern by doing away with the canon of the mass and using the vernacular. It has affinities with the works of the Zurich reformation in its removal of ritual aspects, such as the mingling of water and wine and the use of vestments. As in its Zurich counterparts, most of the spoken parts are said exclusively by the minister. The two exceptions to this are a corporate confession of sin and a congregational response in the pledge of love (*Liebespflicht*).[112]

Included in this one ordering of Holy Communion are two services: a preparatory gathering[113] and the communion itself.[114] Elements of explanation and instruction are woven in with the words and acts of the liturgy itself. Great care is taken to make certain the people understand what they are doing. It is exceptional among Anabaptists that Hubmaier's communion service retains a fixed liturgical form for the celebration of the Lord's Supper. The confession of sin, altered to include the words of absolution as part of the corporate prayer, uses customary penitential vocabulary.[115] The prayer of thanks before communion is similarly cast into prescribed, public language.[116] But here accustomed form is combined with novel content. Together with the words of institution, this prayer constitutes a replacement for the canon of the mass. It makes an extensive allusion to John 3:16.

Such liturgical innovation is rooted in Hubmaier's ministry prior to his crossing over to the evangelical party.[117] *Nachtmahl* is the final stage in that process of the renewal of eucharistic worship. Though radically innovative, it is a liturgy which (by retention of a fixed form, progression, and allusions to classical texts) stands within the tradition of medieval worship. This cannot be said of other extant Anabaptist worship forms of the same period. The best-known of these all have another character.[118] In them there are no prescribed forms or prayers. The rubrics are of a general nature, often identifying the biblical warrant for a practice. In its use of traditional liturgical content and form, Hubmaier's ordering of the Lord's Supper accepts an extrabiblical norm for worship. This stands in contrast to the stringently biblical liturgical sense of the Swiss Brethren, especially as set forth in Grebel's two letters to Thomas Müntzer.[119]

We now proceed to place *Nachtmahl* under the microscope for examination. It opens with a call to brothers and sisters to gather at an agreed-upon time and place to observe the "table of God," just as Jesus had arranged with his disciples for the Last Supper. Pointed instructions are given to the worshipers to dress decently and not to chatter frivolously. This emphasis on the human disposition in the breaking of bread is carried throughout the text. After the congregation has confessed its sin, the "Scriptures of Christ" are to be explained so that the eyes of those in attendance may be opened. The purpose of the sermon is to inflame in the hearts of those gathered around the table such a contemplation of the suffering and death of Christ that the worshipers will respond with devotion, love, and gratitude.[120]

In response to the portrayal of Christ on the cross, the congregation answers with what appears to be a hymn, "Bleibe bei uns," based on the Emmaus road encounter of Luke 24. This text is alluded to in the commentary introducing the sermon. As was the case in Hubmaier's exegetical treatment of this passage, he shows no interest in the peculiar eucharistic setting it portrays—an appearance of the risen Lord. In the present context, Hubmaier uses it as a model for opening the Scriptures to people. As the hymn is the last act of the preparatory service, this call for Christ to be present seems to have no overtones that bear directly on the act of communion. It seems to be a petition that the purpose of preaching, to illuminate the hearers, may be realized.

Although it is not said in so many words, this must be the end of the preparatory service because the next sentence begins with an instruction that on another day the "servant" or presider is to take his text for the communion exhortation from a certain list of biblical passages.[121] The exposition of the text follows. After the sermon, those who have assembled are at liberty, following the order of 1 Corinthians 14, to raise disagreements or deficiencies, presumably in the sermon, though this is not said.[122] The Pauline passage seems to have been the model for the Sunday meeting of the Anabaptist communities referred to, and Hubmaier made it an integral part of holy communion. Hence, it is likely that his church practiced weekly communion.

Thereafter, the priest (*sic*) reads verses from 1 Corinthians 11, warning all the believers not to eat or drink damnation unto themselves.[123] Then the text proceeds to explain in four points what making a memorial consists of. First, it consists of faith that Christ gave his body and blood for us on the cross. Such faith is founded on Jesus' words, "This is my body given for you and my blood poured out for you for the forgiveness of sins." Second, participants should individually examine themselves as to whether they have an inner hunger and thirst for that bread which comes from heaven. The heavenly bread and cup are to be taken in spirit, faith, and truth, as taught in John 4, 6, and 7.

A warning follows that unless a spiritual eating and drinking precedes it, the outer breaking of bread is a deathly exercise. Spiritual eating and drinking occupies a twofold role in Hubmaier's liturgy of the Lord's Supper. On one hand, it is mentioned as part of the whole action of the memorial, a communion with Christ which happens within the Eucharist.[124] Later this communion is described as a relationship with Christ and his members, given in conversion and followed by baptism. It exists prior to the breaking of bread and is its precondition.[125] With only incidental reference to bread and wine, Hubmaier proceeds to his third point, thanksgiving. Each communicant should express gratitude to God in words and deeds for the inexpressible gift of his Son. But because Christ has no need of our well-doing—he does not hunger—we fulfill our works of gratitude, physically and spiritually, toward our neighbor by comforting prisoners and housing the needy. This is doubly required if the needy one belongs to the household of faith.

The concept of living memorial (*lebendige gedechtnuss*) is the development of a cherished notion from the earlier exegetical work of the author, that of the body of Christ in remembrance (*der leib Christi in der gedechtnuss*).[126] The sense of this new version of Hubmaier's interpretive epigram is that the breaking of bread and passing of the cup become a living memorial when they become a sacrament, that is, a promise by the believers to give up their lives for others. This renders in succinct language and places within a liturgical context the concept Hubmaier developed long before *Nachtmahl.*

Whereas the inward reality, the coming of the Spirit, happens prior to the Lord's Supper, the outward reality happens after it. The sacrament is not the cause but the consequence of faith and obedience. This familiar refrain rounds out the argument of these pages. Our communion with Christ is not given through the breaking of bread; it precedes the ritual of the Supper and has been sealed in our inner nature because Christ came in the flesh. His incarnation is a promise of self-offering, fulfilled in the church. It could be called a sacrament just as the believers' willingness to offer their bodies is a sacrament.[127]

Once it is clear to his readers that sacraments are not divine acts but the ultimate, unequivocal response of human faith and love, Hubmaier goes on to say that one cannot be a Christian without them.

> For just as water baptism is a public testimony of the Christian faith, so is the Supper a public testimony of Christian love. Now he who does not want to be baptized or to observe the Supper, he does not desire to believe in Christ nor to practice Christian love and does not desire to be a Christian.[128]

If all one had of the Christian gospel was a right understanding of water baptism and the Supper of Christ, one would have everything—God, his creatures, faith and love, the law and the prophets. With these soaring words, Hubmaier reaches the climax of his theological commentary in *Nachtmahl.*

The liturgy moves on, in its sixth step, to the problem of worthy participation in the Lord's Supper. Those are worthy to come to the Lord's table who confess God's love in the sacrifice of Christ, who are moved by the word of God to sacrifice their lives in a similar manner.

Believers are not only declared worthy to sit at the Lord's table but actually become worthy, at least in terms of a new will and disposition they have received. The central action of the Holy Communion, the passing on of love which comes from God to other believers and to people outside the church, can be carried out by those anointed with the Holy Spirit.

The next and seventh action in the Lord's Supper is a prayer to God that he will increase faith and light fires of love.[129] A period of silence follows this petition to permit everyone to contemplate the suffering of Christ and rest in him. The silence ends with the corporate praying of the Lord's Prayer.

The eighth action in the Lord's Supper commences with an explanation by the priest that bread is bread and not the flesh of the Lord. Immediately following that, the presider asks all those in the congregation who want to eat the bread and drink the cup of communion to take the pledge of love. Thus one kind of real presence is ruled out while another kind is affirmed. It is the real presence of the flesh of each believer, pledged as a self-offering for his neighbors. In order that the pledge of love, which is the essence of the breaking of bread, not become merely a dead letter, the communion proper is introduced by means of a pledge of love. In it the congregation is asked for specific commitments in loving one's brother and sister and, if necessary, disciplining them. Only after this assent is there sharing of the bread and wine. The text of the pledge follows:

> Brothers and sisters, will you love God in the power of his holy and living word, before, in and above all things, serve, honor and pray to him alone and henceforth follow his name; [will you] also subject your fleshly and sinful will to his divine will which he has worked in you through his living word, for life and death? Let each one separately say, I WILL.
>
> Will you love your neighbor and fulfill on him the works of brotherly love, offer your flesh and pour out your blood for him? [Will you] be obedient to father, mother, and all magistracy according to the will of God, and this in the power of our Lord Jesus Christ who also offered his flesh and poured out his blood for us? Let us each one separately say, I WILL.
>
> Will you use brotherly chastisement (*straff*) toward your brothers and sisters, make peace and harmony between them, also reconcile yourself with all those who have offended you, drop envy, hate, and all evil will toward any; willingly desist from all actions and dealings which injure, damage or vex your neighbor, also love your enemies and do good to them; [and will you] exclude [from the church] all those who are not willing so to do according to the order of Christ (Matt. 18)? Let each one separately say, I WILL.

Do you desire, here in the supper of Christ by the eating of the bread and the drinking of the wine, to confirm publicly before the church this covenant which you have just now made and to testify to the power of the living memorial of the suffering and death of Jesus Christ our Lord? Let each one separately say, I DESIRE IT IN THE POWER OF GOD.

Therefore eat and drink with one another in the name of God, Father, Son, and Holy Ghost. May he give us all power and strength that we spend the time according to his holy will, worthy of salvation. The Lord communicate to us his grace. Amen.[130]

The communion service proper then proceeds. The bishop takes the bread into his hands and offers a fixed prayer of thanks for the goodness of God, the death of Christ, and through it the possibility of faith unto eternal life. Then the priest breaks the bread and offers it to those seated around him. He speaks the words of institution from 1 Corinthians 11 concerning the bread. An invitation is issued to commune in memory of Jesus.[131] After a sentence prayer of thanks for the wine, the same sequence follows: words of institution, invitation, distribution.

The tenth and last act of the service begins with another exhortation! In it believers are urged to conform to Christ, the head of the church, and like him to be a person for others. That commitment is a renewal of the oath once made in faith and baptism and renewed in the pledge of love and the breaking of bread. In a strange way the ethical nagging in which Hubmaier gets caught up is the highest tribute he can pay to the Lord's Supper. In it the believer speaks the word of promise to live a life of love. Therefore, unbelievers can rightly judge their faith and their love by how Christians live. Because their lives are the book which the world reads, believers must discipline each other in love. Lead your lives before God and people, the presider concludes, as table companions of Christ Jesus.

Words of dismissal bring the assembly to a close. The congregation is urged to watch and pray lest it fall into temptation. With these words a cautionary identification is made between the church and the disciples at the point where Jesus' followers refused to suffer with him. Three traditional statements of blessing follow.[132]

This concludes our delineation of the flow and elements of Hubmaier's communion service, with explanatory commentary on its style and content. We turn now to a theological assessment of the text and an attempt to judge the extent of continuity between his treatises on the subject and their expression in worship, with particular attention to Christology.

There is an unusual statement in the postscript to *Nachtmahl.*

There Hubmaier asserts, "Thus Christ cannot be eaten or drunk by us otherwise than spiritually and in faith."[133] In all his corpus, this is the first unequivocal reference to a spiritual communion with Christ concomitant with the breaking of bread. This choice of language seems to be a recasting of his ideas into the terminology of the eucharistic debate going on in Moravia at that time.[134]

A concomitancy of actions, which could be read into the flow of the communion service, is ruled out for the following reasons. First, it has no other warrant, either from Hubmaier's writings or the tendency of his thought. Second, the word *communion* (*gmainschaft*) is reserved for realities other than sitting at the Lord's table. It is used to describe a relationship with Christ which precedes and is the precondition for observing the Lord's institution, an inner communion in the Spirit and in truth.[135] Further, communion with Christ and participation in his body is given to those who follow the command of Jesus and offer up their lives for others.

> If one is thus inclined toward his neighbor, he is now in the true fellowship of Christ, a member of his body, and a fellow member with all godly persons.[136]

Hubmaier employs the word *communion* in two ways. Union is with the heavenly, divine Christ, and also with the earthly, human Christ. The former refers to an unmediated faith relationship in the Spirit; the latter speaks of a love relationship with the neighbor which prolongs the earthly presence of Christ. The first communion is mystical and inward; the second is ethical and outward.

That which the Catholic tradition asserts to be given surpassingly in the bread and wine is here the gift bestowed on those who have become Christ to someone in need. As it stands, this explanation is a refinement of a claim that concludes *Messe.*[137] Just as the body and blood of Christ have become my body and blood on the cross, so should my body and blood become that of my neighbor. This is the will of Christ in the Supper. Novel here is the use of classical eucharistic language with reference to a communion which is not sacramental but ethical. This deliberate planting of old language in new ground underscores the radicality of Hubmaier's intentions. It cannot be accidental that Hubmaier uses the same concept, *Wesen* (essence), to describe the mode of Christ's absence and that of the church's presence in the Lord's Supper.

In summary, then, the "doing" of a sacrament is possible only on the basis of the grace and power of the suffering and shedding of the blood of Christ. To make his point clear, Hubmaier restates it. The communion of saints is not established because of the breaking of bread or by means of it; rather, the communion of saints was established by Christ when he came in the flesh. The breaking of bread is then a consequence rather than a cause of that communion. Those who inwardly are communicants and in the Spirit may also outwardly use the bread and wine. Here we observe one of the few places in Hubmaier where inner and outer participation are paralleled. But this is not a concomitancy of actions. The parable of baptism makes this clear. We are not baptized in water in order to believe. We are baptized because we previously (*vorhin*) believed.

Such "inner fellowship in the Spirit" (*inwendige Gmainschafft im geyst*) constitutes the referent for baptism. Each Christian in coming to faith is given this inner communion in the Spirit. It is not specifically related to the Lord's Supper. It is not an isolated, repeated experience but the nature of the Christian's relationship with God. The communion, which in baptism believers confess to have, makes a worthy use of bread and wine possible. These elements refer backward to the suffering of Jesus and forward to the suffering of his people. Both points of reference are historical. The Lord's Supper is the sign that the incarnation is being carried on in the church.[138]

How can a historical event also be a spiritual one? Hubmaier goes on to state that the elements are a living memorial of Christ's suffering and death for us, "spiritually" signified (*bedeuttet*) and signed (*anzaigt*) through the breaking of bread and the pouring out of wine so that people might do likewise for each other. A complicated sequence of clauses expresses the complicated thoughts behind them, each elaborating on and qualifying the other.[139] Here *spiritual* seems to have nothing to do with an inward eating and drinking with or of Christ. It refers to the "inner Christian essence,"[140] the pledge of love by the believer and the church. The breaking of bread signifies the at-once spiritual and material reality of readiness to suffer. From this we clearly see that Hubmaier uses the concept *spiritual* in two distinct senses. In reference to the Spirit as the agent, spiritual reality is immaterial and ahistorical.[141] In reference to the believer as agent, it is material and historical, an imitation of Christ's incarnation.

It has been clear all along that Hubmaier fears sacramentalism. He believes he safeguarded the church against it by not allowing outward things to have salvific power.[142] But he is equally wary of spiritualism. It does not follow from the fact that God works immaterially and ahistorically that humanity does so. The difference in their natures makes their spiritual reality different. All human actuality is historical. Therefore, it has outward form. Sacraments signify sanctified human nature. Their prototype is the earthly life of the second person of the Trinity.

The call for contrite hearts and the proclamation of divine love are building stones of this liturgy, but its cornerstone is the covenant of love. Not only is it the cornerstone of this service; it is also the pinnacle of Hubmaier's theology as a whole. Gathered up in this pledge of love is everything Hubmaier believes concerning redemption, human nature, and the church. The sanctified person acquires the will not to sin. The church is made up of people who confess that God has set them free. They covenant with one another to use this freedom in self-sacrifice. The pledge of love in the Lord's Supper makes explicit the inseparability of receiving the love of Christ and offering it to others. The service begins in the past, with a memorial of Christ's suffering. Its climax is a thrust into the future in the form of the church's willingness to suffer in Christ's stead. Its pledge includes not only an abstract willingness to live in love but also a concrete agreement to administer and accept church discipline and excommunication, where love is lacking.

In conclusion, we turn to an examination of Hubmaier's use and development of technical theological terminology in *Nachtmahl.* There is a striking contrast between the compactness of the liturgy itself and wordiness of the commentary and instructions.[143] Hubmaier's commentary in the *Nachtmahl* employs terms and nuances of expression which are absent—consciously and deliberately, one senses—from the other writings on the Lord's Supper in his corpus. The author speaks of being table companions of Christ Jesus.[144] The plain meaning of this term is that a communion exists between the host and the guests at his table. The context of this comment suggests that the nature of this solidarity is not mystical but ethical. To be table companions of Jesus is to live out one's baptismal vow, one's pledge of love. In Hubmaier's scheme of things, this is not a reducing of spiritual reality to the human. It is an assertion that the ethical is the mode of the spiritual.

The most important change in phraseology, however, concerns Hubmaier's interpretive key for the words of institution, "the body of Christ in remembrance" (*der leib Christi in der gedechtnuss*).[145] In *Nachtmahl* it becomes "living memorial" (*lebendige gedechtnuss*), used three times in relation to Jesus' suffering with the adjective *living* and once in relation to his body without the adjective.[146] In both uses the meaning is changed from the original. In *Einfältiger*, Hubmaier constructs the phrase so that the bread is the body of Christ in remembrance or memorial.[147] The purpose of this construction is to remain close to the wording of the biblical text. When he recasts these words for liturgical purposes, the literal use of "this is my body" is given up. The line is further removed from its origin by association with the suffering of Christ, and not the body of Christ. The accent is thereby taken completely off *body* and placed on living memorial.

This living memorial is the willingness of believers to give up their lives for each other now as Christ then did for all of them. Such a shift and definition move Hubmaier even farther from traditional formulations than he had been. Of equal significance is how he merges the two originally separate acts of remembering in faith and acting in love. That is to say, to partake in the living memorial of Christ is to imitate his love.

This leads us to a final comment on the language of *Nachtmal.* It was composed for a church threatened with persecution and possible martyrdom. As such, it faithfully expresses the thrust of Hubmaier's theology as a whole. It teaches that faith is the beginning of a new life in which the believer both wills and is sustained by grace in obedience unto death. However, in the pledge of the communion service, his rigorous ethic reaches its most concentrated form of expression. By means of the phrase, *living memorial,* Hubmaier merges his two principal points of eucharistic dogma: faith in the work of Christ's sacrifice and imitative obedience to it.

The Power of the Keys and the Lord's Supper

Although a general commentary on and liturgy for the ban, which follows those of baptism and communion, exceeds the boundaries of our study, there are christological and ecclesiological references in the text of *Bann* which shed light on the Lord's Supper. The avowed intent of this discourse is to show convincingly that in the keys, Christ gave the church his power to retain and remit sins.[148] Before his resurrection, this authority was exercised by Christ alone. After he was raised, he passed on this power to the church until he comes again. The guarantor of this authority is the Holy Spirit, whom Christ gave to the church. Whereas, once people saw the Spirit visible above Christ at the Jordan, on the day of Pentecost they would see the Spirit visible above themselves.[149]

Most striking about this set of claims is that it leads Hubmaier straightaway to the matter of the Lord's Supper. The gist of the argument is this: if Christ were present in the bread, it would mean that he has taken back the keys which he gave to his church. But we know that he has given the church the keys to the kingdom until he comes again. In other words, Christ cannot be present in the bread and wine because he has left the plane of history. Hubmaier draws an explicit conclusion from this assertion: by understanding the power and use of the keys, one knows the meaning of water baptism and the Supper of Christ. This meaning, as expected, is that water cannot save and that Christ is not bodily present in bread and wine.[150]

In these paragraphs we encounter again the dualism within the material world which characterizes Hubmaier's thought. A page earlier in *Bann,* he has claimed that baptism is the first key of the church. By means of it, the church admits the believer to itself and to the forgiveness of sins.[151] Further down, he emphasizes the role of the visible church as the mediator of Christ's power to forgive sins. The claim made by Hubmaier about the dominical ceremonies—that nothing outward can save—stands in complete contrast to the calling of the church, a visible, historical institution, which admits people to the forgiveness of sins.[152] This dualism can exist within Hubmaier's thought because the church, in his view of it, is composed only of believers who collectively and individually bear the Spirit as well as the commission of Christ.

During Christ's absence from history the church acts in his stead. Its outward existence prolongs the earthly life of Jesus. This is not to say that it acts in its own might. Its authority, the power of the keys, was received from Christ before his ascension. The power with which the church has been entrusted is the outer form of the same power which inwardly is the Spirit. By the Spirit, people are born again and set free to imitate Jesus Christ. Hubmaier's ecclesiology allows him to distinguish the church from all other historical realities. Because it is composed only of believers, it is literally the embodiment of faith and love. This is the realm of spirit within history. Only spirit can mediate grace. Therefore, ceremonies, which are material but not personal entities, cannot be means of grace.

On the basis of the church's power of the keys, *Bann* makes the church's calling as the prolongation of Jesus' earthly ministry tangible and vivid. The church is the real presence of Christ's humanity on earth. Hubmaier says nothing to describe the role of Christ in his divine nature between his two advents on earth. From it he derives nothing of the divine presence and power on earth in the interval between advents.

Conclusions

Two pairs of questions remain at the end of this examination of the eucharistic thought of Balthasar Hubmaier. One pair deals with his motivation: Is the revolutionary content of his claims the uncalculated result of a desperate attempt to sever the Lord's Supper from the belief that in it Christ's body is "physically" and "substantially" eaten?[153] Or, did he deliberately reconstruct a theological system whose consequence was a radically new conception of the sacrament? The second pair of questions deals with the result: Was Hubmaier's teaching concerning the Lord's Supper primarily a nonspiritualistic alternative to sacramentalism or primarily a nonsacramentalistic alternative to spiritualism? To put the same issue another way—was it an opposition to the very idea of a sacrament as a medium of grace, which sought also to avoid the complete individuation and internalization of religion? Or, was his teaching an opposition to the very idea of spirit as inwardness whose goal was to find an innovative way to speak about spiritual reality as external? We will allow this set of questions to guide our evaluation of Hubmaier's eucharistic and christological thought and then return to them at the end.

As our study has unfolded, we have identified reasons and sources for certain of Hubmaier's thought forms and convictions. But what was it which made his premises plausible and his borrowings convincing to him? What were the underlying assumptions guiding his eclectic choices and original constructions? The most that can be ventured in response to such a far-reaching query is an indirect answer. Hubmaier was trying to actualize a Christianity whose main tenets were put forth in certain thought patterns originating in the Fourth Gospel. The reason for my careful phrasing is that it cannot be said that Hubmaier literally appropriated the substance of John's Gospel or fully entered its spirit. One has the sense that it was mediated to him by another thinker or spiritual tradition; he used pieces of it but did not understand the whole. Both Hubmaier's writings and our examination of them are too circumscribed to make extensive claims about the origins and inspirations of his thought. Nevertheless, nothing can explain some dominant tendencies in Hubmaier's thought as well as themes from the Gospel of John are able to do.

The conclusion of the matter is that Hubmaier was indebted to the Fourth Gospel for much of the structure of his thought. On this, nevertheless, two cautions need to be entered. First, Hubmaier did not work directly with John in a sustained way. It is the Johannine world and spirit which left their mark on him and gave him the structures of his thought. Hubmaier's exegetical engagement was undertaken from the vantage point of a Johannine Christology but occurred primarily with the baptismal and eucharistic texts in the Synoptics, and especially Romans and 1 Corinthians, among Paul's writings. Hubmaier knew that the sacramental passages in the Synoptics and Paul were the arena in which the main debate over the Lord's Supper was carried on. Here point-by-point exegesis had to be done and claims of biblical precedent for Hubmaier's positions had to be grounded. This was where the eucharistic wars of the sixteenth century were fought and where Hubmaier also had to stake out his territory.

Second, in relation to his use of the biblical materials, there is a striking omission: Hubmaier made no substantive use of the eucharistic claims in John 6. No doubt he passed over this section because its graphic, extravagant vocabulary sounded too much like that of his arch opponents. In his omission of this contentious piece of Johannine eucharistic theology, Hubmaier's work stands apart from Zwingli as well as Anabaptists like Marpeck and Dirk.[154]

Yet, the above qualifiers notwithstanding, the Fourth Gospel did provide Hubmaier with his metaphysical picture. Its understanding of God as Trinity and, following from that, its ecclesiology and anthropology, were formative sources for Hubmaier's christological and eucharistic thought. Hubmaier shared the trinitarian assumptions of the Fourth Gospel in at least four ways. First, it portrays the sequence of revelation as moving from Father to Son to Spirit. Second, there is a paucity of positive claims for the presence of Christ in the world after his ascension. Where they do occur, as in John 14, Hubmaier made no use of them. Third, Hubmaier made certain christological motifs in John into a critical principle by which he interpreted New Testament and contemporary belief about the Lord's Supper as a whole. Fourth, he related Johannine ecclesiology directly to the problem of sacraments, as he saw it. He thought of the church as the primal sacramental reality. In it Christ's power remained at work in the world.

Let us look at each of these aspects as a way of pursuing the relationship in Hubmaier's writings between Christology and the Eucharist. The Johannine imprint on Hubmaier's trinitarianism is one-sided. Little is made of John's emphasis on the unity between the Father and Son. But much is made of the relationship John posits between the Son and the Spirit. Nothing in the Hubmaier corpus suggests that the Spirit is the present form of Jesus. The distinction between the roles of the Son and the Spirit present in Jesus' farewell discourses in John 14–16 is evident also in Hubmaier's thought: If Jesus does not leave the earth, the Comforter cannot come.

On this foundational premise, Hubmaier builds up christological claims which are inspired by the Fourth Gospel but go beyond it. They are the following: First is the centrality of Jesus' ascension. His absence from the earth means his presence in heaven. Hubmaier speaks not only of Jesus' physical absence but also his essential absence. The Son and the Spirit remain distinct in both their person and function.

Second, whereas Jesus has completed his historical work, the Spirit is active and present. Hubmaier never suggests that the two persons are interchangeable, and only once that the Son has sent the Spirit. At times the outward work of the Son stands in contrast to the inward work of the Spirit. This is the case, for example, with the church's authority over the keys. The work of the Son and the Spirit, however, is not simultaneous or parallel, but sequential: the Son gave the keys, the Spirit guards them through time.

Third, Hubmaier contends that if Jesus were present, he would nullify his gift of the keys to the church. The church is evidence for the promise of the Spirit's presence, as in John. But, and here Hubmaier makes a crucial extrapolation beyond John of immense significance for his eucharistic thought, the church is also evidence for the promise of Christ's absence. The force of the argument concerns the keys: the power of the earthly Jesus is now given form and authority in the keys. Jesus' power remains on earth by means of the keys rather than by baptism or the Lord's Supper. The church legitimately wields this power only because Christ is not present to do so.

To highlight the fact of Christ's absence, Hubmaier uses both these two arguments, the coming of the Spirit to replace Christ and the giving of the keys to the church so it could be his representative. Here again, he is selective in what he takes from John. He uses only that which strengthens the notion that the ascension of the Son means his removal from the world. The invitation of Jesus in John 6 to eat his flesh and the promise of his presence in John 14 are conspicuously absent from Hubmaier's description of Christ. With the idea of the absent Christ in mind, Hubmaier sets about to interpret the institutional narratives as found outside the Gospel of John. This allows him to make as much as he does out of the memorial aspect of the Supper. The sequential working of the Son and Spirit means, from Hubmaier's vantage point, that the Lord's Supper is the testament and departing command of one whose presence is there only in the memory of his followers.

The other assumption which seems to have its origin in the Fourth Gospel is Hubmaier's understanding of the Lord's Supper as an ethical rather than a sacramental reality. The Last Supper, as recorded by John, has no mention of bread and wine. Instead, it concentrates on Jesus' condescending love in washing his followers' feet. The bond established between the Lord and his disciples in John 13 is one of example and imitation. These two characteristics, memorial and imitation, constitute the core of Hubmaier's Eucharist.

The sequential working of God in the world as Trinity is also the basis for Hubmaier's ecclesiology. The power of Christ's incarnate, self-giving, forgiving love is prolonged on earth in the life of the church. This is the power referred to in relation to the keys. The extension of the incarnation in salvation history is not embodied in Christ as the second person of the Trinity but in the church. The Lord's Supper is the surpassing act of the church's self-expression. It is the prototype of the church's life in the world, an action done in memory, gratitude, and imitation of Christ's sacrifice. The power of the church's outer life comes from its participation in the incarnation. But the church also has an inner life, a participation in the Spirit, which is the existential source of its self-offering for the world. Through the Holy Spirit, the church brings the sacrifice of Christ into the present.

Only by means of Hubmaier's ecclesiology can we illuminate the persistent puzzle of his Christology: nowhere does he make claims about how Jesus is present in history. Neither in his eucharistic nor his other writings does he turn his attention to positive claims concerning the role of the second person of the Trinity in the ongoing life of the church and the world. It is not that Hubmaier has nothing to say about God's presence here but that he separates it from his teaching on the person of Christ. By means of Hubmaier's pneumatology and ecclesiology, these questions are addressed. Functionally, the Spirit and the church represent and replace Christ.

For Hubmaier in his day, the attractiveness of this schematization of God's work lay in its ability to solve hitherto insoluble difficulties he had with traditional and contemporary eucharistic and ecclesiological claims. He was convinced that the belief in a corporeal presence of Christ in the elements of the Eucharist was unsustainable only if Christ were understood to be bodily and essentially absent from the plane of history. This conviction was the stone which stood firm against all challenges to his view.

Once the fundamental point had been established, he undertook extensive exegetical work to substantiate it. Its purpose was twofold. One was to remove Christ from the present by picturing his institution of the Supper solely as a memorial to his departure. Hubmaier accomplished this through his hermeneutical key, "the body of Christ in remembrance." The act of remembering has an ethical and not a mystical character: to think on Jesus' sacrifice is to act on it. Hubmaier's second claim about the Lord's Supper, as we have noticed, was tied to his belief about the church as the extension of the incarnation. In both cases the relationship is inner-worldly, with the historical Jesus abstracted from the preexistent and now glorified Christ. This deliberate omission of classical christological affirmations was Hubmaier's way of doing battle with sacramentalism.

But Hubmaier found the pneumatological and ecclesiological frame of reference, within which he had placed his christological and eucharistic doctrines, equally helpful in combating the contemporary challenge of spiritualism. He sided with the spiritualists with regard to the physical and essential absence of Christ from time and space, but he stood against them with his pneumatology and ecclesiology. By means of his teaching on the church as the prolongation, not only of the incarnation but also of the Spirit, Hubmaier had found a powerful argument for the outwardness of Christian reality. With the help of his anthropology, it was possible for him to have a sanctified human community which carries on the work of the sacrifice of Jesus in the world.

In its role as the embodiment of the church's outward life, the Lord's Supper is the *sine qua non* of the church. Hubmaier's emphasis on the outwardness of the church was not only of theological but also of practical value to him. It helped him to find a theology of the Lord's Supper adequate to the needs of a persecuted church threatened with martyrdom. This he achieved by making the focus of the theology and liturgy of the Lord's Supper the living memorial in which the church remembers Christ's sacrifice surpassingly in its pledge to do likewise. Not only did such a eucharistic teaching help beleaguered Christians find meaning in their circumstances; it also prepared them to be loyal to Christ until death.

Hubmaier limited the role of spiritualism in his thought largely to its correcting, negating function and refused to allow its positive claims, that is, that all spiritual reality, including the personal (the church) is inward and invisible. He argued that sanctified human reality, the life of believers in the church, was outward and ethical. Hubmaier arrived at his conclusions by a process at once eclectic in its borrowing and original in its construction. His borrowing and reshaping of numerous sources was undertaken consciously and reflectively. Rollin Armour sums up this eclectic stance as the way of Anabaptism. Armour's conclusion to that effect is applicable in its most extensive form to Hubmaier:

Our study of Anabaptist baptism therefore supports the view that the movement was a third way alongside Catholicism and Protestantism, or fourth, if Spiritualism is added. With the Protestants, the Anabaptists rejected the sacramentalism of the Catholic tradition; with the Catholics, they denied the solafideism [by-faith-alone stance] of the magisterial reformers; and, with both, they criticized the implicit Gnosticism of the Spiritualists. For their own part they attempted to form a church which kept the doctrine of creation they believed the Spiritualists to deny, and a church faithful to the doctrine of redemption they felt both Catholic and Protestant to misinterpret.[155]

In all his revision of traditional Christian thought and practice, Hubmaier declined to give up the church's sacramental language. His originality consists principally in reinterpreting this language to express his understanding of the relationship between grace and faith and between faith and love. Windhorst goes so far as to say that the developmental principle of Hubmaier's theology was his *Sakramentskritik* (critique of sacraments).[156] Hubmaier's resolution and resourcefulness in thinking through an alternative eucharistic theology were monumental. He established the tendency which was to hold sway in much subsequent Mennonite thought: a ceremony is a response to grace rather than a means of grace. Had Hubmaier carried over his criticism of sacraments to all dimensions of the church's life, he would have been a spiritualist. But he permitted the sacramental principle, that of the incarnation, to form his ecclesiology. The church became for him the *res* of which the Lord's Supper was the *signum*. It has been the central concern of this essay to assess the negation and transformation of the sacramental principle in Hubmaier's thought.

The recapitulation of Hubmaier's thought on the preceding pages has left us with the following answers to the questions posed at the start of the conclusion. Hubmaier's theology was the deliberate reconstruction of a theological system whose consequence was a radically new construction of the Lord's Supper. It was accomplished at the enormous cost of adopting an economic trinitarianism in which Christ is only a transient mode of the divine presence. Although Hubmaier violated the canons of traditional trinitarian and sacramental theology, the strong bias of his theology was an opposition to the very idea of spirit as inwardness. Its goal was to find an innovative way of speaking about spiritual reality as external. This, too, was achieved at the immense price of severing the breaking of bread from communion with Christ.

Hubmaier was a person hunted and haunted for the duration of his decisive years as a churchman. No single interpretation of Christianity could contain his ideal or his fears. Even in 1527, after threats and imprisonment had taken him from place to place, Hubmaier had lost none of his passion to reform the church. He continued to seek a setting in which to realize his ideal. When voices arose to protest the unjustness of his execution by burning in 1528, the Austrian theologian, Faber, set out to vindicate the authorities' action. Hubmaier was said to have deserved death as a heretic because of his convictions concerning baptism and the Holy Supper of Christ.[157]

Pilgram Marpeck (1495?-1556)

3

Pilgram Marpeck

Introduction

Pilgram Marpeck (1495?-1556) was born in Tyrol of devout Catholic parents.[1] When and under what circumstances he was drawn to the cause of reform is unknown. It is known, however, that radical theological influences were abroad in the Tyrol and in Rattenberg during Marpeck's time there in the 1520s.[2] Marpeck's baptism as an adult was the result of a deeply personal confession of faith,[3] but there is no evidence that Marpeck had formally studied theology. His writings suggest that he was an autodidact. His profession was that of an engineer, leading to socially protected positions in Rattenberg, Strassburg, and Augsburg. He married and with his wife had one natural child and adopted three more.

Marpeck began his career in the Tyrol, but religious persecution led the Marpecks to move to Strassburg in 1528. He straightaway became the foremost Anabaptist spokesperson in the city, at the same time building timber dams to float lumber down to the city. Four turbulent and decisive years followed, both for Marpeck and for the movement to which he had devoted himself. The next twelve years of Marpeck's life were spent in obscurity, due no doubt to the unrelenting persecution of Anabaptists in these years. Until 1540, Marpeck traveled extensively through Switzerland and Moravia.[4] He was located in St. Gall in the mid-1530s. Scattered correspondence from those years suggests that Marpeck's preoccupation during this interlude was the unity of South German Anabaptism.[5]

During the time before his next move, he wrote pastoral letters, edited and expanded Bernhard Rothmann's treatise on baptism and the Lord's Supper, and developed an elaborate polemic against spiritualism. From 1544 until his death, Marpeck lived in Augsburg, active both as an engineer and church leader. At the beginning of this final time of his life, Marpeck wrote at least the first part of the

Verantwortung (VWG), his response to Schwenckfeld's criticism of his theology of the sacraments and his Christology.

Two characteristics of Marpeck are especially helpful in understanding his thought. First, he accepted the radicality of the Anabaptist dissent from the *corpus christianum* (Christian body, church and state as an inseparable unity). The loss of baptism on confession of faith was for Marpeck the fall of the church.[6] Second, the incarnation defined for him how God meets humanity. Spiritual reality takes material form. With these two principles, he sought to avoid the imbalances he saw within Anabaptism as well as within the larger Christian world of his era. Marpeck feared the legalism of the Swiss Brethren and the dissolution of the church evident in spiritualism. He pursued an alternative to the sacramental life of Christendom because it was not founded on the response of faith. The alternative Marpeck chose was unique in its retention of sacramental realism, the belief in a "metaphysical correlation"[7] of the event of the Supper with the body and blood of Christ. For him, the action of the congregation with bread and wine became a communion with Christ.

In order to remain true to his two principles, Marpeck had a pragmatic readiness to borrow from whatever sources strengthened his position. His theology is aptly described by the German term *Kontroverstheologie*, meaning thought forms worked out in controversy with different opponents. It neither begins nor ends with a fixed system but evolves under the stimulus of challenges. By means of his two guiding principles, Marpeck sought to defend the Anabaptist community theologically. He strove for a theological identity at the heart of a group's self-understanding and apologetic. This stands over against the primary concern of most Anabaptist communities, especially the Swiss and Hutterian, for the ordered and disciplined life of the church as the decisive defense against its detractors.

As noted, Marpeck's biography and his original yet eccentric writing suggests that he was an autodidact. In light of this hypothesis, certain features of Marpeck's thought make sense. His trinitarian scheme, for example, does not follow the laws of inherited theological convention but fills in gaps resulting from his attempt to explain God's activity in sacraments. This and other of Marpeck's thought structures cannot be explained exhaustively because they are not deduced from a formal and coherent system. Marpeck was a person who did not think all his thoughts through to their conclusion. He made use of two different eucharistic views to the extent that they constituted a defense or offense against opponents. But he apparently never concerned himself with their incompleteness or incongruity. The hypothesis that Marpeck was largely self-taught in matters of theology may give room for criticism of him but also credits him with unusual creativity and insight into competing visions of reform. His is the outstanding intellectual defense of Anabaptism in the age of the Reformation.

Influences

The fact that Pilgram Marpeck was not a trained theologian heightens the difficulty of identifying influences which might have shaped his thought. Whence come his eclecticism and originality, his Christology which stretched trinitarian thought almost to the breaking point?

The focus of the present study is the human and divine components in the Lord's Supper and the Christology which Marpeck unfolded to validate his claims about it. One of the preoccupations of the whole Reformation was the search for an ordering principle by which the human and divine and the inner and outer[8] could be brought into a relationship with each other. Which of its thinkers provided Marpeck's frame of reference? As the Marpeck texts are examined, probable sources for their line of argument will be identified. Here I only identify three worlds of thought which constitute the intellectual background for Marpeck's writings on the Lord's Supper. The question of the form and extent of their influence on Marpeck is almost unanswerable because he was not formally schooled in any of them. Yet the following worlds of thought do make their way into Marpeck's writings.

The three primary influences at work in Marpeck's eucharistic writings are mysticism as mediated by the Radical Reformation, sacramentarianism as mediated by Ulrich Zwingli, and the Catholic sacramental tradition as mediated by Martin Luther. Mysticism in the late Middle Ages appeared in a baffling range of guises. Its relationship to the religious innovations of the sixteenth century compounds this complexity. The practitioners of mysticism taught the possibility of the believer's unmediated relationship with God.[9]

The roots of sacramentarianism were fertilized by mysticism, but the soil in which they were planted was the world of late medieval Augustinianism. Christof Windhorst identifies this philosophy by the belief that an "ontological barrier" separated the material from the spiritual world.[10] This spiritualizing of religion was one of the chief factors which brought the Reformation into being. It relativized medieval concepts of sacrament, priesthood, and church, unable to find a "place for external actions as causes in the realm of grace."[11] In its sacramentarian form, this religion of the spirit had a formative influence on Karlstadt and Zwingli, as we have seen. Through their influence it permeated the atmosphere of the Reformation.

The sacramentarian mark is evident in Marpeck's insistence that without the presence of faith, material elements have no spiritual reality. It is also evident in his secondary teaching on the Lord's Supper. Melchior Hoffmann (ca. 1495-1543) is often grouped with the sacramentarians and thought to have had at least indirect influence on Marpeck through Bernhard Rothmann (ca. 1495-1535), from whose writings Marpeck borrowed. But it is clear that Hoffmann's influence on Rothmann begins only in 1534, the year after the publication of the treatise Marpeck borrowed.[12]

Luther's influence on Marpeck was decisive at one point. Through his conflict with Karlstadt and Zwingli, among others, Luther perceived that the corrective spiritualism had brought to the church was being used to eliminate the material world as a medium of divine communication. Everything signified by the incarnation was under threat.[13] Marpeck shared this assessment with Luther. Through Luther's critical retention of Catholic sacramental tradition, Marpeck was able to appropriate it. By means of it, he arrived at an understanding of the incarnation which became the basis for his theology of the church and sacraments.[14]

Marpeck's fateful years in Strassburg (1528-32) are a fortunate exception to the lack of documentation of his early public life. His encounter with Strassburg's political and religious life carved the basic lines of his theology. This Alsatian city was a haven of tolerance, due partly to the fact that the Reformation began later there and was led by the irenic Wolfgang Capito (1478-1541) and Martin Bucer (1491-1551). It provided a cosmopolitan urban setting in which the strict separatism characteristic of other Anabaptist movements in the late 1520s was neither necessary nor possible.[15] Forceful debate with the official church was possible.

Marpeck's controversy with fellow radicals like Hans Bünderlin (1499-1533) and Caspar Schwenckfeld (1489-1561), as it turned out, was even more formative of Marpeck's thought than his encounter with the Magisterial Reformation. The spiritualists sought authentic Christian life in a mystical piety liberated from the fetters of externality—sacraments, a visible church, the letter of Scripture. Marpeck opposed a spiritualism which, in his judgment, evaporated the incarnation and with it a visible church and all of its manifestations. In Marpeck's judgment, neither interpretation of Christianity—magisteri-

al mass church or spiritualistic individualism—possessed a biblical ecclesiology or sacraments.

Schwenckfeld shared with Marpeck a passion for radical reform.
It therefore took novel and sustained theological reflection by both
theologians to identify where these two radical interpreters of the way
to renewal parted company with each other and, as it turned out, contradicted one another. This parting of ways between the two personali-
ties and movements did not crystallize until the end of the decade. To
make his convictions plausible in the debate with Schwenckfeld, Marpeck worked backward from the cluster of assumptions under debate
to the principles underlying them. From his understanding of the Trinity and the incarnation, he defended his claims about the church and
the sacraments. Neither could be grasped without the other.

The preeminent goal of Marpeck's theology was to create an
apology for ceremonies as external works which were of one being with
the inward reality they represented. He based this claim on the fact of
the incarnation and, in turn, presented it as the ultimate defense of the
incarnation. To do this, Marpeck unfolded a trinitarian structure and a
Christology inspired by the Gospel of John.

Marpeck's Chief Writings Concerning the Sacraments

Among the many writings attributed to Pilgram Marpeck, the four
to be introduced in the succeeding paragraphs are decisive for the development of his theology of the Lord's Supper. Many have speculated
concerning their authorship. Only in recent years have the first two
been ascribed to Marpeck. The third treatise is the revision of a borrowed document. The fourth has conceptual inconsistencies which in-
vite the suggestion that more than one hand stands behind it. This, in
turn, has generated the theory of a *Gemeindetheologie* (church theology) emerging out of the Marpeck circle of leadership in South German
Anabaptism. The hypothesis of this study, which will be substantiated
as soon as the documents have been introduced, is that Marpeck as an
individual theologian is the author of all these texts as they now stand.

The purpose of introducing these writings beforehand is to provide a historical and literary outline of the development of Marpeck's
thought. The proposed analysis will, however, proceed thematically
rather than chronologically from treatise to treatise. The choice of categories for this analysis has been guided by the purpose of the present
study. I will set forth the human and divine components of the
Eucharist in relation to the christological views which Marpeck developed to validate his sacramental claims.

The *Clare Verantwortung* of 1531

The *Clare Verantwortung* (*CV:* A Clear Refutation) is one of two early polemical tracts written to refute the spiritualistic tendency within the Radical Reformation.[16] It has as its subject all the "ceremonies" of the New Testament. By this term the author means all external rites given by Christ to proclaim the gospel. Throughout Marpeck's corpus, there are varying lists of ceremonies. None of them lists only the Lord's Supper and baptism. A ceremony is anything out of Jesus' ministry which passes on his teaching and identity. This broad understanding of ceremony fits well with Marpeck's notion of the church as the prolongation of the incarnation in the ongoing community of faith. The ceremonies included in *CV* are baptism, breaking of bread, Scripture, separation from the world, ban, rebuke, exhortation, prayer, kneeling, example of believers, proclamation, and teaching.[17]

The significance of this broad definition of ceremony or sacrament is that it stands in contrast to that of Marpeck's spiritualistic opponents. They worked with a narrower definition of *ceremony*, which excluded the Bible. In sum, Marpeck recast the definitions so as to challenge what he saw to be a fundamental inconsistency of spiritualism, which rejected the concept of *sacrament*. Yet, at least in Strassburg circles, spiritualism retained the Bible as valid external authority for the Christian. This is how Marpeck puts his case: to accept the Bible is to accept the ongoing validity of external witnesses; to reject the mediating role of external witnesses is to reject the Bible. If one abuses ceremonies, that cannot invalidate them for the believer who understands, uses, and practices them in a correct manner. The ceremonies, duly instituted, are valid in themselves.[18]

It is crucial to note the setting in which these positions contended with each other. Christian symbols and rites had become divorced from faith and obedience. This was the exasperated charge the radicals of the Reformation made against both the old church and the Magisterial Reformers. Marpeck dissents from his fellow radicals' commitment to the abrogation of all ceremonies by arguing the inseparability of inner and outer.

CV turns into a discourse on the work of the Holy Spirit.[19] This progression of thought from technical definitions to the realm of the ineffable, makes clear that in Marpeck's thought these two realities are inseparable. Only willing, obedient, repentant persons receive the Spirit in their heart. But nothing spiritual is lost in affirming that spirit is mediated by matter. On the contrary, our spiritual instruction begins with "[Christ's] physical words, works, deeds, and life."[20]

CV expresses the hardening positions Radical Reformers in Strassburg were taking toward each other by 1531. Even though the spiritualists and biblicists were agreed in their opposition to infant baptism and a mass church, they proposed diverging alternatives. Marpeck's proposal derives from the literal authority he grants the New Testament with regard to externals. The cornerstone of this treatise is the argument that the church life of the apostolic era is the enduring norm. The church has a historical, external existence. Its ceremonies reveal God's grace.

Like Marpeck's other writings under examination, CV seeks to anchor one pole of the dialectical movement from inner and immaterial to outer and material, without losing its hold on the other pole. This was the challenge facing the Protestant Reformation as a whole. Marpeck accepted this challenge; his spiritualistic confreres did not. Marpeck's engagement with this central struggle of the Reformation allowed his theology to be presented not only as an alternative to spiritualism but as an alternative to established versions of reform. Marpeck had a distinctive argument for holding together inner and outer which will be in the forefront of our study. That the gospel comes to us externally does not lessen the need for it to be appropriated internally. This comes about only through God's Spirit. When the Spirit is present in the heart, ceremonies become external witnesses of the Spirit's work.[21] This notion is the embryo of Marpeck's later idea of *mitzeugnus* or co-witness.

The *Klarer Unterricht* of 1531

The *Klarer Unterricht* (*KU:* Clear Instruction), addressed to the same opponents as CV, continues the defense of ceremonies but bases it more exclusively on claims grounded in Christ's human nature. "Through Christ's humanity the inward must be revealed and recognized."[22] This claim is set within a trinitarian framework. The Father's drawing of people to himself is revealed through the Son; belief in the Son is possible only when one is drawn by the Father. The Spirit of God becomes known through the humanity of Christ.[23] This is the beginning of a trinitarian rationale for the working of the incarnation and ceremonies which is developed in the *Vermanung* and VWG.

In these paragraphs of *KU*, it is already evident that the *menschheit Christi* (humanity of Christ) is the decisive concept in Marpeck's early Christology. By it he designates not only Jesus' fully human as well as divine earthly existence but also the external realities which continue his revelation. The first of these is the church, but inseparable from it are the ceremonies by which God's revelation in Christ is known. Not only did God communicate himself fully through Christ's incarnation; God's physical presence in the world is extended through time by means of Scripture and the voices and acts of faithful believers.[24] Only through these outward testimonies is the inward testimony of the Spirit revealed.

To illustrate the inseparability of the incarnation and ceremonies, Marpeck quotes his spiritualistic questioners and proceeds immediately to refute them. "What good is water, bread, or wine to me? It is sufficient if I recognize and inwardly believe. Such reason despises the humanity of Christ to which that reason should be captive.[25] Reason is confounded by and must make itself "captive to the humanity of Christ."[26] The ceremonies of the church are like the parables of the kingdom: by means of them we grasp the workings of God. Throughout his discourse, Marpeck reiterates the point that the ceremonies are gifts to help us serve God. They are not our masters. Through them the physical Christ is present in his members so that they are able to pray "Abba" and worship him.[27]

The *Vermanung* of 1542

The surprising origin of the *Vermanung* (*VMN*: Admonition) was brought to light by Frank Wray.[28] It is a heavily edited but not substantially altered version of the *Bekenntnis von beiden Sakramenten* (*BEK*) (Confession of Both Sacraments), written in 1533 by Bernhard Rothmann the Münsterite. For Rothmann, it is a transitional document, written before the onset of his apocalypticism.[29] It reads like the initial articulation of a position decidedly antisacramental but whose concerns are also not entirely represented by sacramentarianism. The unfinished nature of *BEK* and its ambivalent eucharistic doctrine are suggested by the two views it presents of the Lord's Supper and the contrasting tone of the baptismal and eucharistic sections.

It is not known when Marpeck first discovered the *BEK*. He might have hesitated at first to use it because of the notoriety into which the Münsterites had fallen by the mid-1530s. In any case, by 1542 the rivalry between spiritualism as represented by Schwenckfeld and Anabaptism as represented by Marpeck had reached a fever pitch. This is suggested not only by Marpeck's act of daring in borrowing his defense from discredited sources but also by the decisive response it provoked from Schwenckfeld. His *Judicium* (Judgment) was published within the same year.

In its present form, the *VMN* is about 150 pages in length.[30] Two-thirds of the text is devoted to the subject of baptism, though this section deals also with sacramental questions in general. Most of Marpeck's additions come here.[31] He expands on Rothmann's postulates such that there is a sympathy between the original and added text. The fundamental point of commonality between Rothmann and Marpeck was a shared passionate conviction about believers baptism. It was the critical norm by which everything else in the life of the church was interpreted. By it, everything that was meant by the concepts *sign* and *ceremony* was illustrated. The concentration of Marpeck's additions to the *BEK* introduction and to the section on baptism illustrates this Anabaptist commonality. The position hammered out on the anvil of baptism shaped the eucharistic thinking of both authors. In Rothmann's text as well as Marpeck's additions, the Lord's Supper is often used to illustrate the sacramental argument just presented.[32]

Rothmann's enduring contribution to Marpeck's thought is that he had worked out a sacramental reality more fully than Marpeck had in *CV* and *KU*. The path of that reality ran between sacramentalism, in which active faith was not essential; and sacramentarianism, in which faith replaced any sacramental reality.[33] At the same time, Marpeck's theology of the ceremonies definitively went beyond that of Rothmann.

VMN was published ten years after the original debates between the Marpeck circle and the spiritualists in Strassburg. The vulnerability of Anabaptism to a spiritualistic tendency had become clearer as time went on. By 1542 Caspar Schwenckfeld, its most brilliant spokesperson, and Marpeck had become each other's foremost opponents. Marpeck's initial addition to Rothmann's work depicts a beleaguered conventicle desperately in search of an apologetic for its convictions and sorely in need of comfort in its sufferings.[34] By 1542 the debate between South German Anabaptism and the Magisterial Reformation had become clearly secondary to its encounter with spiritualism. Schwenckfeld saw Anabaptism as the most insidious threat to his views. He wrote a refutation of *VMN* in the same year it was published, 1542.

Neal Blough challenges the view made popular by William Klassen, that spiritualism and Anabaptism, as represented by Schwenckfeld and Marpeck, fundamentally diverged in 1531. The hypothesis Klassen puts forward is made on textual grounds, that *CV* and *KU* were written by Marpeck against Schwenckfeld.[35] Blough presents evidence that the two theologians saw themselves engaged in a common task and even shared basic assumptions in and after their Strassburg years. They did not become antagonistic to each other until after 1538, when

Schwenckfeld repudiated the creatureliness of Christ's humanity and when both men perceived themselves to be competing for the loyalty of the same people.[36]

Schwenckfeld's 1542 tract, entitled *Über das neu Büchlin der Tauffbrüder,* or *Judicium* (*JDM:* On the New Booklet of the Baptism Brothers, or Judgment),[37] is a modest forty-six page response to *VMN.* A tendentious spirit is present in the first part, but it takes a more irenic direction as the document nears its conclusion. At many junctures Schwenckfeld and Marpeck still have much in common. For example, over against Catholic and Lutheran conviction, these protagonists agree that the outer element of a ceremony is of no value in itself.

JDM undertakes a careful unraveling of the positions set forth in *VMN.* Its most stinging rebuke to the Anabaptists is that their religion is one of mere externals. *JDM* is not content with specific criticisms but challenges the principles behind the particular points of contention. It alleges the chief of these to be the false Christology *VMN* espouses.

JDM goes on to challenge the ecclesiological principle undergirding Marpeck's structure. In *VMN* Marpeck claims that after 1400 years of decay, baptism has been restored to its true meaning. He reiterates this argument late in *VWG.*[38] In response, Schwenckfeld asks, "When, how, and where [has] Christ commanded them [the Anabaptists] to reestablish such a great work"?[39] Schwenckfeld assumes that there is no continuity between the apostolic age and the present; Marpeck rejoins that the command of Jesus has never been abrogated.[40] The gist of this altercation is both biblical and historical. Schwenckfeld repeatedly buttresses his position with Scripture, but in the end, his spiritualistic theological critique prevails. At various times he argues both that the church must be without sacraments because they have been so abused and also that it may be without sacraments because Christ's work in the heart makes them superfluous.[41]

The *Verantwortung* (*Verantwurtung über Caspern Schwenckfelds Judicium*)[42]

In 1544 Marpeck undertook a vehement and exhaustive response to Schwenckfeld. He intended it to be a convincing argument against spiritualism. The *Verantwortung* (*VWG*) is a polemical document. It is part of a series of exchanges in which two by-now clearly incompatible Christologies and ecclesiologies are engaged in a contest of ultimate significance. William Klassen calls *VWG* "the finest single source of theology of the South German Anabaptists."[43] On the nature of the opposing positions, the common claim is that the conflict between

Schwenckfeld and Marpeck was one between spiritualism and biblicism. These designations seem too general to be helpful, even if they
do identify the orientation of the combatants. The conflict between the
two men centered on Christology and ecclesiology. The plumb line for
Schwenckfeld's theology was the glorified Christ and an invisible
church; for Marpeck, it was the humiliated Christ and a visible church.
In addition, these two points of disagreement proved to be decisive for
their respective theologies of the Lord's Supper.

Marpeck's response to *JDM* is in two parts. One of them, *VWG I*,
is 111 pages long and was authored in 1544. The longer section,
VWG II, is 389 pages long. Its date of authorship is disputed and will be
considered below. Marpeck's method of response is to create one hun-
dred small units out of Schwenckfeld's text, quote one (sometimes
incorrectly), give his rebuttal, and then take up the next unit. Each
exchange is called a *red und antwort* (speech and response). Preeminence is given to baptism, original sin, the faith of the patriarchs, and
the Lord's Supper. The Supper is the dominant subject of three chapters, totaling 132 pages, the focus of our interest in *VWG*. However,
many shorter and longer references to Christology, ceremonies, and
Lord's Supper occur throughout the treatise. We will also examine
these preliminary chapters as the frame of reference for our more concentrated attention on the eucharistic chapters.

The Question of Authorship

The question of who wrote the books we identify with the name
Pilgram Marpeck casts a dark but fascinating shadow over the explora-
tion of his thought. The uncertainties of authorship extend to all four of
the documents on which the present study is based.[44] The fact that all of
them were lost from the late sixteenth to the twentieth centuries only
heightens the mystery. The daunting complexity of the writings themselves forbids the temptation to pursue the fascinating question of authorship—except for two points directly related to the Eucharist and
Christology in *VWG*. They are the question of authorship in relation to
its probable theological setting and the problem of a *volte-face* (about-
face) in the concluding pages of its argument.

The fact that Marpeck worked with a circle of colleagues, especially with Leopold Scharnschlager, has given rise to the proposal that
the writings in question are the product of a *Gemeindetheologie.*[45] This
interpretation fails to give three factors their due. One of them is that
the *VWG* is written in the spirit of a personal vindication of an author
against his attacker. Its polemic has the marks of an individual writer,

even though it might have been issued on behalf of a community. A second factor is that, as we shall see, Marpeck's eccentricities of thought are too individualistic to mirror a community at work. Third, the Anabaptist congregation in Augsburg during the 1540s did not have a strong communal life. It met only quarterly, being prevented from undertaking sustained collective activity by harsh persecution.[46] Marpeck was the least harassed among the members because of his professional status, and he could write with a freedom which his colleagues lacked.

The most accessible and vexing problem of authorship comes in fragments XCVII to C, at the end of *VWG*. It involves a contradiction of the specific arguments and the overall orientation of Marpeck's work as a whole.[47] The hypothesis advanced by this study is that Marpeck is the single author of all four of the treatises under examination. The sole exception to this is fragments XCVII to C, at the end of *VWG*. Its author struggled with the same tensions Marpeck dealt with but was inadequate to the scale and significance of the debate between the two most profound representatives of the divergent poles of the Radical Reformation.[48]

Throughout all four of the documents under consideration, we see striking developments in the doctrines Marpeck defends. It will become clear, as they are examined, that the challenges put to Marpeck and his community demand the extension of his beliefs in directions not previously thought through. But, even in the midst of these adaptations of arguments to novel circumstances, conceptual continuity is evident. Such continuity is outstanding in three areas, all of them unique to this set of writings: the inseparability of inner and outer reality,[49] the ceremonies as analogies of the incarnation,[50] and the elastic application of the notion of co-witness to God's revelation of himself in time and space.[51] The most persuasive explanation for the intellectual cohesion in these writings is a single, common author.

Marpeck's Theology
A Preface on the Gospel of John in Marpeck's Thought

Marpeck's theology cannot be understood apart from its affinity with and reliance on the Fourth Gospel. This claim is of major proportions and must be substantiated. It is not an easy task to do so for three reasons. First, Marpeck's use of John varies. At times the Johannine spirit shines like a full moon over all Marpeck's thoughts; at other times it is in almost complete eclipse.[52] Second, the Fourth Gospel has been the object of radically divergent interpretations through the centuries.[53] One senses that Marpeck is spiritually at home in the world of the Fourth Gospel: the mystery of God in the flesh and God as spirit has shaped Marpeck's picture of reality. At the same time, that world has been mediated to him by an already existing interpretation of it. His understanding of the "humanity of Christ" is not an exegetical deduction from the text but a complex theological elaboration on it.[54] Therefore, it cannot be said that there is a simple correlation between Marpeck and John. The term *Johannine tradition* will be used to describe the stream of interpretation on which Marpeck depends.

There is a third reason for the difficulty involved in identifying Marpeck closely with the theology of the Fourth Gospel: his use of trinitarian language. It has often been assumed that John is the direct source of the trinitarian formulations set in place at the (First) Council of Nicaea (325) and the christological claims of the Council of Chalcedon (451). The two are not that closely related. Though Marpeck does not make much use of later confessional terminology of the distinct persons of the Trinity,[55] he does embrace other aspects of it. At the same time, the Spirit is often described more as the agency of the Father's work or the Son's, suggesting a binitarian picture of God.[56] In this study the term *trinitarian* will be used not as a claim for the Fourth Gospel but to describe Marpeck's appropriation of it.

The most pervasive evidence for the Johannine character of Marpeck's writing is the centrality of a theologically explicit understanding of the incarnation. The Synoptic Gospels assume a unique relationship between Jesus and the Father, but only the Fourth Gospel spells out the content of this relationship. In particular, the Gospel of John is the origin of Marpeck's concern for the distinctive work of Christ in his divinity and humanity[57] and for the relationship, ontological as well as functional, between the Son and the Spirit. This is present in Marpeck's Strassburg tracts, but it becomes dominant in the trinitarian scheme of *VMN* and *VWG* and in the discussion of Christ's two natures in *VWG*.

Marpeck's interest in John's Gospel consists only secondarily of its exegetical value to him. His primary interest is in John's towering theological constructs. What he takes over from the Johannine tradition are its speculative claims about the nature of things, including God as three persons and the relationship between spirit and flesh, inner and outer reality. Sometimes, especially in *CV* and *KU*, Marpeck relies on the explicit words of a given biblical text as his authority. This is also the case in *VMN* and *VWG* when Marpeck is engaged exegetically with the institutional narratives. Occasionally this becomes an exercise in proof-texting. However, in the construction of his theological system as a whole, Marpeck's train of thought is seldom derived from a serious exegetical engagement with specific texts. Though his authority is the content of the biblical revelation, his thinking is theological rather than biblical, conceptual rather than exegetical. He is inspired and guided by the picture of divine and human reality presented in the Fourth Gospel. Through his affinity with the theology of John, Marpeck moves his position forward.[58]

The Johannine trinitarian scheme, for example, is the inspiration behind Marpeck's understanding of the distinctive work of the Father and the Son.[59] In his letter to Helena Streicher, written during the heat of his controversy with Schwenckfeld in the 1540s, Marpeck highlights the role of the Spirit in relation to the ceremonies.[60] Late in *VWG II*, Marpeck enters a protracted and subtle debate with Schwenckfeld concerning the presence of the two natures of Christ in the breaking of bread. Both men cast their thoughts into Johannine categories and use their rival interpretations of that Gospel against each other.[61]

The binitarian tendency of the Fourth Gospel is also mirrored in Marpeck's thought. The two persons of the Godhead seem to be the Father and the Son. The Spirit is sometimes conflated with either of these persons or described as the mode of their presence.[62]

Finally, what Marpeck takes to be John's account of the Last Supper (John 13) plays a formative role in Marpeck's depiction of a true Eucharist. He posits the foot-washing account as an integral component of the institution. This in turn supplies Marpeck with the criterion of love as the foremost characteristic of the breaking of bread. In *VMN* this notion, taken over from *BEK,* plays a more prominent role than the memorial. Its dominance of the eucharistic discussion in *VWG* is even more obvious. There it becomes the distinguishing mark of Marpeck's version of the Supper over against Schwenckfeld's.[63]

God as Trinity

Trinitarian assumptions stand behind Marpeck's theological language in all the documents under consideration. In the early tracts, conventional claims are advanced about each of the three persons. We note the originality in Marpeck's grasp of trinitarian belief as well as its indispensability for Marpeck's theology of the sacraments. This first becomes evident when he turns to it in order to substantiate his bold and innovative claims in *VMN* concerning the sacraments. Thus he says,

> Whoever has the truth in the heart, the truth which is pointed to and signified by the external sign, for him it is no sign at all, but rather one essential union with the inner.[64]

The author seems to realize that such a bold statement cannot be substantiated with the defense of sacraments he has presented earlier. Marpeck then undertakes an excursus, his first substantive theological addition to the received text of *VMN*, more than a page in length. It explains his sacramental claims with reference to the Trinity. Father and Son are at work simultaneously in this event. The Father works internally as Spirit, the Son externally as man.

> Therefore, the external baptism and the Lord's Supper in Christ are not signs; rather, they are the external work and essence of the Son.[65]

Neither of these events can happen without the other because, in Johannine fashion, Marpeck asserts that no one person of the Trinity exists or functions without the other.[66] The church carries on the work which the Son of man did externally. Thus the church is the humanity of Christ, outwardly doing the ceremonies which the Spirit inwardly fulfills.[67]

Marpeck's next addendum returns to the topic of the Spirit. At this juncture in the argument, however, Marpeck has left behind his earlier concern about the present work of the Trinity in the church. Here his contention is that believers baptism follows from the nature of the new covenant. Marpeck focuses on the historical self-revelation of God as Son and Spirit. His goal is to demonstrate the superiority of God's disclosure of himself in the new covenant. When the Son ascended to the Father, the Holy Spirit could build the church in the hearts of believers. Here the work of the Son and Spirit is depicted as sequential rather than simultaneous. Both claims recur throughout the rest of *VMN* and *VWG*.

This relationship of Son and Spirit derives from Marpeck's view of the old and new covenants. Early in this section, he claims that "before the transfiguration of Christ, no one received the Holy Spirit in the same measure as his apostles and all true believers now receive him."[68] The line of argument becomes more radical as it proceeds. True knowledge of the Father began only with the Son.[69] True knowledge of the Son began only with the Spirit.[70] Through the Spirit, people receive "the sonship of the eternal kingdom."[71]

The contrast between how God functioned historically and how he now works is instructive for the concern of this study on the human and divine dimensions of the Lord's Supper. The simultaneous working of the Trinity is unique to the new covenant. The ceremonies become the paradigm for how God works in the age of the church. The simultaneous work of Father, Son, and Spirit takes form primally in the sacraments; through them we learn what the relationship is between the spiritual and material worlds.

Marpeck's tendency to conflate the roles of members of the Trinity is strikingly evident. Two illustrations are typical. One comes from Marpeck's exegetical work. At the apex of Paul's teaching on the Holy Spirit in Romans (8:1-27, especially 8:15), the primal sign of the Spirit's presence is the believer's ability to cry "Abba." Marpeck uses *Abba,* a notion whose pneumatic context is unmistakable, yet attributes the believer's awareness of sonship to the work of Christ. The second illustration concerns Marpeck's attempt to locate Christ in heaven according to his physical being and on earth in his spiritual mode. His shorthand reference to the latter is often to say that the divine nature of Christ is his Holy Spirit.[72]

Christology
Introduction

In the nature of Christian theology, it is not possible to abstract Christology from its trinitarian setting. Our attempt to place Christology under a separate heading will keep that fact in mind. There are two reasons for treating Christology as a distinct category. First, Pilgram Marpeck's writing is not set out in systematic categories. His treatises are all apologetic pieces prompted by challenges to his position. They become occasions for him to work out a defense for his claims. If we separate the categories in which his arguments are cast, that makes it easier to follow their evolution and monitor their internal consistency. Second, the debate over the Eucharist between Marpeck and Schwenckfeld is focused increasingly on technical christological definitions, especially concerning the two natures of Christ.

The Humanity of Christ

The decisive concept in Marpeck's early Christology is the *menschheit Christi,* the *humanity of Christ.* In *KU,* Marpeck introduces the term to interpret what he means by the incarnation and to set it forth as the basis of his theology of the ceremonies. The ceremonies carry on the presence of Christ in the world. Just as inner, spiritual reality is revealed in outer, material form in Christ taking on flesh, so too do the external works of the church reveal the internal reality. Revelation comes in receiving the physical words and voice of Christ rather than in searching behind them. Marpeck sums up his position by saying, "Christ became a natural man for natural men."[73] Natural realities precede spiritual ones and can lead to them.

The dynamic behind this disclosure is the Trinity.[74] The *menschheit Christi* does not infer that Jesus is simply a human being. By this term, Marpeck intends to say that in Jesus' humanness, God is most fully recognized.[75] The church is the prolongation of this mode of revelation. It has the keys to the kingdom; it is Christ's vicarious presence.[76] Its humble, outer life carries on Christ's humble, outer life. Similarly, Christ is shown forth in the humble substances of the natural order, like bread and wine.[77] The ceremonies become analogues of the incarnation. These claims are given fuller development in *VMN* when Marpeck sets out to substantiate his fundamental sacramental claim.[78] The inner and outer become one reality through the work of the Trinity.

Neal Blough illuminates Marpeck's pivotal christological notion, the humanity of Christ, by proposing that its origin is in Luther and that its appeal to Marpeck lay in Luther's use of the concept to combat spiritualism.[79] For Luther, as for the dominant medieval tradition in general, sacraments were an extension of the incarnation. To reject them was to reject the incarnation. The controversy concerning the Eucharist was in the end a debate between contradictory christologies. Blough strengthens his hypothesis about the origin of Marpeck's train of thought in *KU* by citing Luther's emphasis on the external as the way to the internal, and on the inability of reason to grasp this mystery.

A final claim of affinity between the two theologians relies on the fact that Luther did not limit his concept of sacrament to baptism and the Lord's Supper. Preaching and love of neighbor are often included in his list of divinely ordained outward rites. The parallels between the sacramental notions of the two theologians are striking and lend credence to Blough's claim. He acknowledges that Luther and Marpeck diverge at other points in their writings on Christology. But Luther's arguments mediated to Marpeck the traditional beliefs about the incarnation in a way that challenged the spiritualists.

The Glorified Christ

The pinnacle of Marpeck's christological creativity and his most subtle application of it to the Lord's Supper occurs in *VWG*. It was prompted by a change in Schwenckfeld's Christology which had driven the two reformers into a decisive antagonism to each other. Schwenckfeld had drawn the full consequences of his position by 1538 and denied the creatureliness of Christ's humanity even in his incarnation.[80] The fundamental thrust of *VWG* is a Christology and eucharistic doctrine whose purpose is to refute Schwenckfeld's Christology and

eucharistic doctrine. Both theologians, and the movements they represented, established their positions by advancing teachings about the
Lord's Supper. As they contested with the magisterial reformers and
with each other, they were forced to substantiate their eucharistic
claims with christological ones. This is evident in the structure of Marpeck's thought in *VWG*. Here he is more explicitly and systematically
concerned with the two natures of Christ than with a trinitarian
scheme, which is less prominent yet still assumed.[81]

In *VWG*, Marpeck's major debate with Schwenckfeld is prompted by Schwenckfeld's accusation that Marpeck and those like him are
unable to recognize the true Christ. They both agree that recognition
of the true Christ is inseparable from true communion with him. Indeed, fragment XCVI in *VWG* is a ninety-page excursus by Marpeck
on the crown jewel of Schwenckfeld's theology, the glorified Christ.
Marpeck's explicitly directs his protest at one line from Schwenckfeld:
"Also, they cannot know unless they rightly recognize Christ in glory."[82]
At the heart of his long rejoinder is Marpeck's view of the relationship
in Christ between flesh and spirit, and of the saving role of both his
unglorified and glorified self.

All of their debate flows from principles common to the Radical
Reformation.[83] Schwenckfeld and Marpeck are the most articulate representatives of its extreme positions. In the evolution of their debate
with one another in the 1540s, their positions crystallize in their
Christology. It becomes a way for both of them, partly in retrospect, to
legitimate their views.[84] But it also shows them that they hold to fundamentally different starting points for their theology. This difference is
more profound than the positions they hold in common as radical reformers.

"Do we not rightly recognize Christ in his glory?" asks Marpeck
rhetorically. By reciting his creedal refrain from the *VMN*, Marpeck ex
plains what it means to him to proclaim the glory of Christ. That glory
consists of his "love, patience, and humility" and of the fact that he was
"a true, natural person born of the human order" (*geschlecht der
menschen*).[85] Marpeck is adamant that Schwenckfeld's attempts to
honor Christ actually rob him of his glory, which is his condescension.
Because of this, Marpeck concludes, Schwenckfeld does not know how
to judge the true Supper of Christ; indeed, he has never tasted or
touched it.

Marpeck quotes nine pages of his opponent's christological passages out of works other than *JDM*. Schwenckfeld's definitive claim appears near the beginning of *JDM*.

Christ the king, who received the promise of the Holy Spirit, truly indwell-
ingly distributes his body and blood in the Holy Spirit; he [comes] not only
in pictures or thoughts. Therefore, it is also necessary that the body of
Christ have a spiritual being, i.e., that it be what the Spirit is, who alone en-
livens through the flesh. That is a true meal and a living heavenly bread in
the heavenly reality.[86]

Schwenckfeld proceeds to elaborate on his view. The Spirit does
not belong to God only; he is also the Spirit of the "glorified, exalted, divine man Christ." Christ is true God and true man in the Spirit, that is,
the Lord is the Spirit (2 Cor. 3).[87] The glory of the flesh of Christ is that
it now partakes of everything which God is. No longer is Christ of our
flesh, but we are of his, born from above by the Spirit.[88] His flesh is truly
food.

Now the Lord Jesus has put off all creaturely essence and life through his
death; even according to his humanity he has become Lord of all creatures
in heaven and on earth. . . . Internally and externally his flesh has been
anointed and permeated (*durchgossen*) with the Holy Spirit, so that in Jesus Christ the whole fulness of God dwells bodily, Col. 2.[89]

The conclusion of this is that Christ no longer has a mortal, imper-
fect body and blood—here the eucharistic point of the exercise becomes explicit—but a divine, perfect being which can be reached by
faith alone. This faith has to do with inner, invisible things.[90]

Christ has not put off the flesh, Schwenckfeld insists, but only
bodily, fleshly reality (*leiblich, fleischlich wesen*). This subtle distinction
is introduced to show that he really believes that the believer feeds on
the flesh and blood of Christ. When Schwenckfeld quotes 2 Corinthians 5 to the effect that Christians no longer know Christ according to
the flesh, the reader is not certain to which "flesh" he refers—bodily or
spiritual.[91] The overall argument suggests that it is bodily, mortal flesh.

In Schwenckfeld's view of sanctification, the believer is divinized
and participates in Christ's nature. From the following thought, this
seems to mean that the believer is no longer bound by human creatureliness. Not only Christ but also the children of his kingdom cannot be
localized physically. They are hidden with Christ and translated into
heaven. They share a splendid Supper with him; they are actually his
body, embodied in him not by outward means but by means of the Holy
Spirit. Christology, ecclesiology, and Eucharist all, inseparably, derive
their being from this single reality.[92]

We must attend to one final contention of Schwenckfeld for an understanding of his position. At the Last Supper, which he calls the first Lord's Supper (*im ersten nachtmal*), the disciples were truly fed with the body and blood of Christ even though he was not yet glorified. Anyone who is not confined to a historical, untheological faith knows that Christ "is everywhere and always (*allweg*) glorified. In every age Christ is what he is in and with God yesterday, today, and in eternity."[93] To confess anything less is to hold Christ to be an external, created substance.[94] Such an assertion, according to Marpeck's excerpts from his opponent's corpus, is a further demeaning of the incarnation: everything Christ is, he always was. He always had a human nature and came to earth in his fullness, without taking on anything of our world.

After nine pages of citations from different works of his opponent, Marpeck begins his critique. He wants his readers to see the falsity of Schwenckfeld's claims that the glorified body, flesh, and blood of Christ are the spiritual food and drink of the soul in the Lord's Supper. Further, he explains why Schwenckfeld's imputation of ignorance to the Marpeckian eucharistic doctrine is unjust. Marpeck's thinking proceeds as follows: Baptism and the Lord's Supper were instituted to bring near to us not the glorified, immortal body and blood of Christ but his mortal, unglorified reality as he gave it for our reconciliation before his resurrection and ascension.[95] In the breaking of bread, we remember the Lord's death, his mortal body, until he comes. To faith, Christ is present in his divine nature or in the Spirit (the two appear as synonyms) in the Eucharist, as he is in other ways.

A fundamental difference of belief between the lead players in our drama is in danger of being camouflaged here because of their similar terminology. Schwenckfeld has been saying that the believer feeds on the glorified body of Christ. Marpeck, on the other hand, holds that the memorial and the eating in Holy Communion concern his human, mortal self, spiritually received.

> The soul is fed and given drink in communion . . . through faith in the words and proclamation of Christ's death, that he offered his flesh and shed his blood. It is this food and drink alone which the soul tastes in its already-mentioned hunger and thirst.[96]

The whole point of John 6, according to Marpeck, is that eating Christ corporeally is not life-giving. This applies to his unglorified as well as to his glorified body. What sustains us is the spiritual partaking of his unglorified self, that self which died for us. The ethical and sacramental dimensions of Marpeck's theology are of a piece: the suffering Christ, the example we follow, is the very one on whom we feed. The

Lord's Supper is the celebration precisely of the *menschheit Christi* and his death, not his resurrection and glorification. His glorified body could not have helped us. That body which bled for us is now our food spiritually, through the Spirit.[97]

Guessing that Schwenckfeld might question his orthodoxy, Marpeck repeats his adherence to the high Christology of the Fourth Gospel. Marpeck is unequivocal in his confession that Christ is God. But his divinity does not annul his true humanity.[98] In his divinity he is present as Spirit. "The Lord is spirit" does not mean, as Schwenckfeld insists, that he is present in his human nature equally and everywhere that he is present in his divine nature. In his mortal nature, Jesus was glorified on the mountain. But even in his transfigured state, he was present only at one place.[99]

Marpeck is simultaneously contending that the Lord's Supper is a remembrance of salvation and, therefore, of Jesus' mortal anguish on our behalf. His saving body feeds us sacramentally, that is, really but not physically. These are not propositions which follow from one another, but they have been joined together to counter Schwenckfeld's claim that the Lord's Supper is a physical though not creaturely feeding on the flesh of the glorified Christ. The joining of these propositions creates a double linkage. First, it explicitly ties Marpeck's teaching about the humanity of Christ with the memorial notion of the Eucharist which he inherits from Rothmann. Second, it connects his earlier dynamic trinitarian model of the Lord's Supper with the language of real presence from John 6. At the conclusion of *VWG*, this linkage is suddenly broken apart when it does not seem adequate to the defense of Marpeck's position.[100] Nevertheless, in the fires of controversy, it is a spectacular welding together of elements which have heretofore coexisted without an organic unity.

The Two Natures of Christ and Communion with Him

Difficulty with christological terminology bedevils this debate. Marpeck's problem is that he interprets his opponent's claims about the Eucharist in terms of his own assumptions. If Schwenckfeld thought the way Marpeck does, his description would imply a corporeal eating much like that held to by the Catholics and Lutherans. Thus Marpeck makes his own construction of the issues: Since both parties to the current debate agree that a literal, physical eating is unbiblical, Schwenckfeld is contradicting himself. Marpeck's way out of this supposed contradiction is to describe Christ's fullness, his two natures together, as a "spiritual body of the resurrected humanity of Christ." In the forty days before his ascension, many people saw this body.[101] Christ's corporeality, as explained here, was divinized after he offered himself to God as a *sacrifice* in the resurrection. This is a novel formulation; it departs from his earlier insistence that it is the mortal body of Christ which is spiritually received in communion.

This shift in christological conception is the first step in separating the presence of Christ in the Lord's Supper from his unglorified body, understood as the *menschheit Christi*. This is composed both of Christ on earth as a human being and the church as his extension. Bergsten calls it Marpeck's *Kompromissformel* (formula of compromise).[102] In this closing *VWG* debate, Marpeck turns to make conceivable the split between memorial/broken body and real presence/glorified body as two separate kinds of communion.

This shift, however noteworthy, documents a crucial development in Marpeck's eucharistic doctrine. Yet it does not displace the eucharistic realism he set forth in his earlier argument: the oneness between the outer elements and the inner reality of Christ. Also, it does not alter the logic of Marpeck's argument in this passage. This is evident from the next portion of the debate, where Marpeck tries to sharpen the contrast between their two views. As Marpeck sees it, because the eternal Son of God took on creaturely humanness at his incarnation, he could redeem the world, and he continues to mediate redemption. But as Schwenckfeld sees it, the eternal Son of God had two natures from the beginning. Therefore, he did not need to be born *of* a woman, but only *in* a woman. He never possessed true creatureliness but only the perfect humanness of his preexistence.

Marpeck agrees with Schwenckfeld that through his death, resurrection, and glorification, Christ put off his "earthly, natural" life. But again, he insists on his own conclusion to that premise: Christ ascended to heaven, where (according to the creed both disputants share) he shall remain until the last day. Therefore, his glorified body, flesh, and blood cannot come and be in the hearts of believers. Marpeck insists again and again that the human nature of Christ, though glorified, can be present only at one place at one time.[103] He does not take into account Schwenckfeld's claim that even Christ's human body has put off its earthly form and thus cannot be eaten physically or be bound to earthly limitations. Both men are advocating extreme positions: Marpeck, that there is only a limited "communication of idioms," that is, the only attribution of the characteristics of one nature to the other after Jesus' ascension is spiritual and not physical; Schwenckfeld, that the communication of idioms is such that the distinction between the two natures disappears.

Both theologians buttress their positions by borrowing from Christologies they otherwise find inadequate on many grounds. These strange borrowings are necessary for them to sustain their respective interpretations of the Lord's Supper. Schwenckfeld turns to the mainstream of medieval theology, possibly as it was mediated by Luther. According to it, the human nature of Christ was transformed at his glorification such that it lost its earthly limitations. Therefore, Christ could be present sacramentally in both natures. Marpeck takes recourse to late medieval sacramentarianism, mediated to the Reformation most significantly by Karlstadt and Zwingli. In that view, Christ's glorification did not do away with the limitations to human nature which Christ took upon himself at the incarnation.

Schwenckfeld's position allows the glorified Christ to be present in communion in both his natures. Marpeck's position does not follow as directly from his premises as does Schwenckfeld's. In order for Marpeck to make as full a claim as Schwenckfeld does about Christ's presence, he needs to bring a conceptual shift into play: physically Christ remains in heaven, but spiritually his glorified humanity is present in communion. Marpeck qualifies the concept of the two natures, for example, speaking of "the glorified body of his human nature" and "Holy Spirit or divine nature." In the process of this shift, he replaces the human–divine nature contrast with that of physical–spiritual nature,[104] thus reducing complex categories of "human" and "divine" to much simpler ones of "physical" and "spiritual." This allows Marpeck to get to his point, that Christ is spritually but not physically present in communion. If he puts the matter in those words, Schwenckfeld can hardly disagree.

Only by making the pairs of concepts at issue interchangeable can Marpeck retain his central theological assertion in the eucharistic debate: God saves us through the humanity of his Son. The church and its ceremonies continue to reveal this truth by their outwardness. Because he really took on our flesh and made it part of himself, he cannot be physically present on earth. But his spiritual presence here mediates the saving power of his incarnation.

Both men realize that the foundation of everything they believe is at stake. Marpeck remains firm in his claim that salvation happened in history. The Lord's Supper is the commemoration of an event in time and space and not an eternal truth transacted within the Trinity, as he thinks his opponent believes. However, in order to do away with a corporeal presence—which follows from the christological assumptions he shares with classical Western theology, namely, that the heavenly

Christ retains his two natures—Christ in his physical reality needs to be localized in heaven.[105]

Schwenckfeld, as shown above, believes that Christ now is who he always was: nothing was added to him in his incarnation; nothing was added by incarnation to God's saving work. Nothing creaturely can be the cause of grace. Because of his fervent conviction that the believer is given communion with Christ, Schwenckfeld retains the language which claims that the whole Christ is present. In turn, he rescues himself from eucharistic deductions implied in the classical belief about the two natures—a corporeal presence—by having Christ's humanity so transformed that it no longer has physical attributes. Therefore, Christ can be present bodily without being present corporeally.[106]

Competing Claims of Orthodoxy

One novel christological claim of Marpeck occurs in the pages of repetition and summary which follow. Though Christ was always God, it was through the uniting (*verainigung*) of his bodily character (*leiblichkeit*) with the word of God that he became fully God (*völliger Gott ist worden*). Before his resurrection, Godness (*gottheit*) was not fully in him, though he was God as (*nach*) spirit and word. The fullness which came about in the resurrection was the unity of the Lord's two natures: his humanity was henceforth inseparable from his divinity. This claim is the direct opposite of Schwenckfeld's view: Christ's complete divinity came when he put off his physical nature.[107]

Marpeck ventures a summary of his Christology as he has presented it in the foregoing pages.

> We affirm and believe the glorified human being Jesus Christ with his one, undivided person, according to Holy Scripture, to be the true, almighty God in or with his two united natures.[108]

His unveiled intention is to show that an orthodox Christology, which he confidently believes he has, is compatible with the belief that in his human nature, Christ can be present only in one place at one time. So intolerable is the alleged claim that Christ is humanly, physically present in communion that it must be shown to be an impossible contention. This mentality sets the parameters of most non-Lutheran reformation debates on the Lord's Supper. It also makes clear that at this fateful point, Marpeck sides as decisively with the spiritualistic tendency of the Reformation as does Schwenckfeld, though by a different route.

When Marpeck turns to do exegesis on a biblical text, he imposes the definitions of the preceding debate on his reading of the Corinthian institutional narrative. The words, "For as often as you eat this bread and drink the cup, you proclaim the Lord's death until he comes" (1 Cor. 11:26), mean that Christ is not present according to his "glorified body of human nature" but according to his "Holy Spirit or divine nature."[109] It is difficult to assess whether this conflation of Son and Spirit, a fixture of Marpeck's thought, was a theological convention of the day or whether it was an original attempt by Marpeck to make his view of the Lord's Supper unassailable. Even if this christological motif was old, the application Marpeck gives it is novel because his eucharistic doctrine is novel. It rules out the last obstacle Schwenckfeld has put in his way, that of a bodily but not physical presence of Christ in both his natures. If Christ is present only in his "Holy Spirit or divine nature," there can be no such thing as a bodily presence in any mode.

In a final bid to assert his conviction, Marpeck refines his claims about the two natures of Christ. His human nature is part of his divinity. His divinity is present as Spirit; therefore his humanness is part of that presence, even though his body, flesh, and blood are in heaven. This formula, Marpeck concludes, is the only way of doing justice to the claims of Scripture.[110]

Marpeck's summary of his opponent's position illustrates the surpassing fear he had of a corporeal presence in the Lord's Supper, whatever its definition. He misrepresents Schwenckfeld in a curious way, claiming that the latter holds to a glorified bodily presence in relation to the element of bread. He seems to see Schwenckfeld as a covert Lutheran. Yet throughout their confrontation, it has been clear that Schwenckfeld's Eucharist is dissociated from material elements and that Christ's human nature has no creaturely or physical attributes. Marpeck's strenuous opposition to conventional beliefs about the real presence prevents him from seeing that he and Schwenckfeld are proposing parallel and not contradictory solutions to a commonly perceived problem.[111] The guiding intention of Schwenckfeld's celestial-flesh theology through its stages of evolution was to show that our creaturely human nature cannot be a means of grace. His two central assertions are of a piece: just as Christ could not save us by taking on our fallen creatureliness in his incarnation, so he cannot come to us now by means of creaturely bread and wine.

Like Marpeck's dynamic trinitarianism, his opponent's Christology of glorification was occasioned by profound dissatisfaction with the theology and spirituality of the contending eucharistic doctrines of the

day. Both Marpeck and Schwenckfeld thought the Catholic and Lutheran interpretations seemed to vitiate faith as the only mode of apprehension for grace and reduce Christ to a material reality. On the
other hand, the Zwinglian view—as seen by its critics—seemed to both
men to reduce the Lord's Supper to a human action which emptied
New Testament claims, particularly as found in the Gospel of John, that
the Lord's Supper was a real participation in Christ.

The great irony of the controversy between the theologians was
that although they espoused contradictory Christologies and
eucharistic doctrines, they were agreed that Christ's gift of himself in
communion was not corporeal in character. But they had opposing reasons for defending that belief and ways of doing so. Marpeck was unable to give Schwenckfeld his due because of his passionate conviction
that the latter's alternative was a counterfeit. This was so for two reasons. First, for Marpeck, Schwenckfeld's terminology about Christ's
glorified, bodily presence could be no more than another version of
medieval belief about a corporeal presence. The second reason had to
do with Christology. In Marpeck's eyes, Schwenckfeld's position evaporated the incarnation as the way in which God saves. For Marpeck, the
incarnation both opened a new covenant and perpetuated the work of
Christ through history in the life of the church.

Thus it is more striking when Bergsten notes that the concept of
the church as the unglorified body of Christ on earth disappears in the
second part of *VWG*. He reasons that Marpeck undertakes such radical
reconstruction of his own conceptual framework so that there can be
no ambiguity to the claim that physically Christ has ascended to the
right hand of the Father until his return in glory. As Bergsten sees it,
Marpeck has broken through to a *Kompromissformel:* the undivided
Christ is present through the Spirit in the breaking of bread, but his
body, flesh, and blood remain in heaven. With this formula,

> he tries to hold fast to a Zwinglian position as concerns Christ's physical
> attachment to heaven, and at the same time, to hold onto the view that
> Christ is present in his church not only as God but as a human being in the
> Lord's Supper and the hearts of believers on earth.[112]

Bergsten notes that this compromise formula is "a similar doublet
to the one in Marpeck's doctrine of the Lord's Supper" criticized by
Schwenckfeld in *VMN*. He suggests that the same mind was at work in
both treatises, borrowing from incompatible sources to come to terms
with christological and sacramental issues which no one theology was
able to address satisfactorily.[113]

This formula is successful only in what it negates and not in what it affirms. It guards against the accusation of a complete separation of the two natures of Christ and makes any claim concerning a corporeal presence impossible. But in its christological affirmations, Marpeck's compromise formula is of the same order as the one it criticizes. Both views radically reinterpret the Chalcedonian teaching of Christ's two natures—against Chalcedonian intention.[114] Marpeck divides Christ's human nature into separate spiritual and physical realities such that the physical is confined to heaven and the spiritual is subsumed under the being and work of the Spirit. Schwenckfeld removes what Christian tradition has defined as Christ's human nature by eliminating its creatureliness.

Schwenckfeld accuses Marpeck of verging on transubstantiation because he posits a relationship between communion with Christ and the elements of bread and wine. Marpeck makes the same accusation against his opponent because Schwenckfeld claims that the believer communes with the whole Christ, human and divine, physical and spiritual. As soon as Marpeck brings Schwenckfeld's concept of *body* in relationship with material elements—as he is bound to do because of his view of revelation—this problem is present. They perceive each other's doctrines to be a betrayal of the Radical Reformation because they do not provide an unambiguous alternative to the dominant current sacramental views.

JDM and *VWG* are attempts to warn each other of this danger and to convince each other that the writer has the only adequate defense of belief which both of them hold in common, that Christ is spiritually eaten. For Marpeck, this means that material elements can have no relationship to Christ's physical body; for Schwenckfeld, it means that Christ's physical body can have no relationship to material elements. Thus Marpeck believes in the permanent physical character of Christ's human nature and, therefore, that it is localized in heaven. When the action of the Supper is carried on in faith and love, its elements, in analogy with Christ's incarnation, spiritually become the medium of his presence. Schwenckfeld believes that Christ's physical nature is present to the believer but that this communion has no connection to bread and wine.

A Theology of Ceremonies

The term *ceremonies* is used by Marpeck to refer to the rites of the church. He introduces this term in *KU*, where he first explains what he means by the "external works" of the church. There we see how *cer-*

emonies is an organic concept derived directly from the *menschheit Christi*, his primary christological and ecclesiological notion at that time. *Ceremony*, in contrast with the term *sacrament*, was a concept Marpeck could fill with his own meaning. This was less easily possible with the concept of sacrament because it bore centuries of definition, much of which was rejected in Anabaptism. When, for example, Marpeck inherits the term *sacrament* in the text of *BEK*, he sets out first of all to contract its meaning by pursuing the etymology of the term. He undertakes this paring down of the conventional definition of *sacrament* in order to highlight the role of human action in the external works of the church. Once he has done that, he is free to expand the concept in ways which express his theology.

Marpeck's primary innovation in defining sacrament is the notion of *mitzeugnus* (co-witness). The beginnings of this concept may be found in *CV* and *KU*. In *CV*, Marpeck writes about objective, external witnesses to the gospel. He parallels the role of the Lord's Supper and baptism to that of a preacher, all as agents of proclamation.[115] In *KU*, the author writes about outward witnesses as the way in which unbelievers are first brought to knowledge. "Only when there is belief in this outward teaching and instruction does such outward teaching become spirit and life in the inward man."[116] A sacrament or ceremony is not a static element; it comes to life in the presence of faith.

In *VMN*, co-witness is the term coined to describe this reality. Initially, it is a linguistic adaptation. Where Rothmann writes *teken* (*sign*), Marpeck adds or substitutes *mitzeugnus* (co-witness). This change in terminology involves a conceptual shift from *sign* as an external indicator of an internal reality of which it is not a part, to co-witness as a material element which, together with faith in the power of the Spirit, witnesses to the presence of grace. The explanation of how this happens is the trinitarian dynamic in which God works internally as Spirit and externally as Son to create one reality of inner and outer. The significance for the Lord's Supper is clear.

> A true Lord's Supper is held and should be seen as a true sign of the memorial of the death of Christ and a true participation in the suffering and blood of our Lord Jesus Christ.[117]

The concept of co-witness undergoes expansion in *VWG*.[118] There it is applied to a variety of agents other than baptism and the Lord's Supper. The term is also engaged to describe how the Father and the Spirit show each other's presence and how the Bible and preaching vouch for each other as media of the word. The principle underlying each particular manifestation is that an external reality vouches for faith and becomes its medium to the internal reality. In his response to the XXXII fragment of the *JDM* text, Marpeck argues for the identity of inner and outer by expanding the concept of co-witness. Apostolic baptism is that in which

> the Holy Spirit and the blood of Christ washes and purifies the heart and conscience through the co-witnessing of the outer word when it is believed. . . . The whole person, spirit, body and soul, is presented to obedience in Christ . . . through the concomitantly preached word. . . . This waterbath in the word of Christ, the only saviour, through his service and through his outer service worked in the baptisand through the Holy Spirit.[119]

This cluster of claims recurs throughout *VWG*. Although not every element is included each time, the principle Marpeck is trying to establish remains intact: through baptism the person is saved when the offer of Christ is believed. Then the Spirit and Christ are present—the verbs appear in the singular to suggest that their work is a single, common action. The term "waterbath in the word" suggests the inseparability of water and the word as co-witnesses to the saving divine presence. By means of his novel notion, the co-witness Marpeck seeks to find an alternative to sacrament as either mere sign or as an objective reality independent of faith.

We now proceed to the other components of his sacramental teaching. The initial defense of sacraments in Marpeck's writings is based squarely on biblical authority. Because Christ commands us to break bread, we do so.[120] This is the bedrock of his doctrine. But his apologetic for ceremonies derives from his belief about the incarnation. That belief undergoes a crucial elaboration. The ceremonies are natural signs which hold the natural person. In redemption the created order of things is neither contradicted nor abrogated. It is translated again into the supernatural. "Thus Christ became a natural man for natural men."[121]

Here *KU* is taking issue with those spiritualists who claim for the elect a participation in a kind of realized eschatology in which they are no longer part of the natural order of things. This idea retains a firm place in the substructure of Marpeck's sacramental thought. It expresses a foundational assumption which later pits Marpeck against Schwenckfeld: the church and the Christian continue to live within history and within their creatureliness. That order is their medium of

communication with the supernatural.[122] The incarnation is the claim
that *grace* is revealed externally; the church and the ceremonies are
the claim that *faith* is revealed externally. Without Christ's humanity,
we are not able to recognize God.[123] Christ's humanity discloses him as
savior and leads us to his divinity. Where there is belief "in the outward
teaching," it becomes "spirit and life in the inner man."[124]

   Early in the text of *VMN*, the term *sacrament* is introduced and its
meaning specified. A sacrament is "anything done in connection with
an oath," "a sign of something holy."[125] Paul and the other apostles, Marpeck elaborates, do not place value on the elements but consider the
total usage. A sacrament is not static; it is not a material entity in and of
itself.

> Thus you can see how both baptism and the Lord's Supper are called sac-
> raments, namely, because both of them take place with a commitment and
> sanctification, which is actually what a sacrament is. . . . Only then is bap-
> tism a true sacrament, that is, when the content and action of baptism hap-
> pens with the commitment to a holy covenant. It is the same way with the
> Lord's Supper.[126]

   The significance of the oath is that the person vouches for the fact
that the sign truly represents what is being signified: faith.[127] The notion
of the oath accentuates the other pole of the sacramental dynamic, that
of human response. Without it, no event of grace takes place. This is
not, in Marpeck's eyes, a claim that it is the human response which
makes the sacrament. Instead, a sacrament is an encounter between
God's grace and an existential human response of faith. God is sover-
eign; he acts on human hearts and in human affairs beyond what we respond to. But that is not the meaning of a sacrament. A sacrament is an
event in which *faith*, given by the Spirit, responds to *grace*, given by the
Spirit. It vouches for the fact that this encounter is really taking place.

   Hence, water, bread, and wine have no significance in and of
themselves. It matters what is done with them and in what spirit that
action is done. When, however, the right spirit is present, that is, when
faith in Christ is evident, then "baptism is a burying of the old being
and a resurrection of the new."[128] The candidates cannot assure themselves of salvation. But God uses their faith to make an otherwise lifeless element into a means of revelation. Marpeck adds an elaboration to
the explanation.

Whoever has the truth in the heart, the truth which is pointed to and signified by the external sign, for him it is no sign at all, but rather one essential
union with the inner.[129]

The author appears to realize that such a bold statement cannot
be substantiated with the argument presented this far. Here Marpeck
undertakes the famous excursus, introduced in relation to our discussion earlier in this chapter concerning the Trinity. Father and Son are
at work simultaneously in this event. The Father works internally as
Spirit, the Son externally as man.

In *VWG*, Marpeck reiterates and expands the trinitarian dynamic
within which ceremonies, the *signa* (signs), are united with Christ, the
res (reality). In *VWG I*, the baptismal section, "Von der Taufe," follows
the pattern of *VMN* in dealing with the sacraments in general and de-
veloping baptismal theology as well as the notion of co-witness. But it
totals only 109 pages. By contrast, the eucharistic section, "Vom
Nachtmal," and the related chapters which flow from it, run to 132
pages in *VWG II*. It is the setting for Marpeck's most ingenious
eucharistic speculation. At this point in the encounter between Anabaptism and spiritualism, the Lord's Supper has become the more profound point of contention. This is the case, in part, because christological considerations figure more extensively in the Lord's Supper.

In "Von der Taufe" (On Baptism) fifty pages are given over to a
weighty christological debate which bears directly on the two opponents' beliefs about the church and its ceremonies.[130] Schwenckfeld's
substantive challenges to *VMN* are all introduced forthwith. His first
accusation is that Marpeck's comparison between the inward working
of the Father as Spirit and the outward working of the Son as man—this
jeopardizes the whole person of Christ, as God and man. Further,
Schwenckfeld refutes the claim that Christ was born with a humanity
capable of sinning. To speak of the outer work of the Son in relation to
the ceremonies is to reduce Christ to the elements, as the sophists do in
transubstantiation. After his glorification, Christ was not known by outer signs.[131]

Marpeck enters a number of rejoinders concerning the nature of
Christ. These are repeated at various junctures in the debate on
Christology, but new arguments are not added. As the foundation of his
present position, Marpeck begins by quoting his christological formula
from *VMN* on the inner working of the Father and the outer working of
the Son.[132] According to Marpeck, Schwenckfeld misunderstands this
as necessarily a diminution of either the Father or the Son. It is neither:

as the Fourth Gospel makes clear, the Son does only what he sees the Father doing; he and the Father are one.[133]

Marpeck is certain that if Schwenckfeld had a right knowledge of Christ, he would look not only at the glorified, reigning Lord but also at how he worked on earth prior to his glorification and still works through his unglorified body. The church does outwardly what the Father does inwardly.[134] The glorified Christ rules in his body on earth through his and the Father's Spirit. His rule expresses itself in teaching, baptism, communion, acts of love, and other signs.[135] By positing an inseparability between the church as Christ's unglorified body and his glorified, reigning body at the right hand of the Father, Marpeck tries to refute the accusation that he is reducing Christ to the outward signs of his presence.

At this point Marpeck returns to an early theme of *VMN*. The Lord's Supper is not sign but essence; this is not a claim for the elements of bread and wine but for the action of Christ's members with them. When outward *words of witness* and an inward *disposition of faith* are in concord with the *act of eating,* then the ceremony becomes an event. The event consists of the coming together of these three things; it is dynamic and not static in nature.[136]

In Marpeck's reiteration of his position, the role of the Holy Spirit in relation to the work of the Father and the Son becomes more important. This is also the case with the dynamic involved in making an element part of an event. Marpeck pursues the matter in his letter to Helena Streicher.[137] In this epistle to his antagonist's follower, Marpeck is at pains to explain his understanding of Christ's word as spirit and truth. Just as the physical voice of Christ came by the power of the Spirit when he was incarnate, so also are external word and Spirit inseparable today.

Here emerges a more tightly trinitarian description than has been present in any previous writings. There is a pervasive role for the Holy Spirit. Physical reality, the world we know by nature, becomes spirit and life through faith in Christ.[138] Through it our creatureliness is spiritualized but not done away with. The Spirit and faith bring about the unity between inward and outward. Without Spirit and faith (the condition of unbelievers), the elements can do nothing.[139] There is also a pneumatic elaboration on the co-witness. The ceremonies belong to the rule of the Spirit; in the Spirit, believers become co-witnesses to one another that they belong to the body of Christ.[140]

According to Schwenckfeld, the Marpeckians are erring spirits because they say that anyone who does not confess the external work—the ceremonies of Christ the man—denies the Son and does not belong to the Spirit of the Father. If, he argues, the church continues to be the bearer of the New Testament works of Christ, why is it not raising the dead and driving out demons, as Christ himself did?[141]

Schwenckfeld is attempting to break Marpeck's claim of indivisibility between the earthly ministry of Christ and the ministry of the church. On that oneness hangs Marpeck's ecclesiology and his rationale for the ceremonies. Marpeck's answer to his accuser lies in his definition of external works. They do not consist in the two most common Reformation sacraments (baptism and Eucharist) but in all acts of "external, physical obedience" to the commands of Christ. This definition of ceremony originates in *CV*[142] and is carried on through Marpeck's later writings. It is of a piece with his ecclesiology. In it the incarnation is prolonged in history through the suffering love of Christ's body, the church. All acts done in faith actualize Christ; they share his essence. The Lord's Supper is the primal act of love; in it the church is remade again and again into the body of Christ.

Even though Marpeck's notion of ceremony includes any external event which witnesses to God's work, his focus, from the tracts of 1531 through the *VWG II*, is on initiation and Eucharist. Nowhere, however, does Marpeck offer a reason for the primacy he gives to these two dominical ordinances. In addition, his definition of ceremonies does not deal directly with Schwenckfeld's challenge to the claim that traditionally baptism and the Holy Supper were believed to mediate salvation in a manner that other external rites of the church did not.

Three considerations deserve attention in explaining this incongruity. First, the controversies of the day, in which both antagonists were caught up and whose terms were set by the Magisterial Reformation, focused almost exclusively on baptism and communion. Second, Marpeck used his broad teaching on the ceremonies to diffuse Schwenckfeld's preoccupation with the Eucharist. Third, Marpeck seemed to be much less concerned than Schwenckfeld with the challenge posed by sacramentalism to the Radical Reformation. His preoccupation was with the extreme opposite of that, the spiritualism represented by Schwenckfeld.

For Marpeck, the reform of Christian tradition had gone too far. He feared that the principle of incarnation—that history and matter mediate eternity and spirit—had been overturned. Marpeck set out to vindicate this cardinal affirmation of the church. He believed that his formulation of the truth incorporated Schwenckfeld's reasons for rejecting *ex opere operato* sacraments. Without the Spirit and faith, there is no sacramental reality. Marpeck was one with Schwenckfeld in giving spirit absolute primacy over matter. For him, the line of division between true and false ceremonies was drawn on the basis of faith. Schwenckfeld shared this supposition but found it necessary to defend it from abuse by denying ontological reality to anything material.

The Theology of the Lord's Supper
The Increasing Prominence of the Eucharist

The evidence presented thus far suggests that Marpeck's eucharistic doctrine has a dialectical character. In other words, it both derives from and determines the development of his theology as a whole. The Lord's Supper determined Marpeck's theology because it became the *primus inter pares* (first among equals) of the ceremonies. Surpassingly in the Eucharist, his beliefs about how God works in the church and in each believer came to expression.

It goes without saying that this is true also for Schwenckfeld! What has remained unsaid beneath all the specific altercations between the two theologians is the categorically different content they pour into the same vocabulary. An unarticulated difference obscures what is at issue: for Schwenckfeld, the Supper is an ongoing, mystical participation in Christ, unrelated to particular historical moments or material means.[143] He confuses the issue by making a tactical concession to his opponent, allowing ceremonies to have a role as human acts of witness. By contrasting the human action of these external works with the divine action which takes place inwardly, he hopes to undo the unity of internal and external which Marpeck has been carefully promoting. Schwenckfeld makes it clear that these ceremonies, for example, the Supper of remembrance and love, have no relationship to or participation in divine reality.

Marpeck is obviously aware of this difference between them but seems to be unwilling to expose it. As long as Schwenckfeld has some place for external works, Marpeck can argue with him about the inadequacy of his definitions. But this deliberate obfuscation dooms the debate. For Marpeck, as for Catholic and Protestant eucharistic views at large, the intention of a sacrament is to establish a meeting point within this world of the senses between the divine and the human. Schwenckfeld denies this possibility in principle.

Though the Lord's Supper came to stand at the center of both men's theology, it represented two quite different realities. Some light may be shed on Marpeck's increasingly high esteem for the Eucharist, not only by paying attention to its strictly theological significance (as shown above), but also by noting changes in his community's circumstances in the course of the 1540s. As the persecutions of the sixteenth century grew and the religious fronts in South Germany hardened, there were fewer and fewer conversions to Anabaptism. The initiation of converts into the community by means of baptism on confession of faith marked off the Anabaptist congregations. Because of less observance of the rite, it became less controversial toward the outside and less decisive toward the inside. This is true specifically of the congregation in Augsburg to which Marpeck gave leadership after 1544.[144]

Thus it can be imagined that the Lord's Supper replaced baptism in many Anabaptist congregations as the basic rite of communal life. These groups were looking for sustenance and comfort in their suffering. The communities under Marpeck's influence believed that in the breaking of bread they experienced again that they were the humanity of Christ on earth.

Marpeck's Two Teachings on the Lord's Supper

Turning now from general historical and theological factors shaping Marpeck's Christology and Eucharist, we examine much more specific but equally formative factors. When he borrowed Rothmann's *BEK,* Marpeck inherited two eucharistic doctrines. The first one has been described above in relation to the theological factors which shaped it. Chief among them are a trinitarian dynamism inspired by the Fourth Gospel as well as a Christology based on the humanity of Christ. This first eucharistic doctrine is characterized by a kind of sacramental realism in which a ceremony becomes a co-witness with faith that grace is present.

In *VMN*, the christological grounding this concept was given in Marpeck's Strassburg tracts is recast into an explicitly trinitarian mode. In *VWG* a further shift takes place to the two natures of Christ. This progression of models for the Eucharist suggests that the constant interest in Marpeck's thought was a theology of the Lord's Supper which could serve as the primary line of defense against opponents of Anabaptism. In that sense the Lord's Supper determined the evolution of Marpeck's theology as a whole. We have already established that this development was dialectical in nature. Out of the ensuing debate came both a sturdy eucharistic doctrine and a highly nuanced Christology. How that came to be is the central concern of this section. In order to pursue that concern, it is necessary to present a profile of the second eucharistic doctrine to which Marpeck held.

Marpeck's second eucharistic doctrine was a memorialist view derived from the German-speaking Reformation in Switzerland.[145] Marpeck found it expedient to retain this interpretation because it made two contentious issues unequivocally clear. It ruled out *ex opere operato* sacramental reality by depriving material elements in and of themselves of any spiritual power. On the basis of this assertion, it claimed that whatever God gives his church is received only by faith.

This view and the positions which flowed from it are reintroduced periodically throughout *VMN* and *VWG*. But it remains a secondary teaching in Marpeck, even more decidedly than in Rothmann, because it is not organic to his theology and barely usable within his trinitarian framework for the Supper. This second view remains a borrowed and self-contained statement. Its chief virtue in relation to Marpeck's theological ideas is that it stands like a stone against all eucharistic notions which claim power for the elements or which offer a relationship with God on any other basis than an existential response of faith. When Schwenckfeld continued to accuse Marpeck of unclarity on these issues, he—or his epigone—took recourse to the memorialist view a final time, explaining himself as much as possible in his opponent's categories.[146]

The Meal of Love

In *VMN* Marpeck systematically presents a theology of ceremonies. His most creative work, as has been demonstrated, occurred in the general section of that treatise where he elaborates his trinitarian dynamic and his idea of co-witness. These concepts are foundational, not only for the section of *VMN* on the Lord's Supper, but also for the *VWG*. The first matter of substance which the section on the Lord's Supper takes up is the event character of the Supper. It is a *leiblich* (corporeal) and *lieblich* (loving) gathering.[147] Both of these characteristics are seen by the author to come to their most sublime expression in the Johannine rather than the Synoptic or Pauline accounts of the Last Supper. It is not clear from the account itself in John 13 or in the history of its interpretation in the church that this passage is a warrant for the Eucharist. Yet Marpeck considers it to be an institutional narrative and works from it to the other accounts. In Jesus' mysterious act of condescension, when he rises to wash his disciples feet (John 13), we see the fullness of his communion with his followers. In this action the Eucharist becomes the model of love. The old church also practices such a corporeal gathering in its Maundy Thursday liturgy, but it lacks love.[148]

If love is missing, then Christ's example is completely counterfeited, and the communion cannot be referred to as the Supper of the Lord.[149]

Marpeck asserts that love is that without which there is no Lord's Supper. This is the juncture at which he takes the Corinthian institutional narrative into the flow of his argument. The gathering recorded in that account was not a Lord's Supper because they had forgotten love.[150] The acts of remembering, eating, and drinking—these "represent a bond of love among Christians."[151] In such acts the church "should be one body of Christ in love."[152] Where love is present in the gathered assembly, those who eat and drink become one body of Christ. This description goes to the heart of what Marpeck means by Eucharist.

A striking linguistic distinction is lost in Marpeck's translation of Rothmann's text from Dutch into German. In reference to *body* as a description of the flesh of Christ, *BEK* uses *liues*, but when the reference is to the church as his body, the term employed is *lijf.*[153] The background of this distinction may be Augustine's premise that Christ is sacramentally present in the communion elements and mystically present in the communicants.[154] Perhaps the distinction is unimportant to Marpeck because of the historical continuity he posits between the Christ's earthly existence, his sacramental existence, and the church. All three of them are described as the unglorified body of the Lord.

VMN tries to ground its concept of the Holy Supper as a gathering in love in the New Testament texts. However, Marpeck cautions readers against technical disputes concerning the nature of the elements. What matters is the function which these elements are given.[155] An efficacious communion begins with the individual's self-examination. One's worthiness consists in loving other believers—here Marpeck adds friends and enemies to Rothmann's list—according to the example of Christ.[156]

After elaborating on this point to make its serious nature clear, Marpeck observes, "Thus the entire force and impact depends on the heart of the individual, and not at all on the external, like bread and wine."[157] This pejorative use of *external* has a specific point of reference. It refers to a static object outside the dynamic of divine and human action. In his own trinitarian interpolations into the received text, Marpeck always uses *external* in a favorable sense, as the realm of the Son which becomes one with the realm of the Father through the work of the Spirit in the presence of faith.[158] This positive reference to the outward is evident in the passage at large. It underscores what has been put forth above: the Lord's Supper is an event which begins to happen in the presence of faith and love.

In brief, this is the cast of the chronologically earlier view of the breaking of bread in *VMN*. It is congruent with the trinitarian framework established by Marpeck early in the baptismal section of the same document. It makes *inner* and *outer* part of the same essence. It speaks of faith and love as the disposition of the participants which is integral to the dynamic of the Supper as a transforming event. Its ideas have their origin in the Christology and institutional narrative of the Fourth Gospel. At the same time, scriptural texts decisive for the later memorial view of the Supper, are also part of the structure of the earlier view. This is evident beginning with the section entitled "Die beschreibung, was das nachtmal sei" (The Description of What Communion Is)[159] and continuing through the next two divisions of the text. As noted above, *VMN* introduces the Corinthian narrative, not in its own right, but as a buttress for an edifice built on Johannine theology. Its role is to underscore the fact that love is the primal characteristic of the Eucharist.

The chronologically later view first appears in fragments found toward the close of the chapters on baptism. It gives a minimal value to the elements, builds on the memorial of the Supper, and finds its bearings in the Pauline narrative. Its character is Zwinglian and Karlstadtian. Near the end of *VMN*, the memorial view is presented on its own. At that point the concerns taken out of the Corinthian institutional narrative are of a different nature. For example, the Supper is for the solace of the soul; its remembrance nourishes believers and acknowledges that Christ died for them.[160] The earlier theme of love has a role in this exposition of Corinthians, but it is secondary and derivative.[161] This experience of the Eucharist is a significant component of Rothmann's and Marpeck's thought in that it functions as a line of demarcation. It makes clear to the reader that the dynamic, trinitarian model is not to be understood as leading to a spirituality based on a corporeal eating of Christ. Marpeck sides with this tropistic reading of the Supper, not for what it asserts but for what it denies. It seems to be a necessary but not a welcome ally.[162]

At its close the eucharistic treatise in *VMN* goes on to compare "the principal contradictory" opinions concerning the words of institution. They are transubstantiation, consubstantiation, and tropism. The received text praises the latter view as set forth by Zwingli and Oecolampadius but actually advances the exegesis put forward by Karlstadt.[163] Nevertheless, Marpeck's summary statement goes beyond the claims of tropistic exegesis and makes assertions which follow more easily from the first view of the Eucharist included in *VMN*:

And those who do this act of remembrance with a true faith and heart participate in the body and blood of Christ. . . . If the heart is true it is in communion with the body of Christ through the breaking of bread.[164]

The larger lines of Rothmann's and Marpeck's thought as preserved in *VMN* make it clear that they reject transubstantiation and consubstantiation as the transformation of objects, a change in which faith is not indispensable. But at the same time, the Reformed assertion of sacrament as a sign of grace to faith is inadequate for what they want to say. Their active view of faith as not only *gift* but also *response* allows them to believe that where faith is present, so also is the reality it knows.

VMN's teaching on the Lord's Supper ends abruptly at this point. It is evident that the original document, Rothmann's *BEK*, was an amalgam of ideas and references which drew on two different understandings of the ceremonies. The received text of *BEK* and Marpeck's revision of it give precedence to a dynamic view of sacrament in which the presence of faith and the Spirit make the sign one with the thing signified. It is drawn from the spirituality and Christology of the Gospel of John. This view is strengthened by Marpeck with his scheme of the Father's inner working as Spirit and the Son's outer working as man. In this Johannine perception, the Eucharist is the sacrament of love.

A second view, to which faith is also indispensable, makes use of tropistic readings of the words of institution that are not all of a piece. Marpeck identifies with the exegetical stance of this position but distances himself from its reductionist conclusions. For him, a ceremony is not a mere symbol or an outward sign unrelated to an inward reality. The chief value of the figurative view is that it is an ally of the first view in insisting that without faith, a ceremony is a mere artifice. That in Rothmann which attracts Marpeck is the oneness he postulates between internal and external. This is arrived at by describing the Supper as a gathering of love. It is based on a Christology of example and imitation. When Marpeck undergirds this position with a trinitarian rationale, he finds in it an adequate theological response to his spiritualistic critics and to the spiritualistic tendency in his own community. The memorial doctrine, on the other hand, helps to counter opponents at the opposite end of the spectrum and to assure spiritualist challengers that he has no part in materialistic views of the Eucharist.[165]

Dynamic Trinitarianism and the Incarnation

Not until Marpeck is confronted with Schwenckfeld's challenge in *JDM* does he turn unreservedly to the dynamic trinitarian position as his foundation for the Holy Supper. On its basis, Marpeck takes up new christological speculations. With these two theological lodestones in hand, he further develops his eucharistic doctrine. Even in *VWG*, Marpeck retains one emphasis he still shares with the tropistic view: insistence that without faith, outward things by themselves are of no value.

Only on the basis of this unassailable common ground with the spiritualists could Marpeck enter discussion with them on matters over which they disagreed. The shared *pistic* (believing) starting point made the Anabaptist debate with spiritualism distinct from a Lutheran or Catholic one. Marpeck's goal in *VWG* is to defend his view of the Lord's Supper by repudiating Schwenckfeld's Christology as it has emerged in their debate with one another. The straw which broke the camel's back was Schwenckfeld's inevitable denial of the creatureliness of Christ's humanity. The structure of Marpeck's thought in *VWG* is more explicitly and systematically christological than it is in the *VMN*. The trinitarian scheme recedes, though it is still integral to his working assumptions.

The most profound difference between Marpeck and Schwenckfeld in arriving at their eucharistic doctrines is not how they use the Bible but what they make of history.[166] For Marpeck, the incarnation is the new covenant by which God changes his relationship with the world; for Schwenckfeld, the incarnation is a moment of revelation in which God retains his distinctness from the world. For the former, God sanctified flesh; for the latter, he transformed flesh into spirit. Marpeck believes that the incarnation continues through history in the life of the church and holds the ceremonies to be part of its externalization. Schwenckfeld understands the ceremonies to have been superseded and abrogated at the time of Christ's glorification. At best, they remain outward signs but do not participate in the divine presence. The lesson of history, Schwenckfeld concludes, is that ceremonies stand in the way of God's communication with us.

In *VWG* Marpeck claims that the misunderstanding of the Lord's Supper happens where there is not right faith in Jesus Christ, where faith stands outside the unity (*ainigkeit*) of God. From his earlier writing, it is clear that this unity is constituted by the concomitant acting of the Father and the Son, one inwardly, the other outwardly.[167] This faith is not only internal but also external in that it trusts in the commands of

Christ. To abrogate the commands of Christ is to make an end of faith. Without the Spirit and without the ordinances of Christ, there is no church.[168]

According to Marpeck, the loss of the church is the final outcome of Schwenckfeld's logic. The ceremonies are the permanent marks of the church through which faith, hope, and love are expressed. The church is the bodily presence of Christ on earth until his bodily return. To his accuser's claim that the Anabaptist Lord's Supper is only an "outward thing," Marpeck argues that the spiritual character of the Eucharist is not in its inwardness as an event but in the faith and love believers have in their hearts and actions.[169] The love which they live out is possible only because the Holy Spirit indwells all believers.[170]

With this response, Marpeck takes his view to a new point of clarity: spiritual reality is not inwardness but outwardness given life by the Spirit. In these statements Marpeck strikes at the heart of spiritualistic assumptions. Among them are the following: spiritual reality and the faith which receives it are inward; also, in the nature of things, outward events and actions cannot be forms of spirit. These claims were highly significant in the initiation of radical reform in the sixteenth century. Hence, Marpeck's dissent from them leaves him with the burden of proving that he has not thereby rejected the whole work of reform. More than once, Schwenckfeld suspects Marpeck of Papist sentiments. Marpeck's unequivocation at this point—save for the mysterious self-contradiction near the end of the *VWG*—establishes the consequences of Anabaptist assumptions over against spiritualistic ones.

Schwenckfeld concurs with Marpeck's claim in fragment XCI that love belongs to the breaking of bread. But he insists that there is much more to it than that, namely, a spiritual feeding by faith to eternal life. The spiritual feeding is the real or essential Supper (*wesenliches nachtmal*) and needs to be distinguished from the memorial and thanksgiving.[171] When Schwenckfeld repeats that communion is more than a display of human love, it is clear that the two theologians cannot understand each other. Marpeck tries to explain that human love in a church of believers is the gift bestowed by divine love. First John 4, a favorite text of Marpeck, says plainly that "since God loved us so much, we also ought to love one another" (4:11). Love is not preliminary to the essence of communion, but precisely the means by which Christians are able to recognize its essence. Marpeck's conclusion is unflinching: only he who has love eats and drinks of the flesh and blood of Jesus Christ.[172]

As Marpeck unfolds his position, he takes the love motif he had introduced in *VMN* on the basis of a Christology of example and imitation, and places it within a trinitarian context. He introduces an equation of utmost significance for his eucharistic doctrine: love and God are one; the two concepts are used interchangeably.[173] Love issues from love. This is what the Eucharist incarnates. What more could one want in the breaking of bread, he asks, than to have love and the Holy Spirit, that is, God and Jesus Christ? Is it, in fact, possible to share and eat spiritual food contrary to the love of Christ?

In his thoughts Marpeck ascends to the ethereal; in his words he becomes lyrical. Love is the presence of God in human encounter. The Lord's Supper is the primal point, the concentrated moment of its presence. In it love is remembered, given thanks for, received, and given. Marpeck's trinitarian language is awkward and unorthodox but makes a profound confession. In his conflation of two and sometimes even three members of the Trinity, he is saying that to have communion with the body and blood of Christ is to participate in love, which is to participate in God. Love, in all its concreteness and not as an abstract inward reality, makes the Lord's Supper a communion unto eternal life.[174] Only through love can one come to a right apprehension of the spiritual food and drink.

To underscore his point, Marpeck quotes 1 John (4:8): "Whoever does not love does not know God, for God is love."[175] To know Christ is to recognize his love and to believe that it led him to die for our sin. He gave his flesh and blood as our food and drink. Such knowledge makes us worthy of the table of the Lord. This, Marpeck exclaims, is what he had been trying to say throughout the *VMN*.[176] Jesus, the friend of all true believers, offered up his life—his whole divine and human nature—for us so that out of the same love we could offer up our bodies as a true thanksgiving.[177]

Schwenckfeld argues that his adversaries preserve only one side of the whole Supper. All they do is remember the command Jesus gave to love; they neglect to remember what he did for us and that he feeds our souls. Schwenckfeld is suspicious of the outwardness of love. His fear reflects his belief that all spiritual reality is inward. This gives the ethical, which is by nature external and concrete, no essential place in the Supper. Marpeck's swift rejoinder is that none of these claims minimizes the eating and the mystery involved. In eating we remember the Lord's broken body and shed blood; it gives us joy, comfort, and strength. It feeds us as bread and wine feed the body. We know that two things must be remembered in the Lord's Supper: what Christ has done for our sakes and what we, out of gratitude, should do for his sake.[178]

A subtle conceptual development comes into focus at this juncture. Marpeck uses the differentiated language from the memorialist part of the eucharistic text in *VMN* to gain common ground with Schwenckfeld and at the same time to turn those traditional christological claims to his advantage. In *VMN*, it is the memory of Christ's self-giving which feeds believers as bread and wine feed their body. The source of their joy is the remembrance that God gave his only Son to us sinners. The Son gave his "natural, bodily life (which he received through woman's seed as true human seed without the male sperm or sin through the co-operation of the Holy Spirit and through which the Word became flesh)."[179] The Savior we memorialize is not only true God but also a true human being. Had he not become true man, we should have nothing for which to thank him. The "Eucharist" of the Lord's Supper is an act of gratitude that spirit became flesh.

Marpeck repeatedly takes recourse to passages out of *VMN* to prove his point; the elaborations found in *VWG* substantiate and develop his earlier work. An instance of this follows. Schwenckfeld quotes *VMN* as holding that communion is only a sign. Marpeck promptly distances himself from this claim by asserting it instead to be a co-witness for one who has faith. When entered into by faith, the element becomes a co-witness. Its witness is that the sign bears the thing signified, that the ceremony as event becomes the bearer of Christ.[180]

The work of God on the believers is both inward and outward. The Spirit sanctifies them. Their life is hidden with God in Christ (Col. 3:3). But through the Spirit, this hidden life penetrates through to outwardness, revealed in flesh and through bodily works of obedience. The dynamic force through which the sanctifying work (*frombkeit werk*) of God is externalized is the Spirit. Its medium is the flesh. The prototype for this pattern of divine activity is the Lord's Supper.[181] The issue is not what the elements are but whether the divine action takes place. If it does affect the hearts of believers, then "in them Christ with his flesh and blood is eaten, drunk, and partaken to eternal life."[182] Thus, there is only one Supper in which outer and inner are together. Again and again Marpeck asserts this claim, which incorporates the memorialist view into the realist one.

As to the wine or water, they remain elements and creatures; they do not become essence. Marpeck turns to a homely illustration to make his point. "Water is not a bath, but one needs water to bathe. And no one is able to bathe without water."[183] What counts is the activity in

which water is used. The elements have no meaning without the
"guests" or congregation who make use of them. Because we still live
life within the natural world, we use the realm of nature to participate
in the supernatural essence and spiritual activity of God. Otherwise,
how can the whole person, inner and outer, be saved?

The nature of Marpeck's question to Schwenckfeld suggests that
he is aware of the far-reaching implications of their debate about the
Lord's Supper. In Schwenckfeld's dualistic schema, the material world
remains beyond the pale of redemption. The body is not heir to the
promise of resurrection. Now it becomes clear that Marpeck's
eucharistic doctrine, on the contrary, retains the materiality of the
medieval view. It is not that the elements are changed but that, like
Jesus "natural" body, they are the means by which believers become
one with Christ. Marpeck's Lord's Supper is the ongoing sign of the incarnation, which in turn is evidence that God sanctifies not only souls
but also bodies. He reiterates his explanation as to why this is so. Where
there is faith, natural elements mediate Christ. "Through faith the soul
is fed and given drink to eternal life with the flesh, body, and blood
[*sic*] of Jesus Christ when someone believes that such a body of Christ,
flesh and blood, gave itself and shed itself unto death for his sin."[184]

At the end of this section, we find that the whole of it has been
Marpeck's attempt to show Schwenckfeld that he is consistent with
VMN. There he says that symbols or memorial signs cannot be what
they signify. Where the thing signified is in the heart, the signs become
a co-witness and of one being with the inner reality. What changes is
the meaning of the signs and not their substance. To the believer they
become a figure of memory and edification, to the unbeliever a figure
of judgment. Marpeck turns to the Last Supper to compare it with the
Lord's Supper. He wants to illustrate that the former was not a sacrament because the trinitarian dynamic came into effect only after Christ
finished his work. He goes on to compare unbelievers with the disciples at the Last Supper. The meal was only a sign to them and not
reality because Christ had not yet hung on the cross. They could not yet
eat his body and drink his blood. That happened only after Jesus' ascension when the Spirit brought his reality into the heart.[185]

Misunderstandings and Contradictions

To make it unmistakably clear to his suspicious opponent that
what happens in the breaking of bread takes place by the power of the
Spirit, Marpeck takes recourse to an argument which links his view of
the two covenants with his Christology. He declares that the Last Sup-

per was sign and not essence because Christ had not yet given his body and blood.[186] In the *VWG* he adds the resurrection and ascension and sending of the Spirit as the precondition for participation in Christ's body and blood. Through the work of the Spirit, we are given access to the human Christ. Before his defeat and victory, the disciples could not understand the essential or real participation (*wesentlich niessung*) referred to in John 6 until the Spirit came and made it present to them.[187]

Schwenckfeld has grave reservations about the "master of the booklet's" claim that "the bread and wine of communion become what your heart is."[188] In his response, Marpeck casts this dictum of his into a less enigmatic form:

> If a person believingly and worthily uses and partakes in the bread and wine of the Supper with a right heart, understanding and disposition to the salvation of his soul, the love of his neighbour, and thankfulness to Christ, . . . then the bread breaking and drink of the cup is a true communion of the body and blood of Christ.[189]

Schwenckfeld partially misunderstands Marpeck in that he interprets "heart" to mean external, human action. For him, it is something necessarily incapable of spirit. He goes on to propose that the power lies entirely in the spiritual nourishment offered. In his frequent casting about for arguments against Marpeck, it is as if he has no more than an intimation of where the problem lies. But he has exposed Marpeck's Achilles' heel: the absence of the human response of faith means that there is no communion. Only when spiritually and ethically blameless can a person feed on Christ. Marpeck is, in fact, the subjectivist Schwenckfeld has suspected him of being all along! There is no reality to the Lord's Supper without outward, human action. And, in fact, Marpeck's point has been that the means of sacramental reality is not the element but the faith of the believer.

To Schwenckfeld, this way of guarding against an *ex opere operato* understanding of sacraments places the possibility of feeding on Christ entirely on the human respondent. For Marpeck, divine initiative and human response are meaningless if separate from one another. God is the agent, but his action can be appropriated only by faith. The outer eating then becomes a co-witness with the proclaimed word of the inner eating.[190] Finally, another significant element in their debate has been made clear. Their different understanding of faith has to do with their different picture of the human response to grace. There is no doubt that the human actor and external event play a concrete and conspicuous role in Marpeck's scheme. They cooperate with the Spirit. In Schwenckfeld's design, faith is absolute inwardness and receptivity; it is not an action which can cooperate with God's activity.

Therefore, Marpeck's extreme efforts to show by the place given to faith that his sacramentology has nothing in common with an *ex opere operato* view cannot satisfy Schwenckfeld. In the end, however, Marpeck takes recourse to his pneumatology to show that the Lord's Supper he advocates has not become a completely subjective event. The response of faith by itself can do nothing; the ceremony becomes a reality only where it becomes one with the Spirit. In his conclusion of the matter, Marpeck suddenly adds that where the Spirit mingles (*vermengt*) inner and outer, it remains as one, unbroken. The Spirit is the primal co-witness.[191] Marpeck's final attempt to demonstrate the spirituality of his sacramental teaching involves a paraphrase of passages from John 6. It is a confession that

> the Lord gives food and drink to the soul and the inner person with his holy flesh and blood and that the food and drink of our spirit and soul must be spiritual alone and that though natural bread and wine do not give the soul food or drink they may still be used to the remembrance and proclamation of the death of Jesus Christ and thanks giving for him in a spiritual manner and so it turns out to be a feeding and sustaining of our inner person, soul and spirit and also [working] from inside to the outside gives our body hope in a physical resurrection to eternal life.[192]

Marpeck's careful choice of words suggests how pervasive his concern was not to be seen as advocating a mechanical dispensation of grace. The inner-outer unity he has worked so hard to substantiate is itself threatened by his qualified language. He engages John 6 in the same way that he has used it previously: to make unassailable the spiritual nature of communion. But in this description, bread and wine are added as a separate act of memorial. Marpeck tacks onto the end of his argument the old dynamic of spirit working from the inner to the outer realm, the reason for hope in the resurrection. That assertion leaves only a thread of consistency in the position Marpeck has spent hundreds of pages defending, namely, that inner and outer are inseparable where the Holy Spirit and faith are present.

Not until the *JDM* fragment XCVII does Schwenckfeld assess the exegesis of the words of institution as the *VMN* has presented them. The gist of his accusation is that the Anabaptists want it both ways. First, they say "this is my body" is to be understood figuratively. Then immediately, they follow Karlstadt and claim that by body they understand, "naturally and essentially his true (*rechtem*) body which sat at the table."[193] Christ does not speak in double entendres. In any case, neither of these meanings is correct. When Schwenckfeld proceeds to give his interpretation, it is evident that neither party is doing exegesis. Each is using the text of Scripture to prove an already-assumed point. Schwenckfeld disputes both the Zwinglian and Karlstadtian versions with his alternative:

> [Jesus] is speaking to the believing soul, saying after the breaking and eating of bread, "This is my body"; through the parable of broken, eaten bread, he demonstrates what kind, nature, and characteristics his body had and that it was a true meal for our souls.[194]

Most striking about Marpeck's response is that, though he cites Zwingli as his authority, the tropistic interpretation is significant for Marpeck only when he is fighting off corporeal presence. Throughout most of *VMN* and *VWG*, little is made of this hermeneutical key. Marpeck further marginalizes Zwingli's dictum by setting it beside Karlstadt's. He takes two different hermeneutical proposals to solve the same problem, what Jesus meant when he said, "This is my body." Marpeck uses these proposals together in a way contrary to their original purpose. This adds to an already-ambiguous use of terms in the fragment under scrutiny. He quotes from the eucharistic section of *VMN* that "this is my body" has a "natural, essential" meaning: it is his body as he sat at supper. But the bread and wine have a figurative meaning: they are a memorial of Christ's sacrifice.[195] Even though bread remains bread, believers do partake of (*niessen*) the natural body of Christ in the Holy Supper, that body which sat at the table and which died for us. Thus both meanings of the words of institution are true.

Marpeck is more coherent and original when he thinks theologically rather than exegetically. Only when his foundational dictum is challenged, that bread remains bread, does he return to the Bible to argue it. But Marpeck's real interest in all his extant writings, from *CV* to *VWG*, is the oneness of the outward ceremony with the reality it signifies, where the Spirit and faith are present. Only the Johannine institutional narrative and eucharistic spirituality address this issue. The speculative trinitarian thought of that Gospel is the seedbed of Marpeck's creativity. His interest is in what happens in the Eucharist when the Father and Son act together. The Last Supper itself, except for the unique Johannine record of it, is relatively uninteresting to him because it says nothing of this. A final reason for Marpeck's marginal interest in doing exegesis on the institutional narratives is that he holds the Last Supper to predate the Eucharist. The dynamic of that event was possible only after Christ had ascended and begun to work in the Spirit.

All of this makes incomprehensible the sudden turn in the discussion which follows. Marpeck's final assault on Schwenckfeld's position relies on spiritualistic arguments no different in kind from those he opposes. He says the meal is

> the eternal, essential feeding itself, as we have written in this and other testimony; it is no memorial of the past and expended suffering of Christ. But the Lord's Supper has been instituted as a remembrance of such things, to bear in mind and to proclaim his death.[196]

This is a flat contradiction of everything in Marpeck's eucharistic scheme! All that he believes about outward ceremonies partaking of the essence where faith is present is belied by this spiritualistic divorce between eternal, inward realities and historical, outward ones.

The following is a reconstruction and annotation of the steps in the dispute, given to clarify it. Marpeck localizes their disagreement at the point of Schwenckfeld's claim that in the Lord's Supper, Christ is bodily present as food and drink for the believing soul. Marpeck misunderstands Schwenckfeld's terminology about bodily presence. He recapitulates the latter's notion of the presence of the glorified body and blood in an undifferentiated way as *leibliche gegenwürt* (bodily presence).[197] Schwenckfeld's celestial-flesh Christology notwithstanding, Marpeck reads this term as meaning nothing other than the medieval notion of a corporeal (material) presence. Since Schwenckfeld's Christology is false, so must be any deductions he makes from it.

The purpose of Marpeck's substantive change in argument is to deal a deathblow to any claim of a corporeal presence in Holy Communion. Marpeck forsakes the structure of his theological defense and reduces the matter to an exegetical disagreement. He does so because he knows that throughout the debate, the Bible has remained the only commonality in their discourse; their Christologies and much else in each of their theological systems are mutually exclusive. Thus he is left with the single argument that Schwenckfeld's contention goes against the Bible.

Marpeck's drastic solution involves recourse to a Zwinglian hermeneutic. It holds that the Johannine eucharistic discourse has nothing to do with the narratives documenting the institution of the Lord's Supper and nothing to do with the memorial meal for which

Jesus commanded the use of creaturely bread and wine. What Jesus said in John 6 about eating his flesh and drinking his blood, refers not to earthly food and drink except as they are eaten in memory. The "eternal, essential" meal is not given through the Lord's bodily presence after his glorification.

Marpeck insists that the only warrant Scripture gives the church for its outward life is that it proclaim the Lord's death until he comes. This is what we call the Lord's Supper (*abentmal*). The Corinthian narrative is not a command (as Schwenckfeld holds) to proclaim the Lord's glorified and present body. *That* eating and drinking is described in John 6. It is an inner participation, unrelated to the Lord's Supper because the Johannine text nowhere says that what it talks about is a memorial of the Lord's death, nor is it called a thanksgiving (Eucharist) for that death! The inner participation is not a figurative meal of bread and wine but an essential meal. It is not a remembrance but that which is remembered, not a proclamation but that which is proclaimed.

Let us note what is happening here. All along, Marpeck has taken issue with Schwenckfeld at two points. First, there is only one Supper: the bread is made of one essence with the body of Christ. Second, the believers' participation is in the human body of Christ spiritually present. This contention is of inestimable significance for Marpeck's theology because it is of a piece with his notion of the humanity of Christ, which unifies his Christology and ecclesiology and comes to surpassing expression in the event of the breaking of bread. The final piece of the puzzle is that throughout his writings, Marpeck has moved freely between the institutional narratives of the Synoptics and Paul and John. In addition, he has used John 6 directly in interpreting the Lord's Supper.[198] Indeed, his whole argument for the union of inner and outer in one reality derives from his treatment of John.

Throughout their disagreements, Marpeck has not understood Schwenckfeld's terminology as he himself explains it. Marpeck insists that Schwenckfeld is talking about a corporeal presence as a material presence of Christ in the manner of Catholic or Lutheran teaching. In order to rescue the Eucharist from its misunderstanding as a material presence of Christ, Marpeck is willing to sever it from an inner reality. Marpeck takes refuge in Schwenckfeldian language, calling Christ's body and blood, "the eternal food and drink of God's elect."[199] Now he makes use of that very separation between outward ceremony and inward reality which Marpeck has fought for a score of years. Bread and wine become a parable and memorial of the essential food and drink. In the process he nullifies his most creative hermeneutical act, his interpretation of the Synoptic and Pauline institutional narratives from the vantage point of John 6 and 13.

Just as abruptly as he began it, Marpeck leaves the subject of the believers' relationship with Christ in the Lord's Supper. Having presented his rebuttal convincingly, at least to his own mind, Marpeck goes on to other matters. The final pages of *VWG* are filled with brief summaries of the points at issue and a last claim to have proved that Schwenckfeld's position "is contrary to the teaching and command of Christ and the Holy Spirit."[200] But still persisting are the riddle of this text, its overturning of all that has gone before, and its sudden change of vocabulary. The reader is left with the distinct thought that another hand is at work here, someone trying to think Marpeck's thoughts after him and sharing his stake in the issues at hand.[201]

To the last, Marpeck's writing was *Kontroverstheologie,* theology forged in controversy. Its final statement was not a deduction from what had gone before but an assertion put forward to dislodge his opponent's most painful criticism, that in Marpeck's eucharistic doctrine there was no Spirit. Marpeck was eclectic in his borrowing and ingenious in the recasting of what he had borrowed. At the same time, his theological originality was profound: his teaching on the humanity of Christ and on the dynamic working of the Trinity gave direction and coherence to his whole theology.

Examined from this vantage point, the contradiction at the end of *VWG* can best be explained as an inconsistent response to an intolerable personal accusation. There is one warning of such an outcome earlier in *VWG*, where Schwenckfeld accuses Marpeck of advocating a Supper to which there is no spiritual reality.[202] For the first time, Marpeck separates the inner feeding of the soul from the outward feeding of the body and identifies John 6 with the former. At the end of that passage, he sets limits to this divorce of the body from the soul.

These two puzzling instances illustrate the temptation faced by Marpeck, his followers, and all those who sought a way between sacramentalism and spiritualism. They were constantly being asked to prove the spiritual reality of their communion with Christ by despising his humanity.[203] In his years of struggle for a true Lord's Supper, Marpeck sometimes lost confidence in his own convictions. Yet his writing as a whole and his teaching concerning the Lord's Supper stand as evidence that they remained "captive to the humanity of Christ."[204]

Summary and Conclusions

Introduction

Pilgram Marpeck belonged to the world of Christian theology and piety inherited by the sixteenth century. He pursued his theological task from within its classical locus, that of God as Trinity and the incarnation as the surpassing mode of revelation and encounter. He understood the Bible and the gospel from within the Christian tradition as it had developed until his time. For example, the elaborate trinitarianism Marpeck saw in the Fourth Gospel, came not from a historically unconditioned reading of the text but from participation in the living tradition of many centuries. The world he had inherited made sense to him. He remained firmly situated in the frame of reference within which Catholic theology had developed.

For Marpeck, belief in God as Trinity and Christ as the incarnation of that God were that without which theology and the life of the church were not possible. Nor did he, like certain of his contemporaries in the Radical Reformation, hold these tenets merely as formal principles. He identified with their content and saw the challenge of reform as bringing the life of the church into conformity with them. Marpeck's theology in general, and his sacramentology in particular, was an attempt to vindicate traditional teaching concerning the incarnation.

This claim that Marpeck sought to do his theological work in faithfulness to the classical Christian confession of God as Trinity is not an assertion that his thinking was an uncritical recapitulation of the received tradition. That tradition, in fact, came into the sixteenth century in highly differentiated ways. Not until after the Council of Trent (1545-63) did an exclusive definition of orthodoxy characterize the Roman Catholic Church. The conclusion of this study is simply that Marpeck understood and identified with the doctrines of the Trinity and the two natures of Christ as the creeds and councils had defined them. He shared their conviction that these two doctrines were the indispensable guardians of the deposit of faith. It is true that his eclecticism and his lack of theological training often led him to departures from that core. But they were in the nature of attempts to recast it.

Marpeck's appropriation of tradition can be more clearly grasped when he is placed alongside some other proponents of Radical Reformation. Some of them, like Hans Denck, were more at home in the world of ethical mysticism with elastic theological boundaries. Others, like Menno Simons, placed themselves within the bounds of orthodoxy but were unable to accept the implications tradition had drawn from the doctrine of the incarnation. Their way around this challenge was to adopt a Christology which subverted its chief claim, namely, that God had taken on the conditions of ordinary human existence. The spiritualists, like Schwenckfeld, did likewise. Unlike Menno, who still built his ecclesiology on incarnational thought, Schwenckfeld was consistent in his "demythologizing." For him, the incarnation was only a historical moment, neither adding fundamentally to the revelation of God nor prolonging historically how Jesus had mediated God during his life on earth.

At the same time, Pilgram Marpeck was a child of his age and a proponent of radical reform. This commitment set him at variance with the Catholic Church because he concluded that it had betrayed the pristine Christian tradition by the false practice of infant baptism. All the other deviations from true tradition had followed from this singular act of betrayal.[205]

Marpeck shared the spirit of the Reformation in its rejection of the authority of the Roman Church and in the novel and exalted status it gave to faith as the only means to a relationship with God through Christ. He was caught up in the Renaissance interest to return *ad fontes* (to the sources). That his restorationism was less biblicistic than that of other Radical Reformers may be seen in his sacramental thought, which derives as much from theological principles concerning the incarnation and faith as from exegesis of the biblical texts. His goal was to reform the tradition from which his identity was inseparable so that the church in his day could think and act like the earliest generation of Christians.

The pinnacle of the Anabaptist movement was to find in the practice of baptism the key to the church's reform. It brought faith, which had been given preeminent status in the Reformation, into correspondence with baptism. The Magisterial Reformers retained infant baptism and thus avoided having to answer how the principle *sola fide* (faith alone) related to the rite of initiation. For the Anabaptists, faith and baptism were inseparable; one could not speak of one without the other. Marpeck used baptism as the prototype for ceremonies in general. Therefore, faith and the element—or as he preferred to say, the event—were placed in a dynamic relationship to one another and together to God.

In his writings, Marpeck's structuring of the relationship between faith and sacrament is different from that of other Anabaptists, sometimes in degree and often in kind. For them, the relationship between faith and sacrament is at most sequential or concomitant. For him, the two form an indissoluble unity, ontologically and temporally.[206] The novelty of Marpeck's sacramental thought lies in its applying to faith what the sacramental tradition applied only to grace. God's act, that tradition held, is ontologically and temporally united with the elements which mediate it. To that unity of grace and matter, Marpeck adds faith. In his thought, faith is both gift and response. As a gift, faith is imparted by the Spirit.

The importance of this claim is underscored by the fact that in most of his formulations of the subject, Marpeck lists faith and Spirit together. In its response mode, faith is a human act of involvement with the receiving of grace. In the presence of faith, a twofold dynamic is set in motion by the Father acting inwardly and the Son acting outwardly. In this dynamic of indispensable correlates, the sign becomes united with what it signifies. The material element has no meaning by itself. Its substance is not changed. Marpeck is clear that it is not the element by itself which mediates grace. When it is appropriated by faith and thereby brought into contact with the Holy Spirit, it becomes one with the reality to which it points. Therefore, in baptism, salvation is experienced; in the Lord's Supper, there is a communion with the body and blood of Christ.

For Marpeck, faith as active human response was an indispensable correlate of grace in making the elements and event of the Lord's Supper to be a sacramental reality. He preserved this threefold unity in a way that he believed was lacking among his opponents—Catholics, Magisterial Reformers, and spiritualists alike. He achieved this in a way not true of other Anabaptists, including the other two subjects of our study. In the thought of Balthasar Hubmaier, sacrament is excluded from the relationship between grace and faith. In the thought of Dirk Philips, sacrament remains a sign of both grace and faith and is ontologically, if not temporally, separate from them.

Marpeck stood against the spiritualistic tendency of late medieval thought and its appropriation by the Reformation. He rejected an ontological barrier between the worlds of spirit and matter. His theology of the Lord's Supper led him to a belief in the "real presence" of Christ. Yet he found that language unusable because, as it was conventionally employed, it dwelt on the transformation of the elements rather than on the action of the community and its transformation.[207]

The preeminent goal of Marpeck's theology was to create an apology for ceremonies as external works which were of one being with the inward reality they represented. He based this claim on the fact of the incarnation, and in turn he presented it as the ultimate defense of the incarnation. To do this, he unfolded a Christology and a trinitarian structure inspired by the Gospel of John.

Throughout the evolution of his thought, Marpeck remained consistent in his defense of the incarnation. But he allowed his own fear of transubstantiation and his spiritualistic opponent's accusation that his position was one of spiritless externality, to force him to take refuge in arguments which admitted an ontological barrier between spirit and matter. This involved a fatal self-contradiction! Both he and Rothmann must have been aware of the difficulties involved in the position they sought to establish. Both employed two eucharistic doctrines, one to develop sacraments from the incarnational principle, the other to safeguard the indispensability of faith for understanding and receiving grace. These two approaches testify to the fact that neither the Catholic nor the Reformed interpretations by themselves were able to do justice to the nature of a ceremony as Rothmann and Marpeck understood it.

The mediating position precariously established by Marpeck's sacramental realism can be seen in its broader significance if it is cast into another set of categories. Marpeck's position was an attempt to join together Protestant principle and Catholic substance. The Catholic substance was the teaching of the incarnation as the rock from which all sacramental reality had to be hewn. The Protestant principle, especially in its radicalized form in Anabaptism, was the claim that faith was the *sine qua non* of the church and of each Christian's life. His writings supply abundant evidence that both Catholic substance and Protestant principle were indispensable to his thinking. His attempt to bring both into a single reality was focused in his eucharistic doctrine. What he believed about the incarnation determined his understanding of faith. It was not, as Schwenckfeld insisted, pure inwardness. Instead, it was the recognition of spirit in the external work of Christ, in the humanity of Christ.[208]

Schwenckfeld articulated his controversy with Marpeck in such a way that Marpeck was forced to choose between Catholic substance and radicalized Protestant principle. He allowed himself to be badgered into choosing the latter because he did not want to be accused of forsaking the Reformation. The irony of this choice is that Marpeck's whole theology makes such a split impossible. The initial erosion of Marpeck's wall against spiritualism came when he conceded to Schwenckfeld that it was Christ's divine nature which was present in the Eucharist. By removing the offense of a natural human but spiritual presence, Marpeck hoped to stem the tide. No doubt realizing that he was undermining his own foundations, he reasserted his original position at the close of *VWG*. But the crack in the wall came with his fission of inner from outer as a desperate defense against what he believed was Schwenckfeld's relapse into transubstantiation.

Was this move an existential lapse of a beleaguered and isolated thinker? Was it the editorial work of an epigone unequal to the task or preoccupied with other issues? No clear answer to these questions is possible until more is known of the circumstances surrounding the writing of *VWG II*. This turn in the text blemishes but does not disfigure Marpeck's work as a whole. It stands as an alternative to the theologies of the sixteenth century, which were in danger of choosing one pole of the dialectic over the other. It is Marpeck's tenacious holding together of Catholic substance and Protestant principle which both commends his work to the ecumenical dialogue on the Eucharist today and warns against its pitfalls.

The Development of Marpeck's Christology and His Theology of the Lord's Supper

Marpeck's eucharistic doctrine evolved through several stages. These have been traced in the preceding chapter and will be restated here in order to present a profile of the theological motifs of his mature theology.

CV introduces the concept of the incarnation, and *KU* develops it into the notion of the humanity of Christ, as the basis of the church and of its external life and works. The crucial application Marpeck makes of the notion of the incarnation is its prolongation in history through the life of the church. That is to say, the humanity of Christ refers not only to the human nature of Jesus Christ the person but also to God's way of being present in history throughout the course of the new covenant. The glory of the church is that it shares the humiliation of God. The church is that community whose suffering is the means by which God is revealed and by which he saves people. Steven Boyd sums up Marpeck's christological claims in the idea that Jesus' incarnation made it possible for created reality to mediate divine life. This mediatorial power resided in the church. "For [Marpeck] the gathered community (*leib Christi*), not the supper or baptism, mediated that grace of God in Christ."[209]

Boyd has rightly identified Marpeck's view of the church as the medium of God's presence in the world. As it stands, however, Boyd's claim does not give the ceremonies their due as moments in the life of the church. According to Marpeck, they are part of a dynamic involving Spirit and faith, which unifies outer and inner in one reality. Nor does Boyd's assertion do justice to the status given to the Lord's Supper in *VWG II*, where it becomes Marpeck's dominant means of articulating his understanding of faith and of the church. Our study of the documents leads us to what seems to be a more accurate summary: The church is the primal sacrament. It is the paradigm for all other embodiments of the gospel. The ceremonies, as Marpeck explains them, become manifestations of the humanity of Christ in *both* ways that concept is used. The ceremonies reveal Christ as he took on flesh historically *and* as he indwells his people by means of the Spirit.

This understanding lies behind the primary strand of eucharistic teaching in *VMN*. In it, the Supper is a physical meeting of believers who gather in faith and love. When the believers do this they become one body, that is, they are constituted again as the body of Christ in the world. This claim, however, does not reduce Christ to the historical forms he takes on. The historical body of the church is also given a mystical communion with the ascended Lord through the meal in which bread and wine are shared in nonresistant love. In the sense that this love extends itself to enemy as well as friend, the eucharistic action expands to include the whole world.[210]

The trinitarian dynamic, by which God's presence in the world is explained, is Marpeck's most sophisticated theological creation. It is introduced in the initial sections of *VMN* to undergird the claim of sacramental reality made in *BEK* for baptism and ceremonies in general. It provides the frame of reference for *VMN's* treatment of the Eucharist but is not applied to the Lord's Supper until the *VWG*. In trying to provide a sure foundation for what happens in the breaking of bread, Marpeck makes ever-greater use of the trinitarian scheme derived from the Johannine tradition. His appropriation of that world is not through a simple biblicism.[211] He starts with the idea of Father and Son acting in syncronicity. The Son is present in his human nature externally, that is, historically, in the life of the church.

At this point Marpeck introduces the Spirit by means of an awkward complication. The Spirit is one with the divine nature of Christ. Through the Spirit's power, the dynamic is ignited which brings the external work of the Son together with the internal work of the Father. In *VMN* and in some parts of *VWG*, Marpeck conflates the three persons of the Trinity to two because his preoccupation is with the inner and outer working of the divine. Early in *VMN*, where the Spirit's significance is being established, the Spirit is identified with the Father. This evolves into the following notion: Christ works simultaneously through his two natures, defined here as his glorified existence with the Father and his humiliated existence in the church.

While this scheme preserves intact the humanity of Christ as the church, it misuses the terminology it has borrowed from Chalcedonian Christology. Later, when the notion of the humanity of Christ as the church recedes, the Spirit is more and more identified with the Son.[212] By making the Spirit inseparable from the Son, Marpeck forecloses the spiritualistic tendency to separate Spirit and Son such that the incarnation would have no bearing on the revelation of God in the present. This is the most profound point of distinction between Marpeck's and Hubmaier's Christologies.

Boyd notes Marpeck's tendency "to substitute the Spirit for the Word as the divine nature of Christ."[213] Not until his letter to Helena Streicher and *VWG II* does Marpeck give the Holy Spirit a more defined and distinguished role. This is done to answer his opponent's charge that Marpeck's ceremonies are strictly human in nature.

When he makes deductions from this fluid trinitarianism, Marpeck never leaves the impression that he is innovating. Quite the opposite; his arguments convey the impression that he is invoking the received tradition in order to clinch the point at issue. Was Marpeck's uninhibited freedom to cross conventional thought boundaries the outworking of his theological autodidacticism (being self-taught)? It is beyond the scope of this investigation to try to prove or disprove Marpeck's conformity to trinitarian schemes of the day. It can be said, however, that where his conceptual source is biblical—where he establishes the relationship among Father, Son, and Spirit—Marpeck remains within the pale of conventional hermeneutical boundaries. Where his source is in more speculative theology, as concerns the two natures of Christ, Marpeck moves farther away from traditional dogma. He both bends classical concepts and relies on them for his apologetic task.

Looked at four centuries later and in light of the church's classical formulations from the fourth century, Marpeck's christological leanings are confusing. This is especially the case with the christological disputes between Marpeck and Schwenckfeld in the eucharistic chapters of the *VWG.* It is difficult to avoid the sense that Marpeck uses specific christological motifs opportunistically, that is, in proportion to their persuasiveness in a particular altercation. When, for example, Marpeck is accused by Schwenckfeld of claiming communion only with the divine Christ, he turns around and says that it is the human, creaturely Christ who nurtures us by his spiritual presence. Moreover, in advancing the belief about the two natures of Christ—humanly present in the church and divinely present in the Spirit—Marpeck discovers that he has been unable to offer an alternative to Schwenckfeld's glorified human Christ. In order to counter Schwenckfeld, Marpeck allows the humanity of Christ as his presence in the church to recede from the discussion.

His emphasis shifts to the heavenly Christ in both his natures. Then he goes on to show that, although the Lord is sacramentally present as human and divine, his is a spiritual presence. Physically, the ascended Christ remains in heaven. This is the only alternative he can find to Schwenckfeld's claim that the Eucharist is a communion with the divinized but fleshly, human nature of the Lord. In Marpeck's eyes, his opponent's view is, in the end, indistinguishable from the corporeal presence taught in the doctrine of transubstantiation.[214]

In the second part of *VWG*, a shift with far-reaching christological and sacramental implications happens. The Lord's Supper takes the place of the humanity of Christ as the way of talking about Christ's presence in the church. To be sure, Marpeck's long list of ceremonies does not disappear. In other words, there are many ways in which Christ is revealed, from the Bible to the ban. But the Lord's Supper takes on paradigmatic significance. It enacts most clearly the human-divine encounter. Without ever formally distinguishing Holy Communion from the other ceremonies, Marpeck makes claims for it which are never applied to other external works.

Here is development toward a system of thought whose most profound insights are called forth in the creation of its eucharistic doctrine. This is evident not only in the progression of Marpeck's thought through the documents cited above but also within *VWG*. The letter to Helena Streicher has an unmistakable affinity with the eucharistic chapters of *VWG*. It has the same concern with pneumatology. By contrast, other chapters in both parts of *VWG* have little of the lofty theological speculation and resolution called forth by the problems addressed in the eucharistic chapters.[215]

As "Vom Nachtmal" (On the Lord's Supper) unfolds, the style of discourse changes. This is the first of the three chapters which have been the focus of our studies in the *VWG*. There are fewer flat assertions and more theological leaps. In chapter XCIII, the argument has already moved from biblicistic assertion to theological elaboration.[216] A theological rationale is given for the work of the co-witness in the Eucharist.[217] Marpeck quotes *JDM*, that the problem with the Marpeckian Lord's Supper is that its defenders cannot recognize Christ in his glory. This provides occasion for an expansive theological response which carries on through to the termination of the eucharistic debate. Out of this interchange emerge Marpeck's beliefs about the two natures of Christ and eucharistic doctrine shaped and defended by them.

Early in his writing, Marpeck seems to have been concerned to provide an alternative to the medieval preoccupation with the Eucharist. This may be seen in his various lists of ceremonies through which God works. At this stage in his theologizing, Marpeck focuses on baptism in relation to faith to make it clear that any ceremony is lifeless without the response of faith. These considerations recede once the principal antagonist is no longer the Magisterial Reformation but spiritualism. On this front, it is the Lord's Supper which sustains Marpeck's ecclesiology and Christology as well as his theology of the ceremonies. In the end, Marpeck makes explicit an assumption he has held from the beginning: ecclesiology and Lord's Supper are of a piece. The outward—in this case, the visible church—is one with the inward, the life of God. Spiritual reality is not confined to the eternal and inward but embraces also the historical and outward. That is the message of the incarnation. Any confession which falls short of that claim despises the humanity of Christ. What is posited in *KU* is given elaborate theological development in *VWG*, focused almost exclusively on the nature of the Eucharist.

Marpeck introduces a triad of forces in *VMN* which account for what happens in a sacrament. They are Spirit, faith, and co-witness. These components are present and brought into syncronicity with each other already in *VMN's* early passages on baptism. The term co-witness is introduced into Marpeck's edition of *BEK* without explanation, but its purpose is clear. It makes of Rothmann's static concept of *sign* an action which happens when Spirit and faith are present. What interests Marpeck is not the particular agent (everything from water and wine to the Father and the Spirit are cited as co-witnesses) but the event in which revelation from God is vouched for. The co-witness vouches for the oneness of God's action: what is being done outwardly and materially is one with inward and spiritual reality.

The notion of co-witness is valuable to Marpeck because it highlights the event character of the external works of the church. Co-witness keeps them from being lifeless objects with a mechanical function and makes clear that the recognition and reception of divine acts is not the work of faith alone. To be sure, faith rather than works creates the opening for God to act. The external agent, which or who becomes the co-witness, confirms and aids faith. Where Marpeck speaks of a ceremony like the Lord's Supper, the external agent's work is not the function of a material element in and of itself but as part of a spiritual dynamic. In that dynamic an element is united with faith expressed in love and the Spirit, to create a union between inner and outer.

Where one component of the triad needs strengthening, Marpeck puts aside the scheme. His larger concern is not the scheme itself but the indispensability of each of its components. This is true, for example, of the preeminence given to the work of the Spirit in his letter to Helena Streicher. The enduring significance of co-witness in Marpeck's sacramental theology is not the consistency with which it is used, but that as means of grace, it establishes outward works—never the elements in and of themselves but in the role they are given.

If we remember that all of Marpeck's writings under consideration in this study were an attempt to expose the inadequacies of spiritualism, we can see two things. First, Marpeck realized that only an unambiguous sacramental realism, that is, external events as means of grace, was able to withstand the logic of spiritualism. Second, he constructed his sacramental language to make clear to the advocate of spiritualism that all of Schwenckfeld's concerns about inward reality were accounted for in the scheme Marpeck offered. He undertook whatever measures were called for to take into account criticisms from the spiritualist side. Hence, the seemingly imbalanced emphasis on faith toward the end of *VWG.*

It is historically inadequate to read Marpeck's writings primarily as a response to theological developments in the Magisterial Reformation. Though he initially found in Anabaptism a corrective to Protestant and Catholic reform attempts, he increasingly developed his thought patterns in response to another audience, that of the varieties of spiritualism flourishing in the South German realm in the first decades of the sixteenth century. In this encounter with the most radical of forces unleashed by the Reformation, Marpeck sided with the tradition of the church in its understanding of the incarnation. His originality lay in reshaping its sacramental thought in relation to the role of faith. Marpeck's encounter with spiritualism guided the course of his thought. Without it, he might not have understood the inherent antagonism between it and his own position. Because of his ability as a theologian, Marpeck was able to pursue the difference between the conflicting eucharistic doctrines to their source in Christology.

Marpeck realized that there was an indissoluble unity between christological creed and eucharistic doctrine. What Christology confessed as an abstract belief, the Lord's Supper showed forth in concrete practice. One of them vouched for the truth and reality of the other. Marpeck's dialectical movement between the concrete and abstract forms of his belief demonstrates that he understood the inseparability and interdependence of the two claims. All of this accounts for his defense of the incarnation as the first principle of the gospel, and for his affinity with the tradition at this point. His openness to Luther, especially as a mediator of that tradition, is explained by this need for a radical alternative to existing doctrines derived from the incarnation.

Other Anabaptists had other antagonists, mostly from the Magisterial Reformation, where personal faith was not a given; or from Catholicism, where a mechanical application of the *ex opere operato* view of the sacraments dominated. The inherent opposition between Anabaptism and spiritualism was only gradually perceived by both parties. In Strassburg, Marpeck and Schwenckfeld held more in common than in opposition. Slowly they came to understand that their understandings of inner and outer divided them as much from each other as from the dominant churches.

Schwenckfeld suspended the Eucharist as an external reality and then began the long search for a defense of his decision. He drew the consequences of his belief most fully in his Christology as it unfolded after 1538. Marpeck came to see the Lord's Supper as the paradigm of how the divine and human meet. In order to countenance the spiritualist challenge at the point of its most critical claim, he added an elaborate interpretation of the two natures of Christ to his earlier trinitarian rationale. By means of it, he argued that the incarnation was the abiding key to God's presence in the world.

Anabaptism, Spiritualism, and Orthodoxy

The initial impetus of Anabaptism was ecclesiastical. It sought to recover for its generation the community portrayed in the New Testament. Its theological preoccupation was the idea of the church as a corrective and alternative to the *corpus christianum*. It made common cause with spiritualism—more a tendency than a movement in the beginning of the Reformation—in combating what both movements held to be a false understanding of the gospel. They protested the definition of faith which made religious assent an act of political and social conformity rather than an existential decision.

Neal Blough has made a convincing case that at least until 1538, when Schwenckfeld repudiated the creatureliness of Christ, he and Marpeck had a common vision of the Christian life and saw themselves as allies in its propagation.[218] Beyond the purist and primitivistic similarities which characterized both streams of radical Christianity, Marpeck and Schwenckfeld held crucial assumptions in common which are often obscured by the growing antagonism between them.

The first of their commonalities is also the easiest to overlook. Though they held increasingly divergent positions concerning its nature, both theologians assumed that the Lord's Supper was a real communion with the body and blood of Christ. Second, they both stretched inherited christological concepts to their breaking point and at the same time placed their debate within a trinitarian frame of reference. Within that scheme, they worked out contradictory Christologies, but each of them sought to justify himself as the true representative of orthodoxy. Third and most striking, the theological and spiritual traditions emanating from the Fourth Gospel were the fountainhead of both their Christology and their eucharistic doctrine.

Though they understood the message of John's Gospel in contradictory ways, we should not underestimate their common affinity for John's speculations concerning the Trinity and his description of the existential relationship between the believer and Christ. This common ground gave their debate its peculiar character. It was a controversy between two opponents who both sought to avoid the pitfalls of Catholic sacramentalism and Zwinglian symbolism. This similarity of assumptions made it clear to them that one defense of these assertions was the negation of the other defense.

Through his controversy with Schwenckfeld, Marpeck was pressed to create a theological response adequate to overcome not only the shortcomings of spiritualism but also those of Anabaptism. Marpeck concluded that the reforming, refining power of spiritualistic religion not only stripped away false accretions but did away with the historical character of Christian faith altogether. Certain advocates of spiritualism he encountered in Strassburg, for example, held to the authority of the Bible and preaching but rejected the sacraments. He argued that this was an inconsistent position which could not be maintained over time.

Marpeck's teaching about the outer life of the church emphasized that each external work was cut from the same cloth and derived from the incarnation. He clearly perceived that the role given to baptism among the Anabaptists, often on simple biblical grounds without reflecting on its implications, was untenable apart from a theology of the humanity of Christ. Redefining the sacraments as primarily human acts of obedience—as Zwingli and Hubmaier did—seemed to

Marpeck to be an answer from those who had not taken the question seriously. The question, which the incarnation itself posed, was how matter mediates spirit. To say—as Zwingli and Hubmaier did—that matter cannot mediate spirit, forecloses the question. Even if such a position maintains the outward authority of Scripture or the church, it is an incipient spiritualism, inconsistent within itself.

Marpeck's initial response to spiritualism was to propose the church as the extension of the incarnation, the prolongation of the humanity of Christ. In this proposal, the community of believers became the primal sacrament. Marpeck's thinking throughout his life continued to assume this reality, but it receded in his scheme of things under pressure from Schwenckfeld's christological claims. His ecclesiology, based on the humanity of Christ, threatened his Christology, which in turn thwarted what he held to be true of the Lord's Supper.

In his own eyes, Marpeck had distinguished his thinking on the Eucharist unmistakably and fundamentally from that of Catholic tradition at two points. First, the *sine qua non* (without which there is nothing) of communion with Christ in the breaking of bread was faith and the Holy Spirit, inseparably. Second, his teaching on the humanity of Christ extended the Chalcedonian formula in another direction from the one favored by medieval tradition and emphatically retained by Luther. That tradition claimed that the heavenly Christ in his human (physical) nature as well as his divine (spiritual) nature was present in the Lord's Supper. Marpeck's revision of the received christological formulations made it necessary for him to speak of the human nature of Christ in two different ways. In his glorified humanity, Christ remained bodily at the right hand of the Father. But in his unglorified self (a notion Marpeck had originally developed quite apart from the traditional two natures formulation), Christ remained on earth in the form of his preresurrection incarnation. Marpeck identified the church with the physical, earthly, unglorified man Jesus.

Schwenckfeld did not see these claims as separate formulations drawn up to answer different questions. Contrary to his own intention, Marpeck's notion of the humanity of Christ was applied by Schwenckfeld to the eucharistic debate between the two men. Schwenckfeld used it to accuse Marpeck, claiming that in his thought the communion of the Lord's Supper was with this unglorified physical body of Christ.

In Marpeck's eyes, his two claims were separate applications of the idea of the incarnation in which one neither nullified nor interpreted the other. The humanity of Christ was not to be identified with the person of the heavenly Christ; it was the continuation of God's presence in history through the community he had called forth to carry on Jesus' ministry. The Lord's Supper was the primordial, transforming moment in the relationship of the church to the person of Jesus Christ. Marpeck had written that it was a communion with the body, flesh, and blood of Christ. Schwenckfeld interpreted this to mean a union with the humanity of Christ, his physical, unglorified body. The only meaning of such a claim in the tradition was a corporeal presence. Marpeck's entire corpus is evidence of the fact that this is not what he claimed. Schwenckfeld, however, insisted that Marpeck was refusing to accept the consequences of his assumptions.

Schwenckfeld proposed a draconian corrective to what he believed was a relapse into ancient error. It was a Christology in which Christ in toto, human as well as divine, was glorified, his creaturely humanity having been transformed into a celestial one. By means of this picture of Christ, Schwenckfeld understood the eucharistic reference in John 6:54, "Those who eat my flesh and drink my blood have eternal life." For Marpeck, this was no solution. It had been bought at the price of the humanity of Christ in any meaningful use of the term. Schwenckfeld's conflated Christology resulted from a novel application of Luther's principle of the communication of idioms. In it, Christ's humanity had totally assumed the nature of his divinity.

In Marpeck's mind, this raised fundamental problems in the realms of ethics and dogma. If the humanity of Christ has been abrogated, then the normativeness of his teaching and example must also be suspended. Beyond that, the incarnation as the fullest revelation of God was nullified. Marpeck never tired of pointing out that we know God's glory through Christ's lowliness, that God crosses from himself to us over the bridge of flesh. On a practical, polemical level, Marpeck feared the same danger in his opponent's position as Schwenckfeld had in Marpeck's: a stance which would be unable to resist the old logic of a corporeal presence of Christ in the breaking of bread.

Marpeck's solution to the matter was to develop more fully the teaching of the two natures of Christ. In so doing, he was following the pattern set by Schwenckfeld, though unfolded in quite a different way. Marpeck put aside his past qualifications about Christ being present in the breaking of bread only in his divine nature, as Spirit. Christ was present in communion in both natures. The body in which he had been resurrected and ascended, now remained in heaven in its physical composition. But his human nature, along with his divine, was spiritually present in the breaking of bread. An additional effect of that move was that it countered the tendency of Marpeck's early Christology toward binitarianism. The presence of Jesus in his humanity meant that the person of Christ was present rather than the Spirit, who then returned to being the agent of the presence of Christ rather than merely his form. In Marpeck's thought, this was a role the Spirit had earlier occupied in relation to co-witness.

Both men were at home in the mysterious and elusive world of the Fourth Gospel; neither of them was biblicistic in his cast of mind. Both wanted to account for the stupendous claims on the lips of the Johannine Jesus. By contrast, the Synoptic and Pauline institutional narratives play a supportive and sometimes negative role in the development of both men's eucharistic thought. They set the technical terms of the discussion: the nature of the gathering and of Jesus' instructions. In *JDM*, Schwenckfeld uses especially the Corinthian account to challenge Marpeck.

On the other hand, for Marpeck the Synoptic accounts are placed under yet another limitation. They give the warrant for the church's observance of the Supper, but the event they describe, the Last Supper, is not recognized by Marpeck as the beginning of the Lord's Supper. This is so because the Spirit had not been given before Christ's exaltation. The important negative function of these narratives is that they exclude what is not part of the Lord's Supper. The Supper can not be loveless, it can not be faithless, it can not be a sacrifice. In their use of the Synoptic and Pauline texts to establish a frame of reference, both Marpeck and Schwenckfeld argue biblically, at times exegetically, at other times by mere proof-texting.

However, their affinity is for John and the lofty world of speculative theology and mystical devotion which issued from his Gospel. In addition to the other conflicts each man represented, Schwenckfeld and Marpeck became contenders with one another for the true interpretation of what they saw as the heart of the New Testament, the Gospel of John. They carried on their debate within its world. That is why intratrinitarian relationships had to be elucidated. The contradictory ways in which they understood John were important in setting the course of their debate. Their conflicting interpretations have persisted throughout church history. Schwenckfeld read everything "spiritualistically": Jesus allowed outward things no role in the knowledge of God. Marpeck read everything ethically and sacramentally: the inward was both acted out and known outwardly.

Marpeck's Lord's Supper: A Johannine Theology for the Sixteenth Century

Three characteristics of the Eucharist in the teaching of Pilgram Marpeck stand out as noteworthy. First, his sacramental beliefs, especially those concerning the Supper, are deduced directly from the activity of God as Trinity in the world. Second, Marpeck's doctrine of the Lord's Supper develops out of his Christology, and in turn his Christology is worked out for the purpose of defending what he believes about the Eucharist. Third, for Marpeck, the sacramental and ethical are inseparable. Love is the means by which we participate in God. It takes external form. When we love each other, bread becomes a co-witness to us that Christ is present. The Lord's Supper is the sacrament of love. Explanatory comments on each of these traits follow.

Two decisive transitions take place in Marpeck's thought concerning the ceremonies. The first is found in the middle of *KU*. Early in this document and throughout *CV*, Marpeck argues that the external works of the church have been commanded by Scripture and moved by the Spirit. But halfway through *KU*, Marpeck turns from the fact that the ceremonies are commanded to the question of how it is that they work: "Through Christ's humanity, the inward must be revealed and recognized."[219] In his commentary on *KU*, Boyd spells out the significance of this new train of thought:

> Because Christ shared the nature of the human, that nature was opened or received the capacity (*vermugen*) to share in the divine life. Therefore, created reality, including the material, became, in the person of Jesus Christ, the mediator of that capacity and participation.[220]

Therefore, to refuse the use of water, bread, and wine is to "despise the humanity of Christ."[221] Those who do so refuse to recognize the coming of the new covenant, in which God rescues the created order through Christ taking on its nature.[222] From here on, Marpeck's apology for ceremonies is based on the humanity of Christ, first in Jesus' revelation of God and then in the church's continuation of that role. Though the Father and the Spirit are assigned roles in the drama of salvation, *KU* is concerned that the Spirit not be seen as the unmediated substitute for Christ. At this point of development in Marpeck's thought, the separate roles and natures of the members of the Trinity are clear. These distinct roles work against the conflation of the glorified Son into the being of the Spirit, or simply his being superseded by the Spirit in a kind of economic trinitarianism—the tendency in the spiritualistic circles with which Marpeck contended in Strassburg. The preeminent purpose of this text is to establish the incarnation as God's way to humanity and humanity's way to God.

A decade later, when Marpeck published *VMN*, the issue has changed and results in a second transition in his thought concerning the ceremonies. The focus is no longer on external, material reality as revelatory but on its sacramental unity with internal, spiritual reality. In the first setting, the concern is with the humanward act of God in taking on flesh. It is historical in nature and focuses on the earthly ministry of Jesus. In the second setting, the direction is reversed. It concerns the ongoing external work of the Son in bringing created realities into unity with uncreated ones. This sweeping claim can be substantiated only by showing how the Son is related to the other persons of the Godhead and how his two natures are part of his one person.

Marpeck is not averse to speculation, but his speculation is functional: it supplies the rationale for assertions made by theological instinct or in the heat of controversy. His theological exercises always have a practical purpose in the foreground. As soon as he has established the simultaneous working of Father and Son, in his first schematic description of God's threefold work in *VMN*, Marpeck draws his conclusion: "Therefore, the external baptism and the Lord's Supper in Christ are not signs; rather, they are the external work and essence of the Son."[223] This work of the Son is one with that of the Father and the Spirit. It is in God's nature that none of his persons can be or work without the other. For that reason, baptism is given in the triune name. Whenever God is at work, the external world becomes a partaker of the internal, essential order.

Marpeck's trinitarianism has an eccentric character. This is largely the result of its functional nature. What interests Marpeck about the three-in-oneness of God is not its unfathomable mystery but its practical truth. God as Trinity means that there is a simultaneity between what is done outwardly in his name and what happens in the realm of spirit. Though he cannot be identified with anything outward, he is present in it. The divine dynamic is invoked as the basis of Marpeck's sacramentology; here we find a fluid Trinity rather than the formulated roles assigned to the persons of God by the classical creeds. We have already noticed that Marpeck's interest in the Bible, particularly concerning these questions, is less in the letter of the text than in the spirit of its thought world.

The relatively unfixed and undifferentiated roles of the Trinity in the New Testament, particularly those of the ascended Son and the Spirit, account in part for those characteristics in Marpeck's trinitarian scheme. Yet one senses also that he is working from an extrabiblical frame of reference. His language overlaps with that of the Fourth Gospel but includes other technical terminology. The most striking instance of this is Marpeck's introduction of co-witness as a description of the event character of a ceremony. In addition, the developments in trinitarian language are best explained as the progression within an already-established scheme of thought. When a challenge is put to him, Marpeck alters the scheme without much concern for consistency. Thus, the members of the Trinity seem often to be interchangeable, especially the Spirit. In the opening discourse on the Trinity in *VMN*, the Father works as Spirit and the Son as man. The Son is portrayed as working externally in the church, while the Father works internally in the Spirit.

Later Marpeck takes up an extension of this thought. When the Son returns to be with the Father, the Spirit takes the place of the Son in history. The Spirit is the immanence of the Father, but only after the new covenant has been inaugurated. At the same time the Spirit is equated with the divine nature of Christ. When this more elaborate schematization of the Trinity is applied in *VWG*, Christ as Spirit is the one present in the external works of the church.

This development comes about when Marpeck realizes that an undifferentiated claim about the external work of the Son as the humanity of Christ opens him to the charge of transubstantiation. Schwenckfeld makes this charge by equating the term "Christ in his unglorified body" with a corporeal presence in the Lord's Supper. Marpeck's intention with that notion is to make it clear that the church is militant and not yet triumphant. It has an ecclesiological and ethical but not a sacramental purpose. In order to vindicate himself, Marpeck turns to the language of Christ's two natures and talks about him as spiritually present in his human nature. He is able to use this single formulation as a description of the church and of the Eucharist.

Marpeck's trinitarian terminology is not describing fixed ontological categories. It seems, rather, to paint pictures of the divine, assuming in the simplest possible terms the threeness of God. What interests Marpeck is the dynamic nature of God's relationship with the world and how this can be applied to his problem, namely, how the external and internal are made one. Apparently this view of the Trinity was not a novelty of Marpeck's creation. Schwenckfeld nowhere questions it. Their disagreements concerning Christology, a difference of fundamental proportions to be sure, are located within a frame of reference both of them assume and accept. The assumption of a dynamic Trinity is necessary for both of their doctrines of the Eucharist.

Both grant as a presupposition that there is a movement from God to humanity in the Eucharist. What distinguishes Marpeck's position from that of his opponent is that his concept also includes a Godward movement from humanity. He believes that the created order of people and things can become the bearer of grace and faith. The material and human are united with the spiritual and divine. This happens where Spirit and faith come together. The prototype for this movement is the Lord's Supper.

The basis for this distinction between the two positions lies in the incompatible christological claims of the two theologians. According to Marpeck, Christ takes on the fullness of human nature. He itemizes what this means as its significance becomes clearer in his debate with Schwenckfeld. Christ was born of a woman and knew every limit and pain of mortality and finitude. It is this lowly presence of God which the church embodies. This painfully human Jesus is the one raised from the dead, who ascended into heaven. In leaving the plane of history, he did not lose his humanness; it is forever united with his divineness.[224]

As Marpeck's theology develops to meet the obstacles put in its way, the two-natures Christology becomes more and more decisive for an understanding of ceremonies. Initially, in *CV* and in strands of *VMN*, the humanity of Christ as the prolongation of the incarnation in the church is the basis of sacraments. They reveal God to natural creatures by natural means.

Participation in the life of God remains a secondary motif in the early writings, though it is present in the baptismal doctrine of *VMN*. Its importance is increased by the introduction of the notion of co-witness. The co-witness has two purposes. It vouches for the revelatory character of the event, showing God's presence in the world. But it is also part of the dynamic in which external works become one reality with the God revealed in them. This inclusion of the human in the divine is grounded for Marpeck in the ascension. Salvation is fully accomplished only when the humanness which Christ took upon himself becomes an indelible part of his being. That is why Marpeck makes so much of the descent into hell: in this, Christ took upon himself the deepest of human experiences. The ascension then becomes the unbreakable joining of flesh and spirit.

In his later writings, especially in the eucharistic sections of *VWG II*, the basis for external works is not so much the ecclesial form of the humanity of Christ as the heavenly one. Thus the rationale for ceremonies is shifted from the incarnation and the syncronicity between the Father's and Son's actions to the role of Christ's two natures in mediating the inward and outward to each other. This grounding of the character of a ceremony in the two natures of Christ is worked out almost exclusively in relation to the Lord's Supper. In fact, there is a dialectical movement at work between theological presuppositions and concrete applications, pushing Marpeck's sacramental thought forward. An outline of this progression follows.

In the development of his eucharistic ideas in *VWG II*, ecclesiological and ethical motifs become dominated by christological ones. The church and its life of obedience in the world is never abandoned; instead, Marpeck builds the logic he follows christologically on the assumption that Christian existence has a concrete, historical character. In the debate with Schwenckfeld, Marpeck never relinquishes his earlier convictions. They are of a piece with his christological and trinitarian thought. But, as has been described above, its formulation changes and the discussion comes to focus more and more on how Christ is present in communion. The superlative pursuit of the two Strassburg tracts is the concern with how the church embodies and is made one with that presence. In *VMN* that principle is applied to baptism and the Lord's Supper. *VWG* is preoccupied with the Eucharist to the point where it becomes the prototype for the church rather than the other way around, as in *CV* and *KU*.

There is a similar development in the use of the concept of *ceremony*. Throughout Marpeck's corpus, it means any external work by which God is known and the gospel is shown forth. The trinitarian dynamic, illustrated by the functioning of the two external works under siege (baptism and the Lord's Supper), applies as well to works like preaching and the ban. By the time Marpeck writes *VWG*, the ceremonies (as many means of revelation and encounter) are referred to only by way of example. Similarly, the ecclesial significance of the incarnation—the church as the primal sacrament—is superseded by the Lord's Supper as the prototypical moment in which human and divine, external and internal, are united. In his mature theology, the Lord's Supper has become the workbench on which Marpeck's theology is fashioned. It bears the marks of his theological ingenuity and imagination. The Eucharist becomes the cause célèbre: everything that concerns the meeting of God and humanity unfolds in it.

Marpeck is the only Anabaptist theologian whose circumstances and scope of thought brought the Lord's Supper to the center of his theology. While the Anabaptists as a whole allot a lofty place to the

Eucharist as the primal sign of the church, it is never given the theological and devotional attention accorded to baptism. For that reason Mennonite piety has regularly focused much on decision and responsibility and less on grace and mystery. Pilgram Marpeck's theology evolved from the initial Anabaptist concern for baptism as the ceremony by which the church is ordered, to a focus on the Lord's Supper as the ceremony by which the church is sustained. In the process he laid a theological foundation for the church's life as a participation in the life of God.

Only in relation to the Eucharist were the weaknesses and also the strengths of Anabaptism realized. In his eucharistic doctrine, Marpeck established a trinitarian basis for the relationship of grace and faith, of the inner world of spirit and the outer world of matter. His beliefs are most aptly summarized and characterized as the application of the theology of the Fourth Gospel to another age. Marpeck absorbed Johannine spirituality and its speculative thought on Christology, Trinity, and Lord's Supper. He brought all these to bear on the eucharistic debates of the sixteenth century. Out of them he created a eucharistic doctrine built upon the incarnation and faith, a doctrine which allowed him to transcend the alternatives of sacramentalism and spiritualism.

Dirk Philips (1504-1568)

4
Dirk Philips

Introduction

Dirk Philips (1504-68) was born in Leeuwarden, Friesland, into the family of a priest. During his lifetime, he or others wrote down almost nothing about his early life. There are, however, fragments of oral tradition concerning his upbringing. One is that he was educated by his father and later became associated with the strict Franciscans, an order known to have had houses in Friesland when Dirk[1] was young.[2] Koolman notes that Leeuwarden had a sacramentarian circle in the early 1500s. It is known to have come under the influence of Melchior Hoffmann about 1532.[3] Dirk made only the most general references to his past, and so we are left with nothing more than inferences about his pre-Anabaptist experience. Keeney notes that, "Dirk made a deliberate attempt to deny dependence upon authorities other than the Scriptures."[4] It therefore is difficult to locate the theological as well as biographical factors formative in Dirk's development.

Dirk committed himself to the Anabaptist cause in late 1533 in the town of his birth. He was baptized between Christmas and Light Mass of that year by Pieter Houtzager and ordained as a minister shortly thereafter by his brother, Obbe Philips.[5] He quickly assumed leadership among the nonresistant Anabaptists, whose world had tumbled into disarray with the rise and fall of the violent Anabaptists at Münster. Soon Dirk was ordained as elder, the name given to the episcopal office in Anabaptist circles. He was among the seven elders who charted the course of their church in the next score of years. About 1550 Dirk became the leader of the new congregation of Anabaptist immigrants in Danzig on the Vistula Delta.[6] He remained its elder until 1567, at the same time engaging in a far-flung itinerant ministry. In that year he journeyed to Emden to rule on a division in the congregation there. Dirk remained in Emden and died there a year later.

The most renowned personage among Dutch–North German

Anabaptists was Menno Simons. His role as the preeminent pastor of the movement is undisputed. After he joined the Anabaptists in 1536, he more than anyone else guided their fate. His writings, though equal in length to those of Dirk, are almost entirely occasional pieces written either to defend his community against its detractors or to sustain it in suffering. Menno's references to the Lord's Supper, for example, are usually interspersed with other topics. There is only one sustained treatment of the subject in his works, and even it is not a systematic exposition of the Supper.[7] This lack of focused attention to the Eucharist is characteristic also of most of the scholarly studies of northern Anabaptism which select Menno as their subject. None of them deals extensively with the sacraments and almost not at all with the Lord's Supper.[8]

The theology of the Lord's Supper among the peaceful Anabaptists of the north is most fully articulated by Dirk Philips. Of particular relevance to the purposes of this study is the systematic treatment of the Eucharist in *Van dat Auontmael des Heeren Jesu Christi, onse Belidinghe* (AML: On the Supper of the Lord Jesus Christ, Our Considerations).[9] In addition, Dirk's writing on the incarnation and sacraments in general makes copious references to the Eucharist. His Christology, especially his belief about the unfallen humanity of Christ, supplies the *Vorverständnis* (prior understanding) for his view of the Supper. To this is added an interpretation of Christ's humanity derived from the relationship between the Son and the Spirit as set forth in the Gospel of John. Dirk's writings alone, among those in the movement whose views and stature endured, have a well-enough-developed sacramental theology to compare with the other subjects of this study.

Dirk wrote nearly 700 pages of theological and pastoral treatises in the course of his career. Some of them directly refute views which threaten the Anabaptist communities. Even in his polemical tracts, Dirk's writing is methodical in nature. The Dutch Mennonite historian, van der Zijpp, makes this assessment: "Dirk Philips is without doubt the leading theologian and dogmatician among the Dutch and North German Mennonites of that time. He is more systematic than Menno, though of course also more severe and one-sided."[10] Dirk's writing is characterized by an endless citation of Scripture references and extensive Scripture quotations, usually in paraphrase. Though Dirk systematically addresses his subject matter, he does not think philosophically. His argument proceeds by means of assertions buttressed by biblical quotations. At the same time, his writing betrays a familiarity with classical dogmatic terminology and some grasp of the ancient languages.

In 1564 Dirk gathered most of his writings into a handbook entitled the *Enchiridion* (*ENC*). They were compiled in theological rather than chronological order. Dirk's writings are concentrated in two periods, each about a decade long, from 1534 to 1547, and from 1557 to his death. S. Cramer and F. Pijper, compilers of the only scholarly edition of Dirk's corpus, make the following claims:

> The *Enchiridion* may be given the same status as the most distinguished utterances of Protestant dogmatics in the early period. What the "Loci communes" of Melanchthon was for Lutherans, the *Confession* of Beza was for the French, and the *Leken wechswyser* for the Netherlands Reformed, the *Enchiridion* has been for Mennonites.[11]

Influences

The peculiar form of the spirit of reformation in fifteenth- and sixteenth-century Netherlands was Sacramentarianism. Both Williams and Krahn trace the evolution of reform in the Netherlands from sacramentarianism through Anabaptism to Calvinism.[12] Its theological and devotional center was the Lord's Supper. In its eucharistic teaching, Sacramentarianism emphasized the distinction between flesh and spirit, between inward and outward. Among the unique facets of the Dutch–North German Anabaptist evolution of Sacramentarianism was its peculiar Christology of Jesus' unfallen humanity.[13]

This teaching came from Melchior Hoffmann (ca. 1495-1543), an original thinker and a revolutionary apocalypticist who came to Anabaptism via Lutheranism. His christological views were the seedbed for those of Caspar Schwenckfeld, Pilgram Marpeck's chief theological adversary. Hoffmann held that Christ had only one nature, the divine. He brought his flesh with him from heaven. Voolsta describes this view as a transformation of the divine Christ into flesh rather than a taking on of fallen human flesh from Mary.[14] Hoffmann presupposed that created reality was essentially sinful and therefore incapable of mediating God's salvation. Sinful humanity could not be rescued by anyone who shared its uncleanliness.[15] His view of the incarnation and atonement led him to a negation of the material world per se. This premise, in turn, was compatible with sixteenth-century Sacramentarian thought, which had loosened the spiritual presence of Christ in the Lord's Supper from any material moorings. Though Hoffmann espoused a spiritual presence of Christ in the Supper, its only medium was the word.[16]

Hoffmann's "christological tendency" became the orthodoxy of Dutch–North German Anabaptism.[17] The reason for speaking of a "tendency" is that Menno and Dirk corrected Hoffmann at the point of his monophysitism. As will be shown below, Dirk developed a doctrine of the two natures of Christ. However, he held fast to Hoffmann's underlying claim that only an incarnation in unfallen flesh could be salvific. This assertion was of utmost significance for Dirk's eucharistic doctrine in that it ruled out the mediating role which sacraments—part of the unclean world—had played throughout the Middle Ages.

Though Dirk's sacramental theology goes beyond that of Hoffmann, he breathes deeply of the rarified atmosphere which Hoffmann's Christology inhabits. Its pervasive dualism, which gives the realm of spirit primacy over the realm of matter such that matter cannot mediate spirit, blows like a fierce wind through the structure of Dirk's theology and piety. In the conclusion of his meticulous study of Melchiorite Christology, Voolstra emphasizes its Johannine origins. Its foundation is the preexistent Logos which takes on flesh.[18] This use of the Fourth Gospel as the interpretive key to the various New Testament Christologies and teachings about the Lord's Supper is carried over fully into Dirk's writings.

Together with other reformational movements influenced by Sacramentarianism, northern Anabaptism inherited a problem brought about at the time of the Reformation by the loss of the original theological and liturgical setting of Sacramentarianism. What had distinguished the eucharistic assumptions of pre-Reformation Sacramentarianism from those of the dominant tradition was the claim that at the mass believers could spiritually receive Christ even if they did not receive the host. Prior to its radicalization on the eve of the Reformation, Sacramentarianism had remained a type of *ex opere operantis* theology (the efficacy of a rite being determined by the interior disposition of the administrant or the recipient). That is, the spiritual communion of the believer with Christ added to but was derived from sacramental communion as given in the mass.

At the time of the Reformation, the belief in transubstantiation was jettisoned, and the Sacramentarians were left without a theology of the outward event which Christ had commanded the church to observe. They were left with an undefined juxtaposition between the breaking of bread and the eating of Christ. This is also Dirk's problem. He never arrives at an explanation for the relationship between the outward act of the church and the inward participation of the individual. What distinguishes his position from a purely spiritualistic one is that he retains both the use of bread and wine and an existential communion with Christ as necessary components of the Lord's Supper. How he arrives at this position is the subject of the investigation which follows.

Christology

In Christian theology, belief about the incarnation logically determines belief about sacraments: the manner in which God took on flesh becomes the archetype for the relationship between spirit and matter. This statement is true also in the thought of Dirk Philips, for whom the incarnation was the watershed of his theology. At the outset of this study, one terminological clarification is critical. To describe what Dirk believed about the human nature of Christ, the term "unfallen humanity" has been chosen instead of the more common "celestial flesh." This selection was made because in his eucharistic writings, Dirk uses the term "flesh" almost exclusively to refer to the divine nature of Christ as he gives communion with himself to the believer. In this study *flesh* will be used only in that sense of the divine nature of Christ.

Dirk's christological reflections fall into two categories. First, his picture of reality, including the Lord's Supper, is derived from Hoffmann's view of the incarnation. Second, his thinking on the subject of Christology emerges from his analysis of the Fourth Gospel in relation to the Lord's Supper. It places more weight on the ongoing existence of the human nature of Christ than does his teaching on the unfallen humanity of Christ. Dirk makes direct use of the human, ascended Christ in defining the Lord's Supper.[19] We will take up this second christological scheme in the section on the Lord's Supper.

Dirk's beliefs about the humanity of Christ are concentrated largely in his two treatises on the incarnation, *Van der Menschwerdinghe* (*MNG:* On the Incarnation)[20] and *Van de rechte kennisse* (*KENN:* On the True Knowledge of Jesus Christ).[21] Both of them were first published in 1557, the same year in which Dirk's treatise on the Lord's Supper also appeared in its present form.[22] In *MNG*, Johannine concepts are manifest from the beginning. Jesus is the Word and Son of God, one with the Father, truly God and man. He is the *wesentlijck woort*, the real or essential Word to which all other words spoken by God bear witness.[23] In the opening pages of Dirk's christological reflections, the meaning of "Word" is the Son who "is not a spoken but a speaking Word."[24] This meaning is maintained throughout *MNG*. In *KENN*, the concept of "word" is expanded to include teaching by or about Jesus.[25] But the word as the agency of the Spirit's action is never developed. Dirk does not single out the words of institution as the means by which God acts in the Supper.[26]

Dirk teaches that the Son's taking on of flesh was the way in which he could offer himself perfectly to the Father for our transgressions. It is not in taking upon himself the conditions of the fall that Christ saves but in choosing to die and condescending to death.

> In his humanity he was enabled to offer himself for us a pure, holy, accept-
> able sacrifice, as a sweet-smelling savor unto God, . . . but for us it was the
> forgiveness and washing away of our sins, because he died innocently for
> us, and his human nature is spotless, without sin.[27]

Within a page of this introductory section of *MNG*, Dirk begins to
explain what he intends by the notion, "spotless human nature." Jesus
was born in Mary but not by corruptible human seed.[28] He is the living
bread which came down from heaven. Therefore, his flesh could not
have been formed by Mary. Dirk immediately applies this assertion to
the Lord's Supper by means of quotations and paraphrases of John 6.[29]
This is his argument:

> Now if Christ is the bread of heaven, and if the bread of heaven moreover
> is the flesh of Christ, it is impossible for the flesh of Christ to be formed by
> Mary; for neither the seed of Mary nor that of any earthly creature can by
> any means be the true living bread that comes down from heaven, or be so
> called.[30]

Here are Dirk's Christology and sacramentology—if his image may be
extended—in embryo.

In his exposition of the incarnation, Dirk seems to be aware of the
fact that his position is a dissident one. He anticipates the reader's
question: "If Christ did not receive his flesh and blood from Mary, how
then could he suffer and die?" Rather than answer this question immediately, he replaces it with one which he considers decisive. If his humanity was like ours, "how could Christ make an everlasting atonement
for our sins and pay for them?"[31]

Though his burning interest is in the second question, Dirk does
have an answer to the first one. It is that Jesus could suffer because he
actually assumed human nature, voluntarily humiliating himself.[32] That
nature was finite but not sinful, like that of Adam before the fall. This is
what Dirk means when he talks about the Lord's "true humanity."[33] He
approvingly quotes an ancient anti-Nestorian resolution: "We confess
that God's Word suffered in the flesh and was crucified in the flesh."[34]
Dirk's vocabulary tallies with that of the christological references he
chooses out of the Bible and out of the classical age of dogmatic tradition, but his one-sided interpretation of these references is at variance
with that of the ancient councils.

The problem, seen from the vantage point of Chalcedon (451), is
not an absence of precise doctrinal formulation. This is not outside
Dirk's sphere of competence or interest, as we can see from his careful

formulation of how Jesus was born in Mary. The problem lies in the imbalance in Dirk's attention to the two natures of Christ. This christological one-sidedness has two manifestations. First, he tries to rescue Jesus' humanity from participation in ours. Second, his preoccupation remains on Christ's divinity. At the conclusion of *MNG*, he asserts that it is not enough to confess the human Christ; he must be acknowledged as the "eternal Word."[35] In most of Dirk's christological passages, Christ in his divine nature is the one who is the Father's agent. In his divine nature, Christ is the mediator of both creation and redemption.[36]

Against whom was Dirk arguing his defense of the eternal divinity of the Son? Socinianism became a factor in Mennonite theological life only after his death. All his Protestant and Catholic opponents shared the belief he confessed. One may well argue that Dirk's purpose in restating Christ's divinity so emphatically was to make tenable his dissident view of Christ's humanity. This hypothesis puts his argument together as follows: If the believer were to take to heart the awesome claim of Christ's "glory with the Father before the beginning of the world," it would become devotionally—if not theologically—inconceivable to taint him with the flesh of a fallen humanity. This is an instance of the law of prayer (*lex orandi*) determining the law of belief (*lex credendi*).

Only when Dirk thinks he has convinced the reader that Christ's humanity is fundamentally different from ours does he move to a description of the incarnation. For him, none of the wonder of God taking on flesh is lost if his flesh is different from ours.[37] In it we encounter the unfathomable grace and mercy of God.[38] Through the Holy Spirit's work in us in the new birth, we receive by grace the being Christ had by nature. Our new nature has not only an ontological but also a moral oneness with that of Christ.[39]

Lord's Supper

In this, the central section of our study, three purposes will be pursued. The first is to introduce Dirk's view of the sacraments. Some attention is given to sacraments in general in the eucharistic documents to be explored below. But the subject is most systematically dealt with in Dirk's baptismal treatise, *Van der Doope* (*Doope:* On Baptism).[40]

The second purpose is to formulate the theology of the Lord's Supper which emerges from the writings which are explicitly eucharistic in nature. They are not uniform in style or content, so attention will be given to their commonalities and anomalies. The eucharistic texts are four in number. The principal treatise, *Van dat Auonmaal*

(AML: On the Supper), is a systematic setting forth of Dirk's teaching on the Lord's Supper. Second is a section on ordinances in *Van de Gemeynte Godts (GEM:* On the Church of God).[41] Third is a letter to the church, *De derde vermaninghe (THIRD:* Third Admonition).[42] The fourth, *Een verantwoordinghe ende Refutation op twee Sendtbrieven Sebastian Franck (FRANCK:* A Response & Refutation of Two Epistles by Sebastian Franck), is a reply to letters of Sebastian Franck.[43]

The third purpose of this section is to identify the nature of the relationship between Dirk's teaching on the Lord's Supper and his beliefs about the incarnation. In their introduction to Dirk's work, Cramer and Pijper draw attention to the intimate connection between the two doctrines.[44] But that relationship, as introduced above, is not uncomplicated in its character or its place in Dirk's thought.

Two concepts are essential to an understanding of Dirk's theology. They are "spiritual" and "faith." Neither of them is dealt with methodically by him because they are part of his universe of established assumptions. *Spiritual* is not a term Dirk uses often but it aptly describes his picture of reality. It affirms that grace is not transmitted by material means: spirit mediates spirit. Spirit, however, is a reality which takes on creaturely form. Christians, as mortal, fallible creatures, are spiritual because they belong to the Spirit. Even though they continue to have an earthly existence, they now have a spiritual and not a fleshly nature. This is true also of the church, which is at once an empirical and a spiritual entity.

Dirk cautiously carries this notion over to sacraments late in his career in his refutation of Sebastian Franck. But even here, the relationship between sacraments and spirit remains undefined. A different and even more impenetrable problem is the relationship between Christ's human nature and the spiritual realm. Christ in his divinity is the agent of both salvation and communion. The human Jesus, in Dirk's Johannine picture of him, ascends and recedes from a mediatorial role between humanity and God. The flesh and blood of Christ which feed the believer are from the divine Christ, who comes to us as Spirit.

Faith is also a definitive category in Dirk's theology. To adequately describe the role it plays in Dirk's thought would exceed the bounds of this study. Of interest for our purposes is the following: Faith is a gift of God as well as a human response. As faith is moved by the Spirit, it becomes the means of grace, the primary reality of the Christian life. Only in the presence of Spirit and faith as a dynamic can any outward thing point to Christ. Sacraments gain whatever spiritual significance they have only in relation to people of faith, people who belong to the Spirit.

Dirk's Theology of the Sacraments

Dirk's view of sacraments in general determines his eucharistic doctrine in that his sacramentology supplies the terms of reference for the Lord's Supper. Especially important is Dirk's understanding of the character of a sign, of faith, and of the relationship between spirit and form. In his chapter on the church, *GEM*, Dirk lists the sacraments as baptism and the Lord's Supper. Sacraments, however, are only one category of the larger concept of ordinance. The term *ordinance* refers to six ways in which God orders the life of the church: the ordaining of ministers; the sacraments; footwashing; evangelical separation; love of neighbor; nonresistant, crossbearing suffering.[45] Like many other sixteenth-century reformers, Dirk includes in the essential marks of the church more than the administration of the two so-called dominical sacraments. But the Lord's Supper and baptism have a function which distinguishes them from the other ordinances. Their designation as "sacraments" underscores their special character as concentrated moments in the divine-human encounter by which believers "are made partakers of all that belongs to Christ."[46]

In *Doope*, Dirk ascribes the same character to baptism as to the Lord's Supper. He arrives at this claim in the course of his argument against those who admit children to baptism but not to communion. His contention is that children cannot participate in either because they cannot believe.

A *sacramentlije teecken* or sacramental sign has the following characteristics. To it belong—in addition to faith—confession, mystery or hiddenness, a good conscience, and changed behavior.[47] Hence, the inclusion of the two sacraments in the list of ordinances makes it clear that all the marks of the church have objective and subjective characteristics: all of them come about when faith responds to grace. But only the two sacraments establish the believers in their relationship with Christ. The principal mode of a sacrament is vertical communion, while the principal mode of the other ordinances is horizontal partnership. The breaking of bread as a sign of community plays only a marginal role in Dirk's doctrine. In his writing, Dirk is preoccupied with the union of the soul with Christ. Of the two sacraments, the Lord's Supper is the paradigmatic one; it is the norm against which baptism is measured.[48]

Dirk's use of the term *sign* is twofold. There are sacramental signs (as described above), but Jesus Christ is the only saving sign, the only sign of grace. According to the baptismal treatise, God's covenant of grace "is not linked with any outward sign." "All outward signs point us from them to him."[49] Christ is the only actor in the sacramental drama.

He comes to us "through faith, in the Spirit, by the power of his word."[50] Christ "fulfills in us the signification of the sacraments."[51] The gist of these concentrated paragraphs concerning the Eucharist is that sacramental signs are visible, earthly pointers to the invisible, heavenly sign of grace. That is to say, by his incarnation and atonement, Christ became the effectual sign of God's grace. He is the only means of grace. Faith alone comprehends this and receives it. The gracious relationship of the believer with Christ is signified by the Supper. To take the bread and wine is to respond in faith that Christ gives us his flesh to eat and his blood to drink.[52]

In the Reformation *concomitance* was understood as parallel but not causally related actions; one outwardly takes the bread and inwardly receives the body of Christ. *Concomitance* is too precise a word to describe the relationship at issue, yet Dirk teaches that when Christ is received in faith, bread and wine become signs of his grace. The breaking of bread is a particular instance of confirmation of the relationship the believer has been given with Christ by faith.

Dirk returns to the twofold language of signs in *THIRD* and in his letters against Sebastian Franck. The saving sign of the covenant of God with humankind, according to *THIRD*, is Jesus Christ himself. Yet God has always confirmed his promise with outward signs. For this reason a repentant person should be baptized not only inwardly by Christ himself but also outwardly and with water by a minister in the church.[53] Here the sign points in the opposite direction from its role in *Doope*. There it is a token of God's act of grace; in *THIRD* it signifies the believer's response of faith. The outward sign is a confirmation of what God has done through the individual's faith rather than an invitation to it. Baptism is a sign of the individual's response to God's saving love; the Lord's Supper is the sign of the church's response to his love.[54]

But even in this treatise, there is more to a sacrament than its response character. Both the role of the minister and the active character of the sacrament itself (for example, "we are also admonished by the Lord's Supper")[55] make the sacrament inseparably something received by and something carried out by the believing recipient. Yet, the agent of God's action always remains the Spirit, who works on behalf of the Word, Christ, and through the spoken word as the expression of his power. The elements themselves are never the medium of this power.

Dirk continues his antispiritualist refutation of Franck by claiming the inseparability of the Spirit from the historical forms he takes. His reply to Franck is an attempt to spell out the relationship between the two. Dirk meets Franck's assault on "outward signs as baby-things"[56] by insisting that they in no sense lessen the role of Christ himself. The word of Christ, his teaching, is spirit. His teaching includes the command to practice the sacramental signs. When this is done in faith, the Spirit of God is at work in them. The Spirit gives visibility to the work of God.[57] This is the loftiest claim Dirk makes for outward signs: where faith and Spirit are present, sacraments reveal grace. Though the immediate cause of this affirmation of sacramental reality is Franck's challenge to the validity of dominical commands, it does lead Dirk to make a positive claim for material evidences of an immaterial presence. Despite the sacramentarian tendency of his thought, he refuses to reduce the sacraments and ordinances to images of inner experience.

Franck's position is that those who live in the realm of spirit are adults who have left behind them the childish need for physical attachments. Dirk and Franck have in common a doctrine of sanctification which builds on the belief in the divinization of human nature. By *divinization* Dirk means that the believer is given by grace what Christ is by nature, participation in the being of God. But Dirk is unwilling to follow Franck to his conclusion: that the believer is transformed in such a way as to outgrow the need for outward signs and the obligation to obey Christ, who commanded them.[58] Dirk retorts that the outward acts of the church are not the "dolls and rag babies" of Christians who have come of age and no longer need them. The sacramental tokens are by no means powerless if they are rightly observed with true faith.[59] Dirk explains how it is that outward signs have power by introducing a defense of sacraments from his ecclesiology. The church exists in spirit and truth, yet it is visible.

This claim is profound, even if undeveloped. In effect, it says that *spiritual* and *external* are not necessarily opposites. This is not a tenet of Dirk's christological and eucharistic teachings, but it is the bedrock of his ecclesiology. He believes that the company of believers, those united with Christ, live an external yet spiritual existence. The spiritual character of their visible community is protected by the ban. By invoking ecclesiological assumptions at this point in his defense, he implies that sacraments are an extension of the visibility of the church.[60] This affirmation brings the world of physical reality, as represented by a sacrament, to the threshold of the realm of spirit. But material signs still cannot participate in the reality to which they point. They, unlike people, are not included in the transforming power of the incarnation.

Like his eucharistic doctrine, Dirk's teaching about the church follows two parallel tracks. Going along one of them, he emphasizes the eternal existence of the church as a celestial entity.[61] Going along the other, he speaks of it as a visible, historical reality.[62] The latter notion assumes that the church has an outward reality; the salvation of Christians includes their bodies. If this were not so, there would be no need for the ban—the physical separation of one person from the community. The conclusion of the matter, then, is that Dirk is of two minds on the extent of the work of sanctification. His sacramental doctrine, especially prior to the *FRANCK*, follows from one strand of his Christology: fallen physical reality cannot mediate grace. But his soteriology builds on another aspect of his Christology: the human being, including one's outward nature, can be transformed. What he holds to in his anthropology and ecclesiology, Dirk is willing to extend to his sacramentology only as a last resort in creating a bulwark against the extreme spiritualism of Franck.

Thus Dirk's theology of the sacraments as well as his theology of the Lord's Supper was not spun as a seamless garment; it is a coat of many threads and colors. As challenges to his beliefs arose, he elaborated on them and changed them. The example of Dirk's encounter with Franck illustrates a fundamental trait of his theological method. It also provides a perspective from which to view his spiritualizing tendency in other of his eucharistic writings. In both instances his beliefs about sacraments in general and about the Lord's Supper in particular were not a series of deductions from a single unalterable premise but a setting of limits to spiritualist and sacramentalist positions.

He applied two criteria in setting these limits. One of them was his spiritualism. It involved a rejection of a received notion about sacramental efficacy, that there is an instrumental causality, something other than Spirit and faith alone, which can bring about unity with Christ. The core of Dirk's spiritualism was its affirmation of the spiritual union of the believer and Christ. This union is the one signified and confirmed at the Lord's Supper.

Biblicism is Dirk's other limiting criterion. He used it as a principle of demarcation: anything which violated the clear command of Christ was illicit. These two criteria were applied in opposite directions. Dirk pulled back from the spiritualist extreme when it threatened the visible church and its authority. He pulled back from the sacramental view when it seemed to allow for the gift of grace without faith. Whenever Dirk was threatened by anything which might open the way to *ex opere operato* sacramentology, he emphasized the *sine qua non* (necessity) of faith so relentlessly that the material signs all but disappear.[63] Yet Dirk was confronted by the relentless spiritualism of a consistent sacramentarian like Franck. Only then did Dirk feel safe in making positive claims about the Eucharist as a visible, tangible event.

His fears about Franck's theology had as much to do with authority as they do with sacramentology. Dirk reasserted that Jesus explicitly instituted the sacraments and the early church commanded them—two tenets gainsaid by Franck. Against Franck's anarchistic pneumatology, which rendered the authority of the outward word (both the Bible and preaching) subservient to individual illumination, Dirk emphasized biblical and hierarchical authority. Therefore, he appealed to the ordinances of the church to guard it against the subjectivism of each individual and each generation.

Under the challenge of Franck's consequential spiritualism, Dirk made assertions about the participation of outward signs in the revelation of inward reality. These statements went beyond what is warranted by his Christology of Jesus' unfallen humanity. According to this doctrine of the incarnation, created substances are incapable of revealing uncreated ones. Yet in his rebuttal to Franck and in certain of his eucharistic claims, the outward confirms the presence of the inward and assures believers of its reality.

This leaves us with questions about the grounds for Dirk's divergent sacramental claims as they came to expression in his eucharistic texts. First, was the bond Dirk posited between spirit and form based on a philosophical procedure (the application of a worldview to a particular case) or a hermeneutical procedure? To put the same question in another way, was he saying that sacraments make Christ visible because, as Marpeck put it under similar circumstances, "The inner is known by the outer,"[64] or because the Bible says so? Both are true. Dirk's spiritualism was fundamentally overruled by his biblicism. By exegesis, but even more by simply invoking the authority of Scripture and of Christ's commands, Dirk defended his use of signs against Franck.

According to *MNG* and *KENN*, it is evident that Dirk considered his Christology to be exegetically derived. But he did not invoke his exegetical conclusions about Jesus' unfallen humanity against Franck because their foundational tenet—the exclusion of fallen, creaturely reality from a role in salvation—would only substantiate Franck's position! When faced with a consistent spiritualism, Dirk developed the rudiments of a sacramentology along a separate track from what he believed about the incarnation. It derived from his ecclesiology: Dirk allowed his belief about the sanctification of people as bearers of grace to carry over to sacraments.

Dirk's Theology of the Lord's Supper
Definitions

Dirk's beliefs concerning the breaking of bread were structured by his sacramental thought, including its internal tensions and the adaptations occasioned by them. But his eucharistic doctrine was not simply an application of his sacramental views. This is so for at least two reasons. First, his sacramentology reached its final form a decade after the rest of his eucharistic documents had been written. In comparing statements in *FRANCK* and *AML*, we need to remember that Dirk's confession concerning the Holy Supper was written in the 1540s and revised in 1557. Dirk's theology of the Eucharist had not yet taken into account the challenge posed by a thoroughgoing spiritualism which lacked the constraint of literal biblical authority and a visible church. Though spiritualism was then already part of the setting, the more threatening opponent was sacramentalism. Against it Dirk employed the spiritualistic tendency of his own Sacramentarianism. The full consequences of that tendency were not yet evident to him in the late 1550s, though he sensed the tensions involved in being antisacramentalist yet retaining external rites.

The second reason for asserting the unique development of Dirk's doctrine of the Lord's Supper is that it was shaped by a source which came into play only when the discussion turned specifically to eucharistic matters. This source was a teaching about the existential communion of the believer with Christ as set out on the Fourth Gospel. It is difficult to determine the relationship between this unmediated feeding on Christ, and the Lord's Supper as an event bounded by time and space. Exploring this relationship will guide the following investigation.

We now turn to the most systematic, sustained treatment of the Lord's Supper in Dirk's corpus, his confession on the holy communion. *AML* represents the settled views of a pastor seeking to steer the good ship "Anabaptist" between the rocks of Catholic externality on the one hand and the shoals of spiritualist internality on the other. It begins with a definition of communion.

> At a meeting of Christians bread and wine are to be set forth, and the death of the Lord is to be proclaimed by a minister of the word and taken thoroughly to heart by every Christian, and because of which thanks are to be given to God, after which the bread is to be broken and received and eaten by every Christian, and the wine is to be drunk in true faith and in remembrance of the fact that Christ Jesus gave his body for us and shed his blood for us.[65]

As the document proceeds, additional formal material is presented. Dirk advances more specifically biblical argumentation in this section than in much of the above writing, where theological assertion combined with scriptural allusion cast the shape of his thought.

In the middle of *AML*, Dirk gives the four essentials of a right observance of the Holy Supper: First, a congregation must be assembled which confesses that "just as Christ Jesus gave and left to his apostles and all believers the eating of the bread and the drinking of the wine, so he freely gave them his body and blood."[66] Second, the Supper must be partaken only with "friends of God."[67] They are those who have been baptized in the name of the Trinity, want to lead a Christian life, meditate on him, and are one body with him and with the saints. Third, the breaking of bread is a congregational act. This means that it is not to be carried out by any gathering less than the whole community or without a minister. Every congregant is to partake of both the bread and the cup. Fourth, each is to prepare for communion by examining whether oneself has genuine love for Christ and for fellow human beings.[68]

There follows an attempt to vindicate the definition with which the treatise opens by means of scriptural and theological evidence. Dirk presents four points about the breaking of bread which must be believed: Jesus instituted the Supper, it is a communion of his body, it is a token of remembrance, and it is a new covenant in Jesus' blood.[69] The claim concerning the communion of Christ's body makes use of the most basic eucharistic concept but leaves both *communion* and *body* undefined. The author limits himself to biblical quotation without commentary. We cannot readily grasp Dirk's meaning of *communion* and *body* until they are set in the context of other terminology which he elsewhere uses to speak of the believer's participation in Christ. We will look at such a comparison of terms.

Exegesis

In all his eucharistic discourses, and especially in *AML*, Dirk is grappling with fidelity to the biblical text.[70] He sets out to interpret New Testament materialist language, such as body and flesh, and to develop a pneumatology which will provide the dynamic in the communion between Christ and the believer. There is an unmistakable affinity between this exegetical and theological struggle, and that found in other radical interpretations of the Lord's Supper. But its rationale is neither obviously Karlstadtian nor directly Zwinglian, as these positions have been alluded to in earlier chapters. Nor does it have a substantial affinity with the only other major treatment of the Lord's Supper in the first generation of northern Anabaptism, the writing of Hendrik Rol, *Die Slotel van dat Secreet des Nachtmals* (*Die Slotel:* The Key to the Secret of the Lord's Supper).

Dirk's treatment of the eucharistic narratives is different from that of these theologians. In their explicit theological claims about the Supper, Dirk Philips and Jean Calvin have more in common than any of the other scholars mentioned in this study. Direct dependence is difficult to establish, but in its negations, corrections, and affirmations, the theology of the Lord's Supper in Dirk parallels many of the threads in Calvin's eucharistic cloth.

In his exegesis, Dirk sets forth why the words of institution "must be taken in their spiritual significance." Three lines of thought are advanced to do so. At times inward reality (communion with Christ) and outward event (partaking of bread and wine) are distinguished from each other but not separated. When Dirk puts the case that way, spiritual significance is not a lessening or replacing of sacramental reality but an explanation of it. At other times the relationship between the two has a different character. Sometimes the outer sign is merely a picture of the inner reality. There are also occasions when the graphic language of eating is said to be synonymous with believing. In order to establish the equivalence of these terms, Dirk leaves behind the narratives of the synoptic Gospels and of Paul, with which he has documented the dominical institution of the sacrament. Now he turns to the eucharistic language of the Fourth Gospel. Jesus is that bread which came down from heaven. He is "the pure wine by which the believing soul is refreshed." When believers "eat the bread of the supper, they are admonished and reminded of this."[71]

There is a loose though unmistakable similarity between *Die Slotel* and *ENC* concerning Christ's real and spiritual presence in relation to the Supper. The following quotation from *Die Slotel* suggests this affinity: "So this assembly which gathers in the Lord's Supper is one community and will remain that if they eat this in the faith that they are making memory and that they are there proclaiming the death of Jesus Christ and that they show that they remain in his flesh and blood only by believing that it was given for their sins."[72]

Throughout *ENC* we clearly see the prominent role Dirk assigns to the Spirit in bringing about communion with Christ. But in Hendrik Rol's *Die Slotel*, there is a blunt dissociation between inner and outer eating. At work here is an extreme spiritualism with a distinct vocabulary. Most remarkable of its terms is the notion of eating God and being eaten by him. Direct linguistic parallels are few.

In both parts of his work on the Holy Supper, Rol is concerned with issues which appear in Dirk's writings. The worthiness of communicants is the most prominent instance. By contrast, the words of institution receive greater prominence in Rol than Dirk (or Hubmaier and Marpeck) affords them. Rol, contrary to Dirk, spends most of his exegesis and commentary on the synoptic Gospels. Little of a mystical theology directly derived from the Fourth Gospel comes to the fore. Rol's eucharistic doctrine has more in common with Zwingli's symbolism than with Dirk's realism. Hence, we find it easy to conclude that Rol's writings were not a direct and formative influence on Dirk.

However, as stated above, there is an obvious parallel between Dirk and Calvin on the theology of the Lord's Supper. The two theologians are agreed that faith is necessary to receive what is offered and that Christ's presence is not physical or localized. Following from that, the significance of the sacrament lies in the whole action, including the response of the people. Their definitions of faith differ, largely because of their differing anthropologies. Yet Dirk consistently emphasizes faith as a gift from God and the initiating role of the Spirit. This brings him closer to Calvin than to other Anabaptists outside the Dutch–North German realm.

In passages reminiscent of Calvin, Dirk speaks of Christ himself as the sign of grace and the one who makes the believer a partaker in Christ. The parallel continues when Calvin writes that the bread and wine are signs "which represent for us the invisible food that we receive from the flesh and blood of Christ."[73] Three of Calvin's achievements in the construction of a eucharistic doctrine may also be claimed for Dirk, with some qualification. First, Dirk's interpretation of the words of institution avoids the literalism of his opponents on the right and the reductionism of those on the left. Second, the ascension of Christ and the coming of the Holy Spirit, rather than the working of the rite itself, are the dynamic of the sacramental presence. Third, though Dirk lacked the clarity and depth of Calvin, he holds fast to the real presence of Christ in the breaking of bread while distinguishing that claim from any association with the repetition of his sacrifice.

This parallel of theology on the Lord's Supper is striking not only because of specific similarities but also because both theologians were representatives of the second generation of reformers. Part of their common theological method is the negating of certain negations and the correcting of certain corrections of the generation preceding them.

What fundamentally distinguishes Calvin's and Dirk's views of the Holy Supper is their teaching about the two natures of Christ. Part of the difference is that Calvin's thinking is more systematic and elaborate than Dirk's. Because of that, Calvin is able to affirm that Christ is localized in heaven and yet present in the breaking of bread. He accomplishes this by giving the two natures of Christ a separate existence and function. Dirk nearly conflates the divine nature of Christ with the Holy Spirit and thus weakens whatever presence he claims and separates it from the person of Christ.

Dirk's doctrine of the Lord's Supper is not directly derived from that found in other streams of the Radical Reformation. As to his similarity to Calvin, two possibilities come to mind. One is that Reformed eucharistic teachings including Calvin's were "in the air" in the Netherlands by the late 1540s, when Dirk wrote his first treatises. The other, as mentioned, is that both men were second-generation reformers with different challenges before them than their predecessors faced a generation earlier.

As we return to examine Dirk's writings, it becomes clearer that Dirk follows many routes to the same destination. He never seems to settle on a dominant line of argument. The locomotive propelling him forward is the experience of communion with Christ.[74] Cars are added to the train when they are able to carry the freight of his debate with an opponent;[75] they are dropped when they can no longer do so.[76]

Dirk's lavish use of the language of the Fourth Gospel suggests that only its concreteness is adequate to describe the intimacy of the believer's relationship with Christ.[77] There is a reality which nothing less than "eating Christ" is sufficient to describe.[78] At the same time, Dirk makes it plain that to eat is to believe. On one hand he uses graphic, sacramental language; on the other hand he curtly explains that language in literal, rational terms. This is problematic and begs for interpretation. If what is meant by eating Christ is simply hearing, accepting, and keeping the word of Christ, why does the author not remain with such safely unambiguous words?[79]

The explanation he offers sheds further light on Dirk's understanding of the Lord's Supper and gives a spiritual context to it. Our knowledge of Christ is more than rational assent to the fact of his revelation; it is a participation in his nature and being. The being which Christ has by nature is given to the Christian by grace when the believer is born again. Through receiving the flesh of Christ, one receives his nature. (Hence the emphasis on divinization.) Dirk chooses eucharistic language to describe the oneness which comes about between the believer and Christ through sanctification. Dirk speaks of an analogy between believers and Christ.[80] In short, there is an ontological union between God through Christ and believing human beings. The barrier separating them has been broken. Though it is a spiritual relationship, it takes hold of and transforms the fallen human world of finitude and mortality.

As Dirk moves between the institutional narratives of Paul and the Synoptics and the eucharistic discourse in John 6, he uses both of their vocabularies. Early in *AML*, where Dirk first introduces Pauline language, communion is an outward ordinance commanded by Christ, a communion of the body (*lijf*) of the Lord.[81] This is a historical term referring to the earthly Jesus. Dirk proceeds in the same passage to link that bread of the Last Supper with Jesus as the living bread.[82] But when he goes on to describe the believer partaking of Christ, it is his flesh (*vleesch*) which is eaten.[83] This distinction is lost as the exegetical work of *AML* proceeds because Dirk has established the claim that the true bread is Jesus himself, who is received by the soul.[84] In this train of thought, Dirk is on the verge of absolutely separating the spiritual feeding on Christ from the event of bread and wine. With this conflation of texts and vocabularies, the historical, external, communal setting of the institutional narratives is lost. What is left is the unmediated, invisible communion of the soul with the heavenly Christ.

Everything in Dirk's corpus pertaining to the relationship between Christ and the believer must be understood from the vantage point of Dirk's spiritualistic interpretation of John. In this world, Dirk moves and has his being.[85] Moreover, this hermeneutic is not confined to John 6. It appears again in his reading of Jesus' farewell discourses in John 14–16. From his interpretation of John 16 and other isolated New Testament christological references, Dirk derives claims concerning the nature of Jesus' presence since his ascension. He brings these passages into a direct relationship with the issue at hand: a correct understanding of the Lord's Supper.[86] Though the Lord is "personally and eternally" in heaven, he is with the church in his Spirit. It is evident to any observer that Christ is "not bodily in the bread and the cup." Yet he is "in it" (*sic*) by means of his power or authority. His Spirit of comfort is present.

Lest any affirmation of Christ's presence in relation to the Supper be misunderstood, Dirk is swift to describe the nature of the link between the dominical presence and the event of the Lord's Supper. The Supper is neither the criterion nor the mode of his presence. Instead, the links between Christ's presence and the breaking of bread are faith and love; Christ makes himself known to obedient believers. Dirk proceeds to explain how the Lord is present to such faith: "This spiritual essence (*wesen*) of Christ we understand to be the Holy Ghost, by which he lives and labors in all his members."[87] The Fourth Gospel does not explicitly conflate the Son and the Spirit, but Dirk deduces it in applying the text to his problem. It is more accurate to speak of Dirk's use of Johannine Christology as absorbing the text rather than exegeting it. Dirk does not so much build up a point-by-point analysis as he assumes an affinity between his world and that of the Gospel writer. This is because Dirk perceives John to be addressing the kind of issues Dirk himself is facing.

In assessment, we see that Dirk was attracted to the spiritual, that is, unmediated, communion between Christ and the believer as described in John 6. Nothing less than the language of eating the body and drinking the blood of Christ was adequate to describe that encounter. In the Christology of the farewell discourses, Dirk found the interpretive framework he needed for the extravagant eucharistic claims made in John 6. By equating the presence of Christ in the church with the Holy Spirit, the possibility of a corporeal presence was ruled out. This freed him to use the realist language of the New Testament without following the conclusions drawn about it in Catholic tradition.

In addition to providing Dirk with an interpretation of eucharistic language, the relationship between Son and Spirit, which he drew from John, provided Dirk with a stronger characterization of Christ's two natures. In his Christology of Jesus' unfallen humanity, the incarnation is the human moment in an essentially divine drama. He always speaks of the agent of salvation in the church as the Son in his eternal divinity. But John provides Dirk with a human nature for Christ which endorses rather than undermines Dirk's eucharistic doctrine. The argument has the following contours. If Christ is bodily in heaven, that is, if his humanness is located in a realm remote from the earth, then it cannot have any relationship with the Lord's Supper.[88]

Dirk goes on to explain that Jesus' bodily absence from the world is the precondition for his spiritual presence. Dirk concludes that in his discourse on the Lord's Supper, Christ speaks of this spiritual essence, his postascension presence as the Spirit. The intention of this explanation is to counter the assertion by some that Christ "is bodily in the bread and wine of the Supper, and is thus eaten and received by the wicked as well as the righteous."[89]

Briefly put, Dirk's contention was that spirit could be received only by spirit. That assertion stood like an impregnable wall of defense around everything else Dirk claimed to be true about the Lord's Supper. Like the guard at a medieval fortress, that assertion admitted no aliens and brooked no dissent from those within.

Inner Communion and Outer Breaking of Bread

In the introduction to this chapter, we noted that Sacramentarianism had developed a eucharistic doctrine which resulted in an undefined juxtaposition of the breaking of bread and the eating of Christ. From its origins Sacramentarianism had retained a spiritual union of Christ and the believer, but during the Reformation it rejected the medieval theology of sacraments which was the proper context for such a spiritual union. Sacramentarianism was unwilling and unable to go beyond a negation of the *ex opere operato* relationship of spirit and matter to a positive claim about that relationship. Any positive claim was feared to endanger the absolute primacy of spirit over matter. This was also Dirk's picture of reality, affirmed surpassingly in his Christology. It left him with a command of Christ to observe an external Supper, pitted against a belief that created substance could not enter the realm of spirit.

Dirk came to terms with this dilemma by his interpretation of the institutional narrative and by his understanding of the role of faith. He writes that whoever trusts that Christ was crucified for us receives him "with the mouth of the soul and not literally, with the natural mouth, for spiritual food (that is, the flesh and the blood of Christ) must be spiritually received."[90] In an unusual reference to the Synoptic words of institution, Dirk turns to Karlstadt's interpretation of the narrative: "This is my body" refers to the body of Christ sitting at the table while his disciples ate bread and drank wine. By means of Karlstadt's exegesis, Dirk concludes that the elements themselves have no connection with the body and blood of Christ. The bread and wine became for the disciples an assurance of salvation "which Christ wrought for us with his body and blood."[91]

Clearly the raging debate of the 1520s concerning the words of institution has abated. Dirk states his case and thinks thereby to have solved the hermeneutical problem to everyone's satisfaction. He then proceeds to his more fundamental concern. It is the necessity of faith to receive the body and blood of Christ which is signified in the Supper of bread and wine.

> Judas also ate of the bread and drank of the wine, yet he did not receive the flesh and blood of Christ; for all that God gives us in the use of the sacraments, we receive by faith, and God works in his chosen ones only through his Spirit that which the sacraments outwardly signify.[92]

This is one of the clearest statements in Dirk's corpus concerning the relationship between inner and outer eating. "Outward signs," as Dirk claimed in *Doope,* have the limited function of pointing away from themselves to the only true sign of grace, the Lord Jesus Christ.[93] Where there is faith, not in the outward sign but in the true sign, there Christ's flesh and blood are given. This implied if not defined concomitancy between the sign and the body, happens only when faith is present. Grace is the only necessary condition for receiving Christ; that is established for Dirk in the atonement. But faith is the only sufficient means for communion with him. The work of the Holy Spirit[94] brings about the believers' union with Christ, but it comes to pass only in the presence of faith.

The consequence of the absolute role of faith in the encounter with Christ is expressed in the following contrast. Dirk's eucharistic doctrine does not hold that where the bread is outwardly taken in faith, the body of Christ is inwardly given. Dirk's cautious concomitancy leaves us with a claim that where there is faith in Christ, there he is eaten, and there bread signifies outwardly what has come to pass inwardly. The function of the sacrament is subordinate and subsequent to the reality to which it points. This formulation makes the sequence clear. But the role Dirk here assigns to the Supper, though compatible with his other description of the Eucharist, is not of a piece with it. There its sign function has an objective character which stands prior to faith.[95]

Of the sacrament itself, the meal of bread and wine, Dirk says surprisingly little.[96] The concern of this passage and of most of Dirk's eucharistic references is with the internal disposition of the believer. Dirk is clearly more interested in the dynamic of the event than in the elements. Where faith is present, bread and wine signify what God gives through his Spirit to the soul.[97] Where "the Lord's bread" is eaten "without spirit, without faith, without love for Christ and the brethren, without discerning the body of Christ," those who do so are guilty of his body and blood.[98] Whether the Supper signifies communion or condemnation is determined entirely on subjective grounds, by the disposition of the participant.

In his eucharistic writings, Dirk never resolves his ambiguity and evasiveness concerning the relationship between the outward and the inward Supper. We sense a conflict in Dirk's mind between the poles of his theology—at once spiritualistic and ecclesiastical—and his search for a faithful alternative to what he believed were the errors of sacramentalism (early in his career as an Anabaptist) and of spiritualism (later). Here are two illustrations of the persistence of this ambiguity:

Dirk's chief exposition of John 6 is woven into the fabric of *AML,* his extended discourse on the Lord's Supper, showing that he intends to show some relationship between the inward and outward meal. This is underscored by Dirk's conflation of eucharistic vocabulary from John and Paul, as examined above.[99] On the other hand, outside of the sacramental treatises, many of Dirk's eucharistic citations from John exist in splendid isolation from any reference to a visible event.[100]

Ambiguity and evasiveness extend to the application of the term *communion* itself. Early in *AML* this concept is unmistakably related to the event of the Last Supper.[101] Yet later in the same text, the Lord's Supper is described three times in the space of two pages as the confirmation of the communion which believers are given with Christ at the time of their conversion.

> This communion and incorporation with Christ is also confirmed and renewed through the Lord's Supper in that Christians in the true unity of the Spirit and of faith break the bread and drink the wine which signifies to them, and by which they are reminded of, the fellowship of Christ and the participation of all his merits."[102]

This leaves Dirk with the following conclusion. Though the communion of the believers exists separately from and prior to any external signification, the Lord's Supper is a moment within time and space when visible evidence is given of this communion and the believer is assured of the grace of God.

The nature of communion is spelled out further in relation to faith. In the section of *AML* where Judas' unbelieving participation in the Supper is analyzed, Dirk insists that while the unbelieving, "like Judas, may eat the bread, they do not thereby become partakers of the blood of Jesus Christ."[103] And further, "Christ is not eaten bodily by the wicked."[104] The reason unbelievers cannot have Christ is that they "eat the Lord's bread without spirit, without faith, without love for Christ and the brethren, without discerning the body of Christ."[105] The communion which exists is first of all a bond between Christ and each believer. It is a gift of grace which comes when the penitent is reborn.

Communion and the Church

In addition to the individual communion of each Christian with Christ, there is also a communion among believers. This dimension is conveyed first of all by Dirk's constant use of plural forms: we, they. It also comes out clearly in the conditions Dirk stipulates for a valid communion.[106] This fellowship of believers is implied in his view of the church. But such fellowship is not a point of dispute in the eucharistic controversies which shape Dirk's doctrine of the Holy Supper, save perhaps, in his concluding argument with Franck.[107] The debate through most of Dirk's ministry focuses on the nature of faith and communion, subjects defined in individual terms and in immediate relationship with God. Therefore, the individual remains Dirk's preoccupation throughout his eucharistic discourses. He assumes the corporate nature of the Lord's Supper in his writings on the church and the ban, but he does not add anything of substance to the present discussion.[108]

The one ecclesiological dimension of the Eucharist with which Dirk directly concerns himself is the authority of the presider. That authority is not sacramental in the Catholic sense but functional. It requires proper proclamation of the sacrifice of Christ and seeing to it that sinners, heretics, and unbelievers do not come to the table. Even though anticlericalism was part of the Radical Reformation, Dirk includes the role of the minister as a defining part of a true Lord's Supper; this feature draws attention to itself.[109] The point of the original anticlerical critique, that the relationship between the believer and Christ is unmediated, remains one of his sacramental principles and is assured in his definition of communion. But it is qualified by the need for authority and order in an era of persecution, mutual banning of communities, and challenges from other interpreters of Christian faith. Another of the reasons for the indispensable role of the minister in the Lord's Supper, no doubt, is that Dirk is a second-generation figure in the Reformation, consolidating the breakthroughs of the original reformers. He undertakes a correction of the anticlerical correction.

A second question concerning historical context demands attention. Dirk repeatedly denies, in the introductory section of *AML,* that his eucharistic language has to do with Christ's bodily presence.[110] Against whom is this defense directed? It is doubtful that this insistence has the purpose of refuting Catholic arguments for transubstantiation. By the 1550s the debates of Anabaptists over the Lord's Supper were with Reformed and spiritualistic contemporaries. This is illustrated by Dirk's epistle against Sebastian Franck and Menno Simon's writings against John á Lasco and Gellius Faber.[111] The likely significance of Dirk's negation of a corporeal presence is that his strong Johannine sacramental realism made him suspect to those who held strictly symbolical views of the Supper. Further, as noted earlier, the peculiar evolution of Dutch Sacramentarianism resulted in the recasting of realistic sacramental language in the North in a way that never happened in the South German realm. Some Reformed, Anabaptist, and spiritualist theologians would have challenged Dirk's combination of realist language and the observance of a Supper of bread and wine.

The Two Natures of Christ and the Lord's Supper

We have seen that the human and divine natures of Christ play distinctive roles in Dirk's theology of the Lord's Supper. In a different but equally distinctive way, this is also true for the devotional side of the Supper. Of two alternate eucharistic pieties, one is derived from the divinity of Christ and one from his humanity. Dirk is chiefly interested in the divinity of Christ. This emphasis represents the spirit of the Fourth Gospel, where the ascent to the cross is the moment of glorification. Jesus as the bread of life is the mysterious presence in the believer. All one can say of him is that he comes from heaven. Dirk's favorite christological description from the Pauline writings is "the man of heaven" in the resurrection treatise in 1 Corinthians 15.[112]

To the author of John's Gospel—and to those at home in it—nothing less than the graphic language of eating Christ is adequate to point to the mysterious reality of knowing him. Dirk's extravagant use of Johannine language is possible for him because the Christ it describes is a divine being who draws to himself those to whom he gives divine life, through the new birth in the Spirit.

Dirk's position needs to be distinguished from those with which it shares certain linguistic characteristics. Its Johannine spirituality is framed differently from either the Catholic use of John in its assertion of a corporeal presence or the John-inspired complete inwardness of spiritualism. In the former the language of eating Christ is to be taken literally; in the latter the language is detached from any visible signs.

Thus far we have examined the dimension of Dirk's teaching on the Supper of the Lord which emanates from the Fourth Gospel. It exults in the glorified Christ and union with him. In stark contrast to that is a eucharistic piety which meditates on the awesome suffering of Jesus. As Dirk pictures it, the humanity of Christ is an unfallen substance unique to Jesus, subject neither to sin nor finitude. At the same time, this spotless Jesus chose to suffer; his anguish was real. Though the atonement has to do with Christ's victory,[113] Dirk advocates a response of fear and awe because of God's wrath and Jesus' suffering[114] and sorrow by which we suffer with him.[115]

This devotional identification with the nonresistant Jesus leads to an ethical solidarity with him typical of Anabaptism and of the *imitatio Christi* of late medieval mysticism. But only in the ordinances concerning neighbor love and willingness to suffer is emphasis placed specifically on carrying out the teaching of Jesus.[116] In relation to the Eucharist, this ethical response remains a tangent; it is not a central part of the Lord's Supper. In Dirk's writings, most of the injunctions to follow the suffering Jesus are found in treatises unrelated to the Lord's Supper.

The devotional disposition Dirk enjoins on the faithful stresses Christ's misery and mortality rather than his triumph and his uncreated eternity. It is almost as though there are two Suppers: the theologically argued one of existential encounter with Christ the victor, and the devotionally and ethically founded one in memory of Jesus the victim. Although Dirk does not make this association, it is helpful, in comparing both sides of his Eucharist, to see that the first one derives from the table fellowship with the resurrected Lord, and the second one comes from the Last Supper.

From two angles we can illuminate this strange juxtaposition of two motifs, both biblical, which have no rational bond with one another. One is the situation of persecution and suffering in which Dirk's people were placed. Jesus the victim was the one who mirrored the reality they knew. The other vantage point is the medieval popular piety which persisted, with its dread of unworthy communion, into the time of the Reformation. Its tenacity is shown by the fact that none of the reformers was able to institute frequent communion as the ongoing norm. Christ was too awesome for his followers to draw near. This focus on Christ's awesome suffering was heightened in the Reformation when it gave the memorial aspect of the Supper a preeminence it had never held before. Attention to Jesus' suffering encouraged a subjective attitude of awe to compensate for the lost awesome objective reality in which bread became the broken body.[117]

Through the devotional dimension of Dirk's eucharistic doctrine, the humanity of Christ received a centrality which it was never accorded theologically. Together these beliefs shaped his doctrine of the Holy Communion. Though they are placed beside each other in Dirk's writings, the theological focus on the divinity of Christ and his spiritual essence is entirely different from the devotion to a suffering Savior. These two loci flow through Dirk's writings like parallel lines which never intersect.

Conclusions

We have observed a tension among the elements of Dirk's theology of the Lord's Supper. At its core is a Sacramentarian belief in the unmediated union of the believer with Christ. This oneness is experienced in a paradigmatic way at communion. Other components of his doctrine come into existence as a need for them arises. This is true, for example, of the *sine qua non* character of faith as a defense against the *ex opere operato* view of sacramental reality. On the other hand, the command of Christ and the historical nature of human existence are invoked as a protection against discarding all material signs of divine presence. Despite the fact that the believer has a relationship with the glorified Christ and shares his divinity in some sense, Dirk's eucharistic piety centers on the suffering of the human Jesus.

Traditional Dutch scholarship has not given equal attention to the two tendencies—antispiritualistic as well as spiritualistic—at work in the eucharistic doctrines of northern Anabaptists, particularly of Dirk Philips. Dutch scholarship has tended to see the Dutch–North German Anabaptists as spiritualists who maintained a high but not biblicistic view of the authority of Scripture. They are seen as bearing into the modern world the Sacramentarian legacy of inwardness and subjectivity.[118]

More recent scholarship, largely American, has modified this view. It has put forth the position that a Sacramentarian or even Zwinglian symbolism is inadequate to describe the sacraments of northern Anabaptism. William Keeney goes so far as to assert that in the Lord's Supper there is a "real presence" of Christ, that is, an existential communion with him. Alvin Beachy locates the Lord's Supper within the ontological reality into which the believer enters with spiritual rebirth. By means of it, the new creature, the divinized human being, participates anew in the being of God through Christ.[119]

The Lord's Supper, then, is a sign of the believer being drawn beyond the limits of the fallen world into the realm of the new creation. It is a sign which points toward heaven, toward the oneness of the believer with Christ. Neither of these recent scholarly investigations of Dirk's thought on the subject takes into account the ambiguity of Dirk's vocabulary, the tensions among the various claims which compose his theology of the Supper, or the tenuous link in his eucharistic doctrine between the inward feeding on Christ and the outward observance. However, they improve on earlier scholarship by doing greater justice to the two tendencies, antispiritualist as well as spiritualist, of Dirk's writing on the Supper.

Dirk's Christology provides him with two interpretive keys to his view of the Lord's Supper. The first key is his premise that fallen human nature is incapable of embodying grace. Therefore, Christ had to bring his flesh from heaven. This attempt to safeguard Christ's capacity to save humanity is of ancient origin and was revived in the Reformation.[120] For Dirk and his likeminded contemporaries, Christ's humanity is an otherworldly reality with only an outer similitude to ours. He accepted the limitations of pain and death by choice, not by nature. Though Dirk teaches that by becoming human, Christ could offer himself as a sacrifice,[121] Christ in his humanity is not the medium of salvation. Once he has given himself as a sacrifice, the positive emphasis on his unique humanity recedes and the limitations of his human nature emerge. This change of accent is done in two ways, both of them taken from the Fourth Gospel. First, Dirk holds that Christ as man cannot be the universal agent of salvation; Christ needs to ascend so that he as Spirit, without the boundary of human form, can save.[122] Second, Dirk says that Christ is located in one place and limited to it—a negative qualification.

The second interpretive key to Dirk's view of the Lord's Supper is this equation of Christ in his divinity with the Spirit. Christ offers himself in communion with believers. To stress the reality of this union, Dirk uses graphic and physical language: Christ is the bread of heaven; his flesh and blood are eaten and drunk by believers. Such vivid terminology describes the intensity and totality of the encounter. It can be applied with aesthetic abandon because it refers to a divine and spiritual reality.[123]

Thus we observe that the divine Christ shaped Dirk's perception, not only of the Lord's Supper, but also of the church and the Christian. With the church and the Christian, however, the divine Christ's role is not conflated with that of the Spirit. In Dirk's writing it is difficult to ascertain whether that conflation (of Spirit and divine Christ) in the Lord's Supper flowed naturally from his spiritualistic reading of John, without intending any doctrinal revision, or whether it was a bold and deliberate doctrinal reformulation designed to secure an adequate basis for Dirk's eucharistic bias. The former is suggested by the fact that elsewhere in his theology, Dirk retained separate roles for the Son and the Spirit. But Dirk's teaching concerning the unfallen humanity of Christ indicated that he was willing to embrace radical theological revisionism in order to safeguard the spiritual nature of the Gospel, as he understood it. His only orthodoxy was this spiritual reality, embodied in the communion of believers with Christ and paradigmatically signified in the Lord's Supper. The goal of his theology was to validate that by whatever means were necessary.

At this decisive point Dirk transcended the spiritualism established by his Christology and crossed the ontological barrier between spirit and matter. Through the work of the Spirit, the church as a visible community was also a divine reality; through the Spirit's work, Christians were individually divinized in their earthly existence of body and soul. In making this claim, Dirk broke the spiritualistic equation between spirit and inwardness. He allowed sanctified, obedient human nature a place in the realm of spirit.

The outcome of Dirk's encounter with Franck's thoroughgoing spiritualism is that he extended the possibility, however cautiously, of matter revealing spirit through sacraments. But to revise his Christology according to that principle would have dislodged his only safeguard against sacramentalism. Such an unfinished revision of his thought left him with a fundamental theological inconsistency which was inescapable, given his goal of transcending sacramentalism and spiritualism. This inconsistency was that while fallen creaturely realities like people and even sacraments could be bearers of revelation and grace, Jesus could not have saved us if he had taken on our fallen flesh. In the end, against sacramentalism, Dirk retained his Christology; and against spiritualism, he developed his pneumatology and its power to divinize human existence.

Dirk's eucharistic doctrine took its picture of reality from its belief about the person of Christ. But it used this picture selectively, allowing the factors introduced above to channel and control the implications of his Christology. The result is a view of the Supper with the two natures of Christ so clearly separate that no corporeal implications are possible in the claim that Christ's body and blood are given to the believer. This follows not only from the Sacramentarian spirituality of the Dutch world but equally from the soteriological claim that the believer already shares in the divine nature of Christ. Such participation in Christ is what Dirk meant by communion. This communion is related to the event of the breaking of bread in that the latter was instituted by Christ as a sign to faith of his promised presence.[124]

Dirk's struggled to accept and honor the incarnation of Christ but to remove it absolutely from the world of the Fall. This effort was not unique to him or to the spiritual world he inhabited. Throughout the centuries, simple and learned Christians alike have been troubled by the contrast between the glory which the Son had with the Father before creation, and the horror of his crucifixion. Roman Catholic theology resorted to the most dramatic solution of all to this perplexity: the immaculate conception of Mary. Just as understandable, though no more remarkable than the juxtapositions in Dirk's theology, Catholic theology has affirmed both the sinless conception of Jesus and his physical presence in the bread and wine of the Eucharist.

We have identified the intellectual and spiritual sources of Dirk's teaching concerning the Lord's Supper. Exactly how these beliefs were mediated to him is much more difficult to say. There is only fragmentary evidence for direct influence from sources most likely to have shaped him, although we have noted some probable streams of influence. It is noteworthy that Hoffmann's influence carried over into Dirk's Christology but not significantly into his sacramentology. Dirk saw that the Melchiorite Christology by itself was not able to provide a durable ecclesiology or sacramentology. Fellow Sacramentarians like Karlstadt, Zwingli, and Rol furnish Dirk with his overall theological disposition but are not primary sources for his eucharistic doctrine. Within the limits of this study, all we can say of Calvin is that his teaching on the Lord's Supper is paralleled at crucial points in Dirk.

From his writings it is clear that Dirk contended vigorously with the christological and eucharistic thinking of his day. He found none of the existing alternatives acceptable as they stood. This is true not only of the extreme positions of transubstantiation and spiritualism but also for the mediating theologies of Hoffmann, Karlstadt, and Zwingli. It is also evident, on both historical and theological grounds, that Dirk did not take over the understandings of the Lord's Supper of either Swiss or South German Anabaptism. This may be seen by comparing him with their foremost representatives as regards eucharistic theology: Hubmaier and Marpeck. Though his theology of the Lord's Supper grew up within the spiritual world he knew, Dirk Philips undertook an original shaping of the theological influences which surrounded him.

Dirk's eucharistic vocabulary discarded terminology associated with transubstantiation and the mass. Yet it retained the concept of sacrament and the vivid, realistic Johannine language of feeding on Christ. This was true in large measure because northern Anabaptism had inherited from Sacramentarianism a theological and spiritual framework within which the classical formulations had already been recast. Dirk was therefore able to accept a spiritual but real presence of Christ in a way that was psychologically, if not theologically, impossible for radical reformers in the southern sphere of the Reformation. For all of the Swiss Anabaptists, any claim to real participation in Christ related to the breaking of bread inevitably meant corporeal presence.

While Dirk was able to affirm a communion with Christ, he was unable successfully to establish either a causal or temporal relationship between it and the breaking of bread. On the basis of his acceptance of the traditional definition of *sacrament*, that it consists of inner and outer parts, Dirk's eucharistic doctrine must be judged as incomplete: it never substituted an explanation of the relationship between inner and outer for the one it rejected. This resulted in a further incompleteness of his eucharistic thought. He achieved no synthesis of the individual communion with Christ and the collective act of breaking bread. As a result these two aspects of the Lord's Supper lack an essential unity. If in his late writings, there had been continued ecclesiological influence on his view of sacraments, he would have been able to correct this disjointedness.

In summarizing the evidence presented thus far, we see that Dirk's eucharistic teaching has two defining characteristics. One of them is its Johannine sacramental realism. This tower of his thought is grounded in the sacramentarian doctrine of the mystical union of the believer with Christ. It is buttressed by an unfallen-humanity Christology which has two primary functions. One of them is that it removes the possibility of a corporeal presence. The other is that it is the model for the divinization of a person through spiritual rebirth.

The second high tower of Dirk's belief about the Lord's Supper is of quite another sort. It has two turrets. They are the double set of corrective elements he has put in place to protect what he believes from the rival options of Catholic transubstantiation, Protestant correct belief without corresponding ethical behavior, and spiritualist anarchism. His great achievement is that he establishes the institution of the Lord's Supper such that it is protected from alternative interpretations which violate Anabaptist claims concerning faith, human nature, and the church.

5

Conclusion

Introduction

Before outlining the purposes of this conclusion, I will make three general observations which emerge from the study as a whole. First, those who made the Reformation and those who now study that era necessarily view the debated matters from different perspectives. Reading about the passionate defense of rival Christologies and eucharistic doctrines is a tame exercise compared to staking one's life on those doctrines. I have tried to think the thoughts and join in the emotions of Hubmaier, Marpeck, and Dirk as well as to critically distance myself from them. This is a task which always remains unfinished. When I attempt to do the same with those whom they opposed, such an effort yields an even more fragmentary success, if for no other reason than the vastness of the topic.

This leads to a second preliminary observation, concerning the relative immediacy of language. The protagonists of this study, as members of their generation, stood at the front line of a millennium of history of which they were the heirs. For us, who seek to return to the past, that generation's front line is our rear column. With great effort we return to an encounter with them, yet our point of view is so different that we can hardly bridge the gap. We can think toward them with our minds but we can never fully grasp the realities which set the course of their world.

Thus, when Hubmaier reacts against the medieval fascination with external evidences of the divine by completely separating sacraments from grace, the reader is able to take hold of the barren concept but is not able to fill it with the meaning it had for Hubmaier. What unspoken assumptions accompanied this move? Did he need to break the theological and psychological hold of Rome over his world, however unconsidered the consequences of his decision were? Or, on the contrary, did he still have the confidence of the medieval Christian that

Christ was present in the Eucharist as the presupposition of whatever disagreements followed?

The same question, of the different content in the same forms from generation to generation, may be raised as a caution in interpreting Marpeck or Dirk. Was Marpeck's seemingly grand contradiction at the close of the VWG really that? And was there an unarticulated but intuitively known continuity between the seeming discontinuities of Dirk's claims about the Lord's Supper? This fragility of comprehension between two ages does not excuse superficial probing or make another era completely inaccessible. Yet it does mean that empathy, thoroughness, and humility are indispensable virtues for the scholar.

The third general observation has to do with the nature of the writings under scrutiny as understood by their authors. None of them claimed to be doing systematic theology: they did not comprehensively set out all the major claims at issue in relation to each other. Neither Hubmaier nor Marpeck nor Dirk can be said, for example, to have a general doctrine of God or of creation. None of them claimed to have arrived at such doctrinal completeness. At the same time, all of them tried to spell out enough of their belief concerning disputed matters to provide an alternative to positions from which they had dissented. All three believed they were doing this in their theology of the Lord's Supper. They wrote enough to defend the beliefs and guide the practice of their communities. Yet, as we have seen, their convictions evolved as they wrote and left them with inconsistencies.

We wonder if any of these three authors thought he had arrived at a comprehensive theology of the Lord's Supper. By *comprehensive* I mean sufficient to be perceived by each writer as a self-sustaining alternative to the views from which it dissented. Thus, we recognize that Hubmaier's eucharistic doctrine is comprehensive even though a lingering ambiguity remains concerning the extent to which Hubmaier wanted to take his reorientation of the concept *sacrament*. That ambiguity did not functionally hinder the purposes for which he had written. Two classifications of the theological writings of the Radical Reformation will be applied to each of our authors. They are "existential theology" (Robert Friedmann's term) and *Kontroverstheologie* (as termed in current research on the subject).

In this chapter we have a threefold purpose. The first goal is to present a distillation of each of the three eucharistic doctrines under scrutiny in relation to their christological frame of reference, their insights, novelties, and inconsistencies. Because the setting, background, and mind-set of each of the theologians is so different, they will be dealt with separately after their common characteristics have been summarized.

The second goal is to identify their influence on present-day Mennonite Christology and thought and practice of the Lord's Supper. In order to do this, we will examine confessional documents, modern theological statements, and the worship life of the Mennonite church.

The third goal is to assess the potential contribution of Hubmaier, Marpeck, and Dirk to a fuller theology and practice of the Lord's Supper among Mennonites and in the Christian church at large.

Commonalities Among These Three Anabaptist Theologies of the Lord's Supper

Hubmaier, Marpeck, and Dirk share many traits with the general Christian tradition, the Anabaptist movement, and each other. However, our interest here is only in certain characteristics common to the three theologians which were decisive for their theology of the Lord's Supper.

First, their most general commonality is their collective absorption of the tendency toward spiritualism in much late medieval and Reformation religion. They took this belief—that the relationship between God and humanity is unmediated and that grace cannot be transmitted by material means—and shaped and qualified it in a distinctive way through their ecclesiology. For them, the Christian life inseparably consisted of a relationship with God and with the church. Thus the character of the believer's life could not be one of complete inwardness.

Baptism and the Lord's Supper were paradigms for them of the material nature of Christian life in the world. Baptism was based on a covenant not only with Christ but also with the church. The Lord's Supper was based not only on the memory of Christ's self-sacrifice but also on the communicants' pledge to imitate Christ in living with sister, brother, neighbor, and enemy. Hubmaier, Marpeck, and Dirk differed in the way in which they explained and justified both the spiritual (toward God) and material (toward people) dimensions of the Christian life. However, for all three, the Christian life meant a visible church life in which the ceremonies were indispensable.

The second common feature is that Hubmaier, Marpeck, and Dirk discerned the connection between the spiritual and material dimensions of Christian reality and Christology. Though our subjects were all trinitarian in their dogma and in their working assumptions, they had different understandings of what trinitarianism meant for

Christology and for eucharistic doctrine. They tended to conflate Christ in his divinity with the being of the Spirit. Here was the first step in a theological reconstruction of Christ's relationship to the world. In his postascension humanity, Christ retained the limits he had taken on himself in the incarnation. This meant that God's ongoing relationship with the world was as Spirit. But the limits of his human nature retained ongoing positive significance.

As an example and inspiration in suffering, all three theologians were drawn to the human Jesus, who shared our limitations. Only if Christ remained who he had been on earth, was he an adequate moral model for the Christian. At the same time, the limitations of his human nature were decisive for his presence in the breaking of bread. Since he could not be present spatially at more than one place at a time, it was impossible for his physical body to be in the bread. Moreover, such a presence was unnecessary because the Spirit was in and among believers in such fullness that nothing could be added to the relationship the Spirit mediated with Christ, who was one with the Father. In each theologian, this sequence of thoughts connected the Lord's Supper with their Christology in a mutually influential way.

A third commonality of Hubmaier, Marpeck, and Dirk bears directly on their picture of spiritual reality and of Christ: they were indebted to the Gospel of John. Though it was part of their overall frame of reference, the Fourth Gospel was given preeminence in their christological and eucharistic thought. All three used John exegetically and theologically to establish the relationship between Son and Spirit and to interpret the institutional narratives of Paul and the Synoptics.

The outcome of this work, as it bears on the Supper, is severalfold. They used John's explanation of the ascension to maintain the separate natures of Christ. This, in turn, was indebted to the insistence on the part of Reformed Christology that *finitum non est capax infiniti* (the finite is incapable of comprehending the infinite).[1] By means of this view, Christ's human nature remained localized in heaven and was not part of Christ's divine nature as the agency of his presence in the world. By means of these assumptions, all three theologians invalidated a corporeal presence in the Eucharist (John 6). They characterized the Supper as ethical, as part of its essence (John 13); this was taken from John and used to interpret the institutional narratives. For none of our authors were the words of institution the foundation of their eucharistic doctrine. Those declarations became a summary of and a warrant for christological claims which stood behind them. Similarly, a theology of the word and its technical relationship to the dynamic of the Supper remained a marginal concern, especially for Marpeck and Dirk.

The fourth trait our subjects share in common is their formal and substantive holding together of faith and Spirit. Anabaptism, with its emphasis on sanctification, is often said to depict faith as a humanly willed and generated act of response to God. This has led to a depiction of the Lord's Supper as a rational act of remembrance and a humanly willed remaking of covenant. Neither of these assumptions is at work in the writings of Hubmaier, Marpeck, and Dirk, although there is a sequential movement from faith to memory-making in Hubmaier, to which we will return (below). All of them understood faith primarily as a gift of the Spirit: whatever happens in the believer's heart or in the midst of the community comes from God's initiative. Each of them—in his own way—placed various limitations on the nature and work of the ascended Christ. Therefore, their eucharistic thought is more accurately described as pneumatological than christological.

The Influence of These Theologies of the Lord's Supper on Mennonite Thought and Practice

Introduction

Between the mid-sixteenth and mid-twentieth centuries, Mennonites engaged in little formal theologizing. Persecution removed leaders, inhibited reflection, and scattered communities before they could consolidate their existence, physically or intellectually. The instability of this life made it difficult to pass on tradition intact. Hubmaier's communities in Waldshut and Nicolsburg were obliterated; publication of his works ceased after the time of his ministry. References to his thought occur in letters and treatises only during the next generation. Marpeck's communities endured to the end of the sixteenth century. His treatises were copied by hand during that time but vanished from sight without a trace until the twentieth century. Dirk's writings were overshadowed in popularity by those of Menno but were occasionally published and translated through the centuries.

Therefore, after the first generation of Anabaptist leaders, the major extant records of the next two centuries of Mennonitism are confessions of faith and catechisms. Popular literature on the Lord's Supper became more common in the eighteenth and nineteenth centuries. But aside from the Netherlands and North Germany, not until the twentieth century was more reflective theological writing again possible. This attempt to identify the influence of the eucharistic doctrines of Hubmaier, Marpeck, and Dirk will confine itself to the few confessions of faith, catechisms, and worship formularies which attained normative status. For documentation of twentieth-century belief about the Lord's Supper among Mennonites, we will refer to encyclopedias and books of theology.

The Early Documents

In the materials from the seventeenth through nineteenth centuries, three characteristics stand out. First, all the documents are devotional or liturgical in nature, and so are their comments on the Lord's Supper. Second, they are surprisingly free in their use of realist language even though it is not explained. Third, few of them use language and concepts which have an obvious affinity with the writings of Hubmaier, Marpeck, or Dirk. We proceed now to document such affinities as there are.

In a communion sermon, Hans de Ries, writing a generation after Dirk, uses the sign character of the Supper as well as its dominical ordination in a manner reminiscent of his precursor.[2] He refers to the Supper as an outward obedience which God requires as much as the inward response, and this reference has the same quality as Dirk's writing on the subject. But in the next line, de Ries goes on to claim reception of the forgiveness of sins in the event of the Supper.[3] The communion prayer speaks about eating the bread and wine unto salvation and at the same time asking for the heavenly bread.[4] Such terminology goes beyond anything in Dirk's corpus; the presence of Christ is closely tied to the act of breaking bread.

Leenaerdt Clock's communion prayer, from the same time and place as that of de Ries, echoes Dirk in some of its petitions. He prays that through the gift of the Spirit, believers may be fed with the body and blood of Christ, and that they may have assurance of this feeding through the breaking of bread.[5] No liturgical documents which achieved normative status even in one country exist between the mid-seventeenth century and the early nineteenth century. Therefore, we turn our attention to confessions of faith.

The Dordrecht Confession of 1632 has affinities with Hubmaier's Lord's Supper in its treatment of the meal as a memorial of his suffering and love and an exhortation to love and forgive each other and our neighbors.[6] The understated language of the article as a whole is of the same spirit as Hubmaier's. The present state of historical research makes it impossible to assert a direct dependence of this confession on Hubmaier.

The High German Confession of 1660 uses Dirkian realistic language in a similar spiritualistic sense. Christ is described as the heavenly essence, the life-giving bread of the soul in a spiritual communion.[7]

The Ris Confession of 1766 is pietistic in tone. It continues the communal emphasis in Marpeck and Hubmaier but, turning toward the spirit of Dirk, dwells on communion of the soul with Christ and calls the meal a confirmation and seal of the gospel.[8]

The Shorter Catechism of 1690 also evidences an affinity for Dirk's position in its emphasis on the memorial. Yet its language is less guarded than Dirk's when it claims "through faith, the communion of the body and blood of Christ," and the assurance of the benefits of his death.[9]

The Elbing Catechism of 1778 includes the memorial aspect but goes on to point to the Supper as a sign of communion with Christ and with fellow believers.[10] No connection with any of our sources is obvious. An 1896 commentary on this catechism asserts both that the bread is not the real, essential body of Jesus and that the bread signifies that our souls are fed through the body and blood of Christ. This separation of *res* and *signum* is typical of Dirk. This document also describes the Eucharist as a memorial and a meal of unity and reconciliation. It enjoins moral earnestness but warns against judgmentalism. The ecclesial reference is much less stringent than in Hubmaier.[11]

In a 1910 commentary on the Elbing Catechism, the scholarly and pietistic author mentions the communal dimension of the meal, with reference to the practices of the ancient church. But his accent falls on the Supper as "a symbol and an assurance and a vouchsafing of this secretive communion of Christians with their transfigured Lord."[12] The tendency is Dirkian, but the language is more extravagant than his.

The minister's manuals of 1807 and 1841 make a striking combination of claims. They call the Lord's Supper a means of grace and at the same time call for a stringent service of preparation prior to the day of the breaking of bread.[13] In their first assertion, they are closest to Marpeck, though they lack the explanations with which he always accompanied the use of such terms. In their second assertion, they are of one mind with Hubmaier's work in the preparatory service he created.

The 1982 minister's manual focuses extensively on Christ's presence in the Christian life in general and in the Supper through the Holy Spirit. The eating and drinking are themselves acts of memory-making. An affinity for Dirk is evident here. A confession reminiscent of Hubmaier appears at the close of the third service: "When we share the cup, it is a way of sharing the death of Christ, a death that we may be called on to make for each other."[14]

The *Mennonitisches Lexikon* article "Abendmahl," written in

1913, begins with the claim that for faith the Lord's Supper is the saving appropriation of all the "powers of grace and blessing which reside in the life, passion, death, and resurrection of Jesus Christ."[15] The threefold meaning of the meal is as a memorial, a covenant of the communion of Christ, and of love among believers. Patristic sources, Karlstadt, Zwingli, and Calvin are quoted without commentary. The views of Conrad Grebel and the Bernese Anabaptists are summarized approvingly: the Supper is an action of the congregation, the expression of a communion of faith and love. It is also an *Einverleibung* (incorporation) into Christ and a memorial.

The article summarizes Marpeck's position, from the fragments of his writings then available, as something close to a spiritual appropriation of Christ: the congregation does not so much act as that it receives grace. Hans Denck's view is pictured as a union of Christ with believers, of which the elements are an analogy. All that is said of Hubmaier's communion service is that it repudiates a corporeal presence but speaks of eating Christ spiritually and in faith. Hoffmann is presented as advocating a participation in Christ through the word. Nothing is said of Dirk, but his colleague Menno's doctrine is said to include the Supper as a sign of admonition and memory, a gift of reconciliation, and in general, a presentation of its ethical and practical aspects rather than its essence. The writer lists Hoffmann and the Swiss Brethren as the dominant influences on contemporary German practice, although the description of Hoffmann's position embraces the characterization given to Dirk's view in this study.[16]

The article entitled "Communion" (1955) in *The Mennonite Encyclopedia* has a dogmatic Zwinglian-Swiss Brethren bias. Cornelius Krahn begins, "Communion has always had only a symbolic meaning for the Anabaptists and Mennonites." Sacramentarianism is introduced as the source of eucharistic doctrine among northern Anabaptists. In this connection Menno is mentioned, but Dirk is not. As in the *Mennonitisches Lexikon*, Grebel is quoted extensively in favor of a memorial and fellowship meal. Krahn invokes Hubmaier and Marpeck in the same breath as advocating a meal of commemoration. Nothing more is said of their views. The rest of the article focuses on a description of liturgical customs among Mennonites through the centuries but without any theological commentary. Emphasis is placed on preparation for communion.

In his article, "Lord's Supper," Robert Friedmann emphasizes the originality of one aspect of Anabaptist eucharistic views. In the eating and drinking, the individual *fuses* with the community. Friedmann documents the presence of this view in all streams of Anabaptism but the South German one.

In my article "Communion," I summarize and schematize the research presented in this volume. In addition, I highlight developments regarding the frequency of communion. My hypothesis is that frequent communion did not become the norm among Mennonites for two reasons. One is that they, like the church universal, were unable to overcome the medieval dread of unworthy reception. This was reinforced by persecution: congregations could seldom gather, and since communion was the oneness of the congregation with Christ and one another, the condition for the breaking of bread could rarely be met.

Yet the Mennonite Brethren Church, with its emphasis on grace and assurance of salvation, overcame the historical practice and instituted monthly communion.[17]

In summary, it is evident that none of our three theologians— Hubmaier, Marpeck, and Dirk—is the predominant influence on pre-contemporary Mennonite eucharistic conceptions. Dirk's communion of the soul with Christ is the most recurring feature of these statements.

Current Mennonite Eucharistic Theology

Four theological works by Mennonites represent the spectrum of Mennonite theological conviction in North America. We will examine them for their relationship to the Anabaptism represented by Hubmaier, Marpeck, and Dirk, and to the dominant Christian tradition.

First, *Introduction to Theology* is written from an evangelical perspective by J. C. Wenger.[18] Its discussion of the Trinity makes only marginal references to the two natures of Christ. In ways reminiscent of Melchiorite Christology, it speaks simply of Christ's divinity and his incarnation.[19] No functional relationship is established between the Son and the Spirit.[20] Wenger speaks of assurance, sanctification, and union with Christ in Dirkian terms, but nowhere does he relate the Lord's Supper to them.[21] The commentary on the church restricts itself to functional issues. Sacraments are included as a category under this heading, but no relationship between the two is made explicit.[22] Wenger's writing falls short of a systematic explanation of belief; its goal, especially in relation to the sacraments, is to offer correctives to disputed matters of practice. The brief section on the Lord's Supper claims for it a "dual symbolism" of the body of Christ and the fellowship of the church. The rest of it is taken up with a defense of close communion.[23]

Second, Gordon D. Kaufman's *Systematic Theology: A Historicist Perspective* is written from the viewpoint of liberal Protestantism.[24]

Kaufman sets his work within a well-developed trinitarian thought structure. An early claim for this orientation is that it safeguards the present revelation of God in Christ.[25] Nothing is made of this claim in relation to the life of the church or its sacraments. Kaufman affirms both natures of Christ, though he rejects traditional ontological categories. The meaning of the two natures of Christ is that God is both Lord and Sufferer.[26] In the section entitled "The Perfections of the Divine Communing," he makes no mention of the church or sacraments as the setting of communication.[27] Kaufman's interpretation of the resurrection of Christ has a direct implication for the Lord's Supper. His resurrection signifies God's inbreaking into history but is not an actual physical manifestation of that presence.[28] In a way which hints at Hubmaier's and Marpeck's belief about the church as the prolongation of the incarnation, Kaufman describes the church as the "culmination of the Christ-event" and the "beginning of the reversal of those historical powers enslaving and threatening to destroy man."[29]

Near the end of the book, Kaufman places a meager sacramental treatment to close out his section on the church. There the Bible is assigned a "mediatorial role," but this language is not applied to the Eucharist. It is described as a reenactment of Jesus' last meal, symbolic of his death in that it witnesses and participates in it. The Lord's Supper complements the rational role of the Bible in that it "enables participation in the foundational events of Christian faith below the verbal and intellectual levels of the self."[30] All of this means a "real presence" in the sense that here the community comes into renewed relationship with its foundation: "The very power and being of God the Father which came into human history through Christ is effective *ex opere operato* in the community in and through the sacrament." The elements feed the soul with the bread of life.[31] Kaufman explains his use of this language as "mythical" and "poetic." He rejects it as a supernaturalistic notion akin to a physical resurrection of Christ and his presence in the church.[32]

Kaufman concludes with the explanation that in his system, memorial and real presence complement and correct each other. The reappropriation of the church's foundation which happens in the breaking of bread is not complete until it takes up the burden of ministry and a nonresistant stance in the world.[33] The novelty of Kaufman's reconstructionist position is that it allows him to affirm eucharistic claims beyond what the Anabaptist tradition has been able to do. This is possible for him because he demythologizes the "body" of Christ both in his resurrection and in the ongoing life of the church. Kaufman's language tends to be looser and less precise in his writing on the Lord's Supper than it is elsewhere in his work. The Supper is a memorial and is inseparable from the nonresistant life of the church in the world. Both these aspects carry on motifs found in the three subjects of our study.

Third, in *The Theology of Anabaptism*, Robert Friedmann describes himself as a proponent of "existential Christianity."[34] He argues that Anabaptism was at first a "quasi spiritualistic trend" and later became a "biblicism" which constituted a separate stream of reform from Protestantism. Aside from the work of Hubmaier, the theology of Anabaptism, like that of the Synoptics, was spiritually immediate and implicit.[35] This means that while the Anabaptists were trinitarian and accepted Chalcedon, their interest lay in Jesus' exemplary life and death. They built no system of thought on this confession.[36] In Friedmann's interpretation of the evidence, the church derives from discipleship: it is a collective response to grace, a striving for the realization of the kingdom. Nothing is said of the initiative or presence of God through Christ in the church's gathered and outward life. Dirk and Marpeck are among those invoked in defense of this view.[37]

At the end of his book, Friedmann introduces the "ordinances" as "ways in which the church is actualized and maintained." The Anabaptist Lord's Supper is described approvingly as "rationalistic," "Zwinglian," and also an experience of certitude in being part of the true body of Christ. In this sense it is more than a memorial.[38] Friedmann is deliberate in his claim that the Lord's Supper has no basis in Christology and that Christology is exclusively concerned with the suffering and lordship of Christ. Yet he does not define the content of Christ's lordship nor relate it to the ongoing presence of God in the world. Friedmann's reductive reading of both the general Christian and the Anabaptist traditions tends to remove them from the christological and eucharistic debates presented in this study.

Fourth, Thomas Finger has written *Christian Theology: An Eschatological Approach* from an orthodox theological bias and a believers-church ecclesiological perspective. His initial christological comments indicate that the two natures of Christ are central to his system. He approvingly quotes Karl Barth's claim that Christ's incarnation is the only sacrament.[39] For Protestants, this entails a clear differentiation between that event and Christ's presence in the church. Finger's discussion of sacraments focuses largely on the Lord's Supper and summarizes the views of Barth, Rahner, Calvin, Luther, Aquinas, and the contemporary theologian Vernard Eller.[40] Yet he makes no reference to Anabaptist or Mennonite theologians.[41] His description of the Roman Catholic belief that the church is the primordial sacrament and "the extension of the incarnation" has much in common with Hubmaier's and Marpeck's understanding of the relationship among Christology, church, and sacrament. But Finger makes no mention of this similarity.[42]

Like Friedmann, Finger proposes another frame of reference and questions different from those pursued by the dominant Christian tradition. He begins his exposition of the Eucharist from the viewpoint of contemporary Synoptic studies, which tie the origin of the Lord's Supper to the meals Jesus had with his friends and with society's outcasts. To this claim, Finger adds the Lord's resurrection encounters. This means that the breaking of bread was not a religious ceremony but a celebrative communal meal. These feasts were tied to the Last Supper by Paul as a corrective (and nothing more) to the intemperance of certain gatherings.[43]

In reply to the question of how Christ is present in the Supper, Finger says Christ is in the believers and in every aspect of the event for which they gather. By means of a novel exegetical feat, he concludes that in the institutional narratives, the reference to the body concerns the disciples gathered about Jesus. This interpretation is undergirded by Finger's reference to his earlier definition of *body* in the New Testament as church. In conclusion, he turns to a Catholic notion that Christ is present "where the Supper is rightly administered." This rightness must include willing reception in faith, people sharing "of the life flowing from Jesus' self-giving."[44]

Finger's innovation is that he incorporates the work of modern Synoptic scholarship in his view. His own exegetical attempt to build up a doctrine of the Lord's Supper lacks that authority. The absence of reference to eucharistic thought from within his own tradition is noteworthy. Finger vacillates on the question of whether or not to work within traditional categories. He ends up giving them secondary attention as well as revising their content in line with his convictions.

> In his Supper, Jesus, through his Spirit, not only makes present the benefits of his death, but is present in the "already" of his resurrection. The Supper is a real, genuine taste—although not the fulness—of the messianic banquet. God's presence through earthly food is a sign that the kingdom transforms, and does not abolish, matter. . . . And as a concrete sharing of material goods among diverse people, the Lord's Supper flows naturally into sharing such things in daily life.[45]

In summary, the treatment of the Lord's Supper by all four of these theologians illustrates that they are ill at ease in working with the categories of the dominant tradition. Wenger makes no attempt to engage it, Kaufman demythologizes it, Friedmann rejects its binding character, and Finger restructures the focus and content of the debate. None of these scholars takes seriously the theology of the Lord's Supper and its christological context in Anabaptism. Wenger has no elaborated christological frame of reference. Friedmann's presentation is reduced to Jesus' earthly ministry and an undefined claim for his lordship. Kaufman has a sophisticated doctrine of Christ but does not exploit its possibilities to create sacramental and eucharistic deductions implied in it. Finger's frame of reference is historical and systematic; he is most at home with Calvin (whose Christology he finds most applicable to the matter at hand) and contemporary revisionist Roman Catholics. He goes further than others in the Anabaptist tradition in the direction of sacramental realism. His positive view of the relationship between matter and spirit is reminiscent of Marpeck. At the same time Finger's orthodox outlook makes it surprising that classical christological considerations are absent from his treatment of the Lord's Supper.

None of these theologians gives evidence of a thorough knowledge of the theology of the Lord's Supper in Anabaptism. Only Friedmann refers to Anabaptists in a more than passing way, and then in the form of untenable generalizations. Therefore, they evade rather than transcend the limitations and inconsistencies of the eucharistic doctrines of Hubmaier, Marpeck, and Dirk. This is principally the case because Wenger and Friedmann lack the Christology to do so. Kaufman has a developed Christology but rejects traditional interpretations of both the resurrection and the ongoing presence of Christ, in both his natures, in the sacramental life of the church. Finger affirms traditional interpretations from a postcritical perspective but doesn't build his eucharistic doctrine on them.

The Lord's Supper in Mennonite Worship
From this summary of Mennonite eucharistic theology seen from the perspective of the law of belief (*lex credendi*), we turn briefly to its manifestation in the law of prayer (*lex orandi*). The traditional Mennonite celebration of communion is characterized, in both its northern (Dutch–North German) and southern (Swiss–South German) streams, by an ethical earnestness. Hubmaier, Marpeck, and Dirk desired a precondition of faith and love for a true breaking of bread. This uniformly led to the practice of having a preparatory service, whose purpose is confession and reconciliation. In the Dutch-North German stream this is augmented by an awesomeness surrounding the event as a whole.

The disposition of the worshipers suggests a belief in the real presence of Christ in the Supper in a concentrated fashion, setting it apart from Christ's presence in noneucharistic worship settings.

In the larger conferences of Mennonites, who are becoming less and less separatist, both of these characteristics have undergone marked change in the past generation. The preparatory service or counsel meeting has disappeared or been retained without emphasis on reconciliation among believers. If it is practiced at all, the emphasis is on faith rather than love. The common explanation for this change is that the earlier ethical stringency had become graceless legalism.

At the same time, the awesomeness of the occasion has greatly lessened. The earlier sense that the Lord's Supper is a real, if theologically unspecified, communion of the body and blood of Christ, is now being replaced by an emphasis on the Supper as a celebration of the body of Christ as the church. The most usual rationale for this shift is that the devotional emphasis had become too individualistic and funereal in character. What has happened is that the ethically binding horizontal dimension of the preparatory service, where it is still held, has been replaced by a vertical, devotional stress. On the other hand, the vertical orientation of the communion proper has been replaced by a celebration of relationships among believers.

Toward a Fuller Theology and Practice of the Lord's Supper

What is the potential contribution of Hubmaier, Marpeck, and Dirk to a contemporary, ecumenically informed theology of the Lord's Supper within the Anabaptist tradition? The response to this question will begin with a critique of their Christologies and their eucharistic doctrines and result in a proposal which tries to transcend deficiencies in both areas.

Balthasar Hubmaier

The most radical reinterpretation of the Supper occurs in the writing of Hubmaier. The thrust of making the *res* of the sacrament refer to the church rather than to Christ is twofold. It separates the ceremony absolutely from the divine gift of communion with Christ and ties it absolutely to the divine gift of communion with the community of the church. Hubmaier was not claiming that the breaking of bread was an autonomous human action; it is possible only as a response to the gift, previously given, of a right relationship with God through Christ. The outward event of the Supper is the paradigmatic means of affirming participation in the church and its mission to the world. Each believer is called upon to take the pledge of love: Just as Christ offered himself for me, so I now offer myself for my sister, my brother, my neighbor, my enemy.

This ecclesial reality is the prolongation of Christ's incarnation. Hubmaier shared with Marpeck this fascinating and far-reaching application of Christology to ecclesiology. It is the life of the human Christ which continues to receive form in the obedience of the church. Christ is present in the Supper in that sense. It is a corporeal presence, not mediated by bread and wine, but by the very life of the church. This reality does not come about by the presence of Christ in the event of the Supper. It is given in the ongoing relationship of the believer with Christ and mediated by the believers to each other, paradigmatically, in the breaking of bread. Christ takes on flesh in the world as believers continue to live his life of love and sacrifice. Hubmaier goes so far as to claim that when they do that, they become Christ to others.

As to his divine nature, Christ is "physically" and "essentially" in heaven. Aside from a few marginal references to his presence on earth in his Spirit, Hubmaier made almost nothing of the second person of the Trinity in his divine nature between the time of his ascension and return. According to Pauline theology in the New Testament and the christological formulations of the fourth and fifth centuries, this is an omission of fundamental proportions. Hubmaier, it could be said, did not deny the ongoing activity of the Son in his divine nature; he simply did not invoke him. He thereby avoided having to develop a way of talking about Christ's present work such that it can be misconstrued as a sacramental presence.

But in Hubmaier, the problem was greater than that. Christ in his divinity, as Lord, is removed from the life of the church entirely. Second, the two natures of Christ are not only unmixed but also separated. The church does not have the person of Christ, for two reasons. First, the Spirit is the exclusive divine presence. Second, the prolongation of Christ's incarnation in the church is not literally an extension of his person but a carrying on of the power and the reality which he brought. Hubmaier said as much when he argued that if Christ as a person were present in the age of the church, the church would not be the keeper of the keys.

Hubmaier eliminated the problem of how Christ can be sacramentally present by replacing him with the Spirit. At the same time, he created another problem, that of a graceless Supper. Formally, there are evidences of grace in Hubmaier's writing, for example, in his communion liturgy. But its spirit is moralistic; its preoccupation is with being rather than receiving the body of Christ. The pledge of love demands perfect imitation of Christ as well as perfect purity, sought through the ban. In addition, the act of receiving the body of Christ "in memory" is also a deed of human achievement. For Hubmaier, the Lord's Supper dramatizes his theology: Christ is sacrifice and example. The Spirit brings the power of Christ's work into the present and sanctifies the believer. But Christ himself is present in the life of the Christian and in the Eucharist only as a demand. His role as the ongoing embodiment of God's love and forgiveness has been lost because his divine nature has been lost.

In assessment, once Hubmaier completed his arduous theological evolution, not only through the ideology but also through the institutional life of several Christian communities, he never made significant additions or corrections to his system of thought. Such reflective activity was almost impossible because of the upheaval brought by the Peasants' War and the persecution he had to bear. We cannot doubt the ethical profundity of his theology and of the eucharistic doctrine to which it gave birth. But it was an "interim ethic," unsustainable over time because of a Christology in which the human Christ and the life of the church had been separated from the divine Christ.

While Hubmaier made the Supper part of the essence of the church, he removed it entirely from the sacramental realm, from the mediation of divine spirit by matter. What remained was a ceremony which signified the presence of human spirits for each other. As has been shown above, there are lingering and recessive references in Hubmaier to the Supper as an assurance of salvation and to a spiritual communion with Christ. Yet these are anachronistic to the intention of his reformulation. From the standpoint of Anabaptism, he must be credited with two outstanding achievements. First, he eliminated the possibility of a corporeal presence in the Supper. Second, he created a Eucharist which fully expressed his church's ecclesiology: the church is Christ's presence in the world. However, these gains came at a great cost. To make this shift possible, his eucharistic doctrine was reduced from two dimensions to one, and his Christology was truncated.

Hubmaier was a spiritualist in that he believed that matter could have no role in the communication of spirit. It is difficult to assess whether he initially came to this conviction through the perspective of radical Protestant theology in general or through the need to create a new doctrine of the Lord's Supper to assert his movement's theological and spiritual independence from the Catholic Church. In fact, a dialectical movement between those two poles seems to have been the case.

A spiritualistic tendency is evident in Hubmaier at the Second Zurich Disputation long before his mature eucharistic views were in place. At the same time, Hubmaier's evolving theology of the Lord's Supper prodded him toward his conflationist Christology.

Not enough is known of the immense diversity in every facet of theology at the end of the Middle Ages to ascertain whether Hubmaier's position, clearly heterodox by the standards of Chalcedon, was a popular mode of Catholic thought at the time. It is evident, though, that whatever the source of his beliefs, they failed to function as a safeguard against his drastic reinterpretation of the Eucharist, which in turn defined his Christology.

Hubmaier separated the two natures of Christ in a way which preserved the reality and permanence of his humanity. This meant that the ascended Lord remained, in Hubmaier's words, physically and essentially in heaven until his coming again. While there are rare references in Hubmaier's writings to the spiritual presence of Christ in the church, he neither explained this presence nor made use of it. In his divine nature, Christ is equated with the Holy Spirit. With this conflation, he denied the particular nature and role of the Son, that is, his distinctive revelation of God and his ongoing presence in the church. Therefore, God's attributes and work as they have become known in the particularity of Christ are not of continuing significance in the activity of God in history.

Hubmaier made one supremely significant application of this claim in his ecclesiology. In the giving of the keys, Christ gives the incarnation of his power to the church. But Hubmaier made it clear that this passing on of Christ's authority is undertaken because he himself is to be absent from the plane of history. Christ relinquished the functions of his human nature in two ways. First, he passed it on to the church. Second, he ascended and withdrew from any role in the divine economy until the consummation of all things.

Hubmaier's pneumatology, however, shows that nothing of God's power in the world is thereby relinquished. This is asserted by means of the Johannine exchange in which the Son leaves the world so that the Spirit can be present in it. The consequence of this position for the sacraments is that there is no divine presence defined in relation to the incarnation: God is not present by virtue of Christ's body and blood but only as spirit. The bread and wine are thereby deprived of their role as signifiers of God present in the world as Christ. Their only signification is in relation to his historical presence in the church, that is, the prolongation of his power as a human being on earth.

Pilgram Marpeck

This study credits Marpeck with a theology of the Lord's Supper which embodies spiritualist and sacramentalist traits but which is confined to neither. Part of the difference between him and the other figures in our study is simply time. Marpeck perceived early in his theological life that the reconstruction of sacramental thought along Sacramentarian lines was neither straightforward nor complete. It brought with it uncalculated consequences for Christology and ecclesiology. Marpeck and Hubmaier had similar notions of the extension of the incarnation in the church. Marpeck's form of that belief, which he called the "humanity of Christ," was more elaborate and malleable than that of Hubmaier, as the following contrast between them suggests.

In Marpeck, the soteriological and ethical significance of the incarnation has much in common with Hubmaier's emphases: God was revealed through his Son's condescension and suffering; he continues to be revealed through the church's condescension and suffering. Yet in Marpeck the work of Christ in his humanity did not cease at the time of his ascension. He continues to work outwardly in the world concomitantly with the Father's inward working. The primal mode of Christ in his humanity now is in the ceremonies. From this basis, Marpeck draws theological inspiration from the Fourth Gospel.

Marpeck's primary interest was in the working relationship of the Son with the Father rather than the Spirit with the Father. At times he conflated the Spirit with the Son, and at other times the Spirit with the Father. This enhanced rather than dissipated their roles. Because Christ's present outward work is paradigmatically in the ceremonies, the ceremonies become one reality with the triune God. In the *VMN* this union is with the whole Christ. At this early point in the development of his sacramental thought, Marpeck did not differentiate between the two persons of Christ (human, divine). His interest was in the reality of the communion. But even here it is important to recognize that Marpeck's doctrine on the humanity of Christ is only half of his Christology. When ceremonies become part of the dynamic of Spirit and faith, believers are united with Christ in his divine as well as his human nature.

A major development took place in this doctrine when Marpeck entered his controversy with Schwenckfeld. It involved the recasting of the nature and role of Christ's humanity after his ascension. Marpeck had a double emphasis on the humanity of Christ—as the way in which God is revealed and humanity saved in the earthly life of Jesus as well as in the earthly life of his body the church. He realized that Schwenckfeld used this affirmation against him in their debate about the Lord's Supper, arguing that Marpeck held to a physical presence of Christ in the breaking of bread.

The following controversy showed that each of the men had entered this phase of the debate with a different first principle. Marpeck defined his understanding of the Supper by means of his Christology; Schwenckfeld defined his Christology by means of his understanding of the Supper. Although the ultimate bone of contention between them remained the nature of the Eucharist, they turned to a different progression of logic to assert their positions. Marpeck insisted that, though Christ's humanity has been glorified, it has not lost its nature. Christ's two natures are neither separated nor mixed. This became the bedrock of Marpeck's subsequent theologizing in the *VWG II*. He allowed the notion of the humanity of Christ to recede completely in its reference to the prolongation of Christ's humanity in the life of the church.

In his later attempts to speak about Christ's presence in the Supper, Marpeck made two related christological deductions in relation to the Supper. First, Christ, with his "transfigured body, of human nature, flesh, and blood," is not present in the Supper. Second, though the glorified man Jesus Christ is not with and in us bodily, he nevertheless is with us in "both natures united in the Holy Spirit" (*beder verainigten naturen h. geist*). The relevance of these mysterious formulations to our conclusion is that the two natures of Christ are the sine qua non of Marpeck's theology as a whole and of his beliefs about the Lord's Supper and the church.

Here we sense that Marpeck's various lines of interpretation were not all integrated; his thought was unfinished at critical points. Of significance to our discussion is that he always thought and argued christologically. This is the basis for the difference in eucharistic doctrine between him and Hubmaier and Dirk. Christ, in both his natures, is at work in the world.[46] Therefore, he can be present and is present in the Supper, giving us himself. Marpeck preserved the event of bread and wine as the concrete and paradigmatic locus of this presence. The relationship between Son and Spirit was often imprecisely and inconsistently cast, but it remained clear that the Spirit is the means of the Son's presence. For that reason as well, the Supper is not spiritualized, not divorced from the person of Christ.

When he was contending with spiritualism, Marpeck was not thinking in Catholic categories of real presence. His only goal was to establish the significance of the incarnation for the meeting between God and humanity. Schwenckfeld interpreted Marpeck's general claims in the specific categories of transubstantiation. This turned out to be a tragic imposition of alien thought patterns, diverting Marpeck's theology from the path on which it had been set. Marpeck said nothing about a change in the substance of bread and wine. His eucharistic doctrine, however unfinished, was intended to be an alternative to the traditional interpretation of how God works externally. It also countered the novel claim of spiritualism in limiting the incarnation to an isolated moment in the divine self-disclosure. We have seen that Schwenckfeld so redefined the incarnation that he deprived it entirely of its role as a bridge between God's being and our natural and historical existence.

Marpeck was forced to account for himself in terms of Schwenckfeld's alternatives. Both of them involve the presence of Christ in his two natures in communion. Schwenckfeld so divinized the humanity of Christ as to make it one with Christ's divinity. This redefinition meant that Christ's body and blood completely change character. Christ is no longer known by that body in which he came to earth and which he sacrificed: salvation no longer has a material reference point. Schwenckfeld could conceive of only one alternative to his own position: a corporeal presence in the Catholic sense. He disallowed sacraments as extensions of or analogies to the incarnation, that is, as material reference points for a spiritual presence. This, of course, was Marpeck's position.

Since Marpeck's view is ruled out a priori, Schwenckfeld tried to explain his own teaching in a way that could not lead to transubstantiation. This became his preoccupation rather than his original project of an alternative theology of the Lord's Supper with its own frame of reference. Marpeck did not give up his foundational belief in the incarnation and the deductions he made from it. Yet under Schwenckfeld's goading, he undertook to make clear how the external work of the Son does not mean that the eucharistic bread becomes the physical body of Christ. In the process the particular role of Christ in his two natures is specified. In his humanity Christ continues to work outwardly while the Father works inwardly. In his divinity he works inwardly as Spirit and actually takes over the role which the Father has played according to the Johannine scheme. The prolongation of the church as the work of Christ in his human nature recedes as Schwenckfeld forced claims about it into association with a physical presence in the bread.

At this point Marpeck placed his emphasis on the human nature of Christ in heaven. Something amounting to a communication of idioms took place in Marpeck's thought so that Christ is said to be present in the Supper according to both natures. He claimed Christ's human nature was spiritually present, signified by the event of bread and wine. This explanation is another way of saying that through the unity of external and internal, we are given a communion with the body and blood of Christ, that is, a gracious encounter with God as he took flesh in Christ.

Only at the end of the *VWG*, when the ongoing work of Christ in his two natures is dislodged, did Marpeck (or the epigone who brought his treatise to a conclusion) capitulate to spiritualism. As long as the validity of Christ's human nature in God's self-disclosure was maintained, it followed that, in the presence of faith and Spirit, the external works of Christ (the church and the sacraments) are the way to the internal reality of his oneness with the Father and the Spirit. By means of his whole self, Christ brings us to unity with God.

Marpeck's Christology was initially developed to reassert the continuing work of the Son in both his natures. He chose this argument as the only adequate refutation of spiritualism. It is clear that this was not a diminution of Christ's divinity but a claim that there was both a distinction in and a unity of his two natures. By means of their redefinitions, most extravagantly in the celestial-flesh theory, the spiritualists were disputing both these claims.

In this undertaking, Marpeck stood not only against the spiritualists but against Hubmaier and Dirk. Hubmaier limited his ecclesiological claim for Christ to a historical one. Christ's work was carried on in the church not by the human Christ in his ongoing role, inseparable from his divinity, but only in historical continuity with his earthly ministry. In the present Christ's humanity had no role in revelation or in the mediation of grace; therefore, the external life of the church was not a bridge to the inner life of God. When the divine Christ was merged with the Spirit, the particular role of the second person of the Trinity was lost. Dirk, on the other hand, retained the two natures of Christ but separated them such that only the divine Christ had a continuing role. His presence, too, lost its particularity as established in the incarnation by its near equation with the Spirit. The communion of his body and blood became a spiritual reality divorced from his humanity and, therefore, from all outwardness.

Dirk Philips

More clearly than in either Hubmaier or Marpeck, Christology is the definitive precondition of Dirk's theology. It gave particularity to his spiritualistic world of assumptions. Created matter cannot mediate spirit. Therefore, Christ's incarnation had to be into uncreated matter.

Everything in Dirk's theology, specifically his eucharistic doctrine, flowed from this assumption. It predisposed Dirk to a spiritualistic reading of the Fourth Gospel, which in turn provided the basis for his claims about the Lord's Supper. In the early and middle years of his ministry, Dirk aligned himself with Hoffmann, Menno, and northern Anabaptism in general in exposing the deficiencies of sacramentalism. By the end of his life, the incompatability between his ecclesiology and his view of biblical authority on one hand, and spiritualism on the other, led him to a new defense of the outwardness of the Christian life.

This change came about when Dirk discovered that a simple biblicistic rationale for sacraments carried no weight with his opponent Franck. Hitherto this biblicism, as well as the weight of tradition, had secured the place of ceremonies in the life of the church. His early eucharistic thought came to a point of clarity in his exegesis of John 6.

The flesh and blood mentioned in that text concern only the divine nature of Christ. Reality, according to Dirk, is spiritual in nature; therefore, communion between divinity and humanity can only be between two spirits. Our souls feed on the divinity of Christ. The Lord's Supper, as an event of bread and wine, does not constitute this communion. It is a confirmation to faith that this communion happens. The communion itself is not a particular event but a relationship. The Supper is a means of assurance to the Christian that grace is constant and abiding. There is something of a parallel between this function of the Supper in Dirk and the role of a ceremony as co-witness (*mitzeugnus*) in Marpeck. For both of them, external works were meaningless without the presence of faith and Spirit. But, whereas in Marpeck the outer event becomes one with the inner reality, in Dirk outward things have no participation in inward realities.

At this juncture a comparison with Hubmaier becomes obvious. In both of their Christologies, the humanity of Christ as an ongoing agency of God's work ceased to have a role. Both of their theologies proceeded to a conflation of the divinity of Christ with the Holy Spirit. In Dirk, however, this remained more of a description of the nature of Christ than a complete assimilation of the Son into the Spirit. By means of his Johannine description of the Eucharist, Dirk maintained a distinct role for the divine Christ. He is the one who gives himself by means of the Spirit to believers. This self-giving does not happen in any spatial way, that is, in relation to the event of the Supper.

Though Dirk did not make the matter explicit, his description of the communion between Christ and Christians suggests that they are raised beyond the limits of the earth to commune with him in heaven.

Dirk's view of sanctification as the divinization of the Christian and the believer's participation in the realm of spirit underscores this orientation toward heaven. Therefore, Christ is not present in the breaking of bread as a spatial and temporal event. It follows that Christ is not present in believers when they celebrate the Eucharist: they are present to him in heavenly places, and this is signified to their faith by the communal act of eating and drinking together.

This absolute disjuncture between what happens on earth and in heaven is attributable to the absence of a role for the humanity of Christ in Dirk's scheme of things. His particularity has been lost and he has been completely spiritualized, that is, divorced from any relationship to the created order. Through the new birth, Christians gain admittance to the eternal order of spiritual reality; they are no longer limited to their natural capacities.

A decade later, when Dirk was engaged in controversy with Franck, he used this anthropology in a quite different way to ground his argument against spiritualism. His Christology could not help him against Franck because it was based on an assumption he held in common with his antagonist, that created matter cannot mediate spirit. Dirk's eucharistic doctrine was of little help because it flowed from his Christology and was shaped by its world of assumptions. In fact, its claim for the Supper as sign, confirmation, and assurance was not warranted by the Christology behind it!

This claim has another source to which Dirk turned for a defense of sacraments. Dirk argued that "the church of the Lord, although existing in spirit and truth, is nevertheless, also visible."[47] This contention expresses in corporate form that he believed the individual sanctified Christian lives in the Spirit but on earth. The Christian who no longer lives in the Spirit must be banned from the spiritual community as it exists historically.

Similarly, the sacraments participate in spiritual reality when they are used in faith and in the Spirit. This argument remains hesitant; it is asserted more than substantiated. Here Dirk pushed himself to the edges of his own span of reference. Rather than putting all the weight of his argument on a theory of spirit and matter, he relied largely on his initial biblicistic claim that sacraments have a place in the life of the church because Christ commanded them. These two claims together are the culmination of his sacramentology. Dirk never applied it specifically to the Lord's Supper, presumably because his dispute with Franck never forced that issue. Had he chosen to do so, he would have put his own eucharistic doctrine into question, both its christological underpinnings and their application to John 6.

Dirk's biblicism and his ecclesiology shaped the Sacramentarianism he had inherited and established limits for its spiritualistic tendency. His tenacious loyalty to the text of Scripture led him to practice sacraments simply because Jesus had ordained them. In *AML* he introduced the church's Supper of bread and wine as a mirror of the inner communion which the soul is given with Christ at conversion. This relationship is the subject of John 6. Bread and wine are a mirror of this communion because they reflect an event which takes place outside of them. They are a co-witness of sorts, a witness together with the faith of the communicant that Christ has been eaten. But they are attestations of a separate event rather than, as in Marpeck, part of a present reality.

Though he was unable to establish a causal connection between communion with Christ and the Lord's Supper, Dirk did define them in relationship to one another. Nothing less than the breaking of bread was adequate to visualize and confirm the inner encounter; nothing less than the language of flesh and blood was able to describe the nature of the believer's encounter with the God who had broken into human existence by incarnation. This intense concentration on God in Christ is manifest in Dirk's eucharistic devotion, which stood in awe of the crucified Savior and not the celestial Lord.

The present examination of the Christology and Eucharist of three Anabaptist theologians has shown that they faced the supreme challenge of establishing the linkage between a communion with Christ given through faith, and its presence in the outer life of the church. Only Marpeck was able to assert and maintain this linkage without returning to medieval theories (as he was accused of doing) or losing it in a spiritualistic reductionism, at whose brink Hubmaier and Dirk hovered. They were saved from thoroughgoing spiritualism primarily by the two-natures Christology, which was the source of their ecclesiology.

A Critique of Anabaptist-Mennonite Theologies of the Lord's Supper

Any attempt to develop a fuller theology and practice of the Lord's Supper within the Mennonite tradition would have to address, among others, the following issues:

1. The relationship of Mennonite theology as a whole to the Lord's Supper and Christology.
2. The reductive tendency in Mennonite theology.
3. The paucity of references to, and the misunderstanding of, sixteenth-century Mennonite eucharistic documents among Mennonite historians and systematic theologians today.

4. The relationship of Mennonite practice of the Lord's Supper today to its theology.
5. Aspects of Mennonite eucharistic theology which can contribute to the ecumenical practice of the Lord's Supper, particularly as represented by the document, *Baptism, Eucharist, and Ministry.*[48]

Mennonite Theology

Whether there can be an explicit Anabaptist theology has been debated since the beginning of the movement.[49] It is clear that Anabaptism, like the Reformation as a whole, sought to simplify theology and relate it to the practice of the Christian life. We likewise recognize that, with the fleeting exception of Hubmaier's time in Waldshut and Nicolsburg, Anabaptism was never an established movement charged with the task of applying its principles to all questions involved in the ordering of a society. The diversity of the Anabaptist movement and its theologies in the age of the Reformation makes it impossible to generalize about its nature. When we examine the three theologians selected for this study, it is evident that they were trying to think theologically in a way which compared favorably—in intent if not always in content—with representatives of other Reformation movements.

Friedmann is correct in his observation that Anabaptism was focused on practical Christianity. However, this orientation was not interpreted by Hubmaier, Marpeck, or Dirk as something which made theological formulations unnecessary. The eucharistic doctrines of these three men flowed not only from their straightforward reading of the Bible but also from theological presuppositions to which they were committed, and from their own theology creativity. Though none of them created a theological system, each of them responded methodically to the controversies which challenged him. For example, all of them provided a christological rationale for their understanding of the then much-disputed words of institution. Both Marpeck and Dirk, in different ways, shifted the grounds of debate away from biblical exegesis to theological formulation. In varying degrees all three thinkers favored John over the Synoptics and Paul as the source of the interpretive key to the Lord's Supper.

The conclusion of the matter is that the eucharistic writings of Hubmaier, Marpeck, and Dirk are characterized as much by formal theological structure and rational defense as they are by biblical exegesis. The claims of each Christology as it bore on a particular theology of the Lord's Supper will be briefly critiqued, following the theological method common to the three men.

Hubmaier considered his reformulation of the debate successful. He believed his position to be an approximation of apostolic teaching and an alternative to the scholastic preoccupation with the elements in much of the eucharistic debate in his day. Judged by his own goals, Hubmaier appears to have had the most complete theology of the Lord's Supper among the three men. The development of his thought is straightforward and singleminded. Its attractiveness to a church of martyrs is understandable.

Yet by the same token, the reliance of his position on a perfect willingness to imitate Christ could not be sustained over time. This problem arose because of the absence of the heavenly Christ with grace and succor for those who sought to carry on his earthly incarnation. Nevertheless, when placed within an adequate christological framework, Hubmaier's eucharistic thought safeguarded the ethical nature of the Christian life as taught in Anabaptism. Gratitude for Christ's sacrifice consists not of abstract emotion but of concrete imitation in life: worship reaches its apex in mission. In form as well as content, his communion service is a model against which to test old and new eucharistic practices.

Marpeck made two outstanding contributions to Mennonite systematic and eucharistic theology. First, he appropriated a trinitarian frame of reference within which to establish a eucharistic doctrine and, flowing from that, a developed doctrine of the two natures of Christ. The prolongation of Christ's earthly life in the church was complemented by his heavenly ministry for the church. The point of concentration of this ministry was the Lord's Supper. Marpeck's second contribution was his definition of the sacrament as an event flowing from the gathering of a community in faith and love, moving to the co-witness of bread and wine thus shared. As the climax, the community's action of sharing bread and wine was transformed into a sharing of the body and blood of Christ. This dynamic nature of the sacrament derived from the dynamic work of the Trinity.

The problem with Marpeck's formulations is that they were not always thought through to their conclusions. Nor is it clear whether language was being literally or metaphorically used. This description of the Supper, for example, is clear enough in its intention but leaves unanswered questions. Is Christ the immediate agent of the transformation of the action with bread and wine into a communion with himself? The text speaks as if Christ's external work, as in the time of his incarnation, is carried on in the life of the church. But in the same passages, the Spirit is claimed as the cause of the change. Suddenly it seems as if the description of each person's role in the Trinity is in the nature of a picture of how the God who is known in Christ works—rather than a literal and systematic description of God's action.

As Marpeck became embroiled in controversy with Schwenckfeld, the trinitarian dynamic was narrowed to one whose focus was almost exclusively on the two natures of Christ. What began as an excursus to make clear the role of the two natures of Christ in the Supper, became the center of his eucharistic teaching. Marpeck makes a more far-reaching contribution to our understanding of the Lord's Supper when we view his trinitarian scheme as the foundation of his eucharistic doctrine than when his later attempts to meet specific challenges are taken as the norm in and of themselves. These later attempts to exonerate himself from the charge of transubstantiation undermined his earlier work in the *VMN* to transcend the alternatives into which sixteenth-century eucharistic debate had been cast.

Dirk's theology of the Lord's Supper secured two claims for northern Anabaptism which were indispensable for its spirituality and its ecclesiology. First, he held the Eucharist to be both an unmediated communion of the believer with Christ and an outward meal which vouched for the inward reality. He accomplished this at high cost by holding to two unreconciled Christologies. The unfallen-humanity stream to which he subscribed diminished the significance of the incarnation such that it lost its anchor in the world of fallen creation as a safeguard against spiritualism. It brought with it a lingering reservation about God's presence in the world.

Second, Dirk's move, late in his ministry, to compensate for this influence was necessary to give meaning to the outward work of the Spirit in the church. He did this by giving more weight to assumptions which had shaped his ecclesiology. It is not clear whether he divined that these assumptions flowed from a contrary Christology. But he did see that the visible life of the church provided an analogy and an argument for sacraments which his Christology was unable to furnish. From the vantage point of his late theology, Dirk provides an admirable corrective and model for the direction of much Mennonite theologizing on the Supper since the end of the sixteenth century.

Its Reductive Tendency

Mennonite eucharistic theology since the seventeenth century has tended to treat the Lord's Supper as an isolated point of doctrine. It has left it unrelated to the larger claims of theology and Christology. The breaking of bread has been described most often to be the sign of the church as the body of Christ, or it has been treated as an inward communion of the soul with him. In the former case, the body of Christ as the church has not been related to Mennonite beliefs about the two natures of Christ. In the latter case, the inward communion has often existed without any stipulated relationship to the meal of bread and wine. In some circles the memorial emphasis has become the exclusive one. These claims are deficient when compared to all three of the theologies under study. None of them saw the Supper as an isolated point of doctrine, nor did they gravitate to a single definition of the Eucharist, as much as subsequent Mennonite theology has done.

Mennonite Systematic Theologians and Anabaptism

The paucity of references in contemporary systematic theologies by Mennonites to Anabaptist eucharistic doctrine is baffling. In part, modern Mennonite scholars have wrongly thought that their sixteenth-century counterparts were working outside the sphere of methodical theological inquiry. Added to this is the fact that the writings of Hubmaier, Marpeck, and Dirk have been lost to Mennonite consciousness on both a congregational and professional level.[50] Contemporary Mennonite writings on the Lord's Supper have lacked substantive reference to the early tradition. In addition, they have not dealt with their subject with the sophistication it was accorded at that time. For example, none of the four modern theologians whose works have been examined relates his eucharistic claims to his christological presuppositions, as did his sixteenth-century precursors.[51] None of them places his undertaking within the span of Mennonite theological work from its origins to the present.

The Lord's Supper in Mennonite Worship

In traditional Mennonite worship, the theology and practice of the Lord's Supper has been safeguarded much more by the conservative influence of ritual than by theological exposition. Before the twentieth century, the few treatises written on the subject were devotional in nature.[52] The current trend in scholarly thought and pastoral practice has been influenced by the "recovery of the Anabaptist vision."[53] This recovery highlighted the ethical and ecclesiastical characteristics of Anabaptism. Its consequence for the celebration of the Lord's Supper has been a de-emphasis on a eucharistic piety of the sort found in Dirk's *Enchiridion*, with its focus on the individual's inward communion and contemplation of the suffering of Christ. Instead, the current emphasis is on the Supper as an act of remembrance and as a sign of community. In both cases, the focus has been on human actions.

Contemporary biblical scholarship has contributed to this evolution through its research on the relationship between the Lord's Supper and the Gospel record of Jesus' meals with hungry crowds, with outcasts, and with his followers after the resurrection. This broadened picture of the development of the Lord's Supper has led to less stress on the Last Supper as the exclusive model for the theology and piety of the breaking of bread. With this has come a shift away from the exclusive character of the celebration to its inclusive character. If Jesus broke bread with "outsiders," should not we?

Mennonites have appropriated these features in isolation from the traditional sacramental, christological, and ecclesiologial dimensions of the subject. In current Mennonite writing and practice, little is said about God's action in the event: Jesus in his earthly ministry is invoked as a model for an inclusive invitation to table fellowship, but nothing is said of his presence. There is the traditional link between baptism and communion as the events in which the individual makes and remakes a covenant with Christ and the church, but this has been weakened by the emphasis on inclusiveness. Among some Mennonites, this openness of the Lord's Table has been extended to children growing up in the church. Unlike other denominations which practice the inclusion of children in communion by virtue of their baptism as infants, the Mennonite Church does not have a baptismal theology which warrants such action.

Ecumenical Convergence on the Eucharist

The theology and practice of the Lord's Supper among Mennonites stands to benefit in numerous ways from the priority recently given to the Eucharist in biblical, historical, and liturgical scholarship as well as on the ecumenical agenda. The most far-reaching of these benefits is the way this dialogue integrally relates (1) the Supper and the structure of theology as a whole, with (2) how Christians see the Supper as the fullest expression and experience of the church's belief. Thus, true theology leads to worship; and true worship leads to the Lord's Supper.

At the same time, Anabaptist eucharistic theology, as represented by Hubmaier, Marpeck, and Dirk, has its own contribution to make to the "eucharistic convergence" now being guided by the process associated with the publication of *Baptism, Eucharist, and Ministry*. First, the eucharistic doctrine of Marpeck and (to a lesser extent) of Dirk can help correct the historical misunderstanding that the non-Lutheran

Continental Reformation reduced the Lord's Supper to a human act of remembrance. This misunderstanding is present as much within Reformed and Anabaptist denominations as outside them.

A second and related contribution flows especially from Marpeck's work. He furnished an interpretation of the real presence of Christ in the Lord's Supper which is an alternative to those explanations focusing primarily on the elements (transubstantiation and consubstantiation); yet Marpeck did not spiritualize the communion (that is, abstract it from the action of the church with the elements).[54] This he achieved by means of his dynamic trinitarianism. In it, the Father works inwardly as Spirit and the Son works outwardly in the church, which is the prolongation of his incarnation. The church's place in the event of communion is to gather in faith and love around bread and wine. The Spirit takes the elements and makes them co-witnesses with the Spirit. They then become the means of the church's union with Christ, of its participation in his body and blood.

A third contribution comes from Anabaptist theology as a whole, as well as from its eucharistic teachings: an emphasis on faith, reconciliation, community, and mission. All of these come together in Hubmaier's theology of the Lord's Supper in a profound manner. On the basis of its stress on baptism upon confession of faith, Anabaptism can strengthen other denominations in the understanding of an existential response of faith as that without which the body of Christ cannot be discerned.[55] Anabaptism teaches that communion is the surpassing expression of reconciliation of Christians with God and with each other. From this resource, Anabaptist thought can help to emphasize the concrete, relational nature of the breaking of bread.[56] This is underscored by its belief in the communal and dynamic character of the celebration. Finally, Hubmaier explained the Eucharist as gratitude which takes ethical form (as Christ gave himself for me, so I can give myself for others) and links worship to mission. This thrust contributes to a Christian self-understanding which is other-centered,[57] translating faith into love and thanksgiving into sacrifice.

Notes

Abbreviations in the Notes
(For Document Abbreviations, see page 24.)

ARG *Archiv für Reformationsgeschichte*

BRE *Baptist Review and Expositor*

BRN *Bibliotheca Reformatoria Neerlandica* (see Bibliography)

CS *Corpus Schwenckfeldianorum* (see Bibliography)

DB Doopsgezinde Bijdragen

Elsass Manfred Krebs and Hans George Rott, eds., *Quellen zur Geschichte der Täufer*, vol. 7: *Elsass*, part 1 (Gütersloh: Gerd Mohn, 1959)

Dirk Dirk Philips, *Enchiridion*, trans. by A. B. Kolb (Aylmer: Pathway Publishing Corporation, 1978). A scholarly translation of all Dirk's writings with a critical apparatus regrettably appeared too late to be used in this study: Cornelius J. Dyck, William E. Keeney, and Alvin J. Beachy, eds., *The Writings of Dirk Philips, 1504-1568*, Classics of the Radical Reformation, vol. 6 (Scottdale, Pa.: Herald Press, 1992).

Hubmaier H. Wayne Pipkin and John H. Yoder, eds., *Balthasar Hubmaier: Theologian of Anabaptism*, Classics of the Radical Reformation, vol. 5 (Scottdale, Pa.: Herald Press, 1989). This is the translation cited, compared with the original, and amended where shown. For the original, see *Schriften*, below.

JEH *Journal of Ecclesiastical History*

HTR *Harvard Theological Review*

Marpeck William Klassen and Walter Klaassen, eds., *The Writings of Pilgram Marpeck*, Classics of the Radical Reformation, vol. 2 (Scottdale, Pa.: Herald Press, 1978)

ME *The Mennonite Encyclopedia*, vols. 1-4 ed. by C. Krahn, vol. 5 ed. by C. J. Dyck et al. (Scottdale, Pa.: Herald Press, 1955-59, 1990)

MGB *Mennonitische Geschichtsblätter*

ML *Mennonitisches Lexikon*

MQR *The Mennonite Quarterly Review*

RTK *Realenzyklopaedie für Theologie und Kirche*

Schriften G. Westin and T. Bergsten, eds., *Balthasar Hubmaier Schriften* (Gütersloh: Gerd Mohn, 1962). References are to this original text. Citations are from *Hubmaier*, above.

WOR *Worship*

ZTK *Zeitschrift für Theologie und Kirche*

ZdZ *Zeichen der Zeit*

Zwingli E. Egli and G. Finster, eds., *Huldreich Zwingli's sämtliche Werke*, vols. 88ff. of Corpus Reformatorum (Leipzig: M. Heinius Nachfolger, 1904ff.).

Chapter 1: Introduction

1. J. Jungmann, *The Early Liturgy* (Notre Dame: University of Notre Dame, 1959), 114.

2. J. Stayer et al., "From Monogenesis to Polygenesis: The Historical Discussion About Anabaptist Origins," *MQR* 49 (1975): 83-121.

3. D. Baillie, *The Theology of the Sacraments* (London: Faber and Faber, 1957), 56. Baillie is alert to the problem of misunderstanding and misrepresentation. He writes, "But it seems very important to realize that the doctrine of transubstantiation itself was an attempt, however unsuccessful and unsound, to avoid crude and materialistic conceptions of what happens in the sacrament, and even to save the idea of the Real Presence from the crudely spatial interpretation. . . . When the medieval divines, and finally St. Thomas Aquinas, worked out the doctrine of transubstantiation, they were doubtless assuming an Aristotelian metaphysic of substance and attributes which we can no longer accept, but they were endeavouring to spiritualize a conception of the miracle of the altar which was already dominant in the minds of the people, and the result was far less 'materialistic' than we commonly suppose."

4. J. Lortz, *Die Reformation in Deutschland*, vol. 1, quoted in S. Ozment, ed., *The Reformation in Mediaeval Perspective* (Chicago: Quadrangle, 1974), 4. The subsequent generation of Catholic scholarship has greatly qualified the view that the Reformation completely subjectivized religion. See, for example, O. Pesch, *Die Theologie der Rechtfertigung bei Martin Luther und Thomas von Aquin* (Mainz: Matthias Grünewald, 1967), esp. 326ff., 795ff., 866ff.

5. R. Damerau, *Die Abendmahlslehre des Nominalismus ins besondere die des Gabriel Biel* (Giessen: W. Schmitz, 1963), esp. 111-128.

6. K. McDonnell, *Jesus Christ, the Church and the Eucharist in John Calvin* (Princeton: Princeton University Press, 1964), 6.

7. The fourth Lateran Council of 1215 had decreed a minimum of once-a-year communion. Cf. Gregory Dix, *The Shape of the Liturgy* (London: Daccre, 1975), 631.

8. Among the most radical and famous precursors of sixteenth-century eucharistic thought was Wessel Gansfort: cf. *Wessel Gansfort, Life and Writings*, tr. by J. W. Scudder (New York: G. T. Putnam's Sons, 1917), 3-70.

9. H. Oberman, ed., tr. by P. Nyhus, *Forerunners of the Reformation* (New York: Holt, Rinehart and Winston, 1966), 244. The Catholic interpretation of this definition emphasizes that the sacrament derives its power from the person of Christ and his institution of the ceremonies as well as from the life of the church which actualizes Christ in history. In explicating the significance of *ex opere operato*, Catholic theologians emphasize that it safeguards the fact that faith is the condition but not the cause of sacramental grace. See K. Rahner and H. Vorgrimmler, *Dictionary of Theology* (New York: Crossroad, 1961), 350ff., 425f.; M. Schmaus, *Dogma*, vol. 5: *The Church as Sacrament* (Kansas City: Sheed and Ward, 1975), 12-16, 40-41.

10. On this issue Bromiley highlights a striking comparison between Zwingli's and the medieval position on God's sovereignty in the sacrament. Anabaptism, on the other hand, placed the predominant weight in the sacrament on the freedom and response of the individual. "At this point, the doctrine of Zwingli joins hands with its opposite, the *ex opere operato* doctrine of sacramental efficacy, for at bottom both of them are concerned to emphasize the divine transcendence and soverignty. In one case, the divine transcendence and sovereignty are seen in the freedom of God to work only how and where he chooses. In the other, it is seen in the faithfulness of God to work how and where he has promised to do so." G. W. Bromiley, ed., *Zwingli and Bullinger* (Philadelphia: Westminster, 1958), 183-184. In contrast, see also Pesch, *Die Theologie*, 796, on God's freedom, as understood by Aquinas, not to use sacraments in communicating himself.

11. Ozment, *The Reformation*, 7; and S. Ozment, *The Age of Reform* (New Haven: Yale, 1980), 208-211.

12. The role of Augustine, directly and derivatively, is a matter of exceedingly

great complexity. D. Janz in *Luther and Late Medieval Thomism* (Waterloo: Wilfrid Laurier University, 1983), 158-165, offers a succinct summary of the significance of Augustine's anthropology in the pre-Reformation era and of present schools of interpretation. A similar clarity has not been achieved in current scholarship regarding contemporary understandings of Augustine's sacramental theory. J. McCue in "The Doctrine of Transubstantiation from Bérenger Through Trent: The Point at Issue," *HTR* 61 (1968): 385-388, speaks of Augustinian and Ambrosian schools of sacramental interpretation. H. Oberman in *The Harvest of Medieval Theology* (Grand Rapids: Eerdmans, 1967), 271-280, 340-360, documents a spiritualistic approach to sacramental reality which grounds itself in Augustine. This is the tendency which Windhorst describes.

13. C. Windhorst, *Täuferisches Taufverständnis* (Leiden: E. J. Brill, 1976), 195.

14. C. Krahn, *Dutch Anabaptism* (Scottdale, Pa.: Herald Press, 1981), 44-79; G. Williams, *The Radical Reformation* (Philadelphia: Westminster Press, 1962), 27-37, 85-117. But see the contrary view in Stayer, "Monogenesis. . . , 112ff.

15. Ozment, *The Reformation*, 34-39. H. J. Goertz gives a succinct summary of this tendency before and during the Reformation: *Die Täufer* (Munich: C. H. Beck, 1980), 40-76.

16. *RTK*, III, 3:107.

17. P. Althaus, *The Theology of Martin Luther* (Philadelphia: Fortress, 1966), 375ff. An exhaustive and self-critical analysis of the current discussion between Catholic and Lutheran scholars on the Lord's Supper may be found in *Lutherans and Catholics in Dialogue, I-III*, ed. by P. Empie and A. Murphy (Minneapolis: Augsburg, 1967), 1-126, "The Eucharist as Sacrifice."

18. Neal Blough, *Christologie anabaptiste: Pilgram Marpeck et l'humanité du Christ* (Geneva: Labour et Fides, 1982), 65-72.

19. H. MackIntosh, The Doctrine of the Person of Jesus Christ (New York: Charles Scribner's Sons, 1912), 240.

20. W. Koehler, *Zwingli und Luther* (New York: Johnson Reprint, 1971), 1:56.

21. *Karlstadts Schriften aus den Jahren 1523-1525*, ed. by Erich Hertzsche (Halle: Max Niemeyer, 1957), 2:31, et passim.

22. C. Pater, *Karlstadt as the Father of the Baptist Movement* (Toronto: University of Toronto, 1984), 101, 153. See also H. Barge, ed., *Andreas Bodenstein von Karlstadt, Teil 2: Karlstadt als Vorkaempfer des laienchristlichen Puritanismus* (Leipzig: Friedrich Brandstetter, 1905), 146, 148, 161.

23. We have already noted that the impact of the spiritualistic tendency in Anabaptism was blunted by factors such as ecclesiology. This is most extensively the case with Marpeck, but see also M. Brecht, "Herkunft und Eigenart der Taufanschauung der Züricher Täufer," *ARG* 64 (1973): 147-153.

24. Hertzsche, ed., *Karlstadts Schriften*, 20, 37.

25. R. Sider, ed., *Karlstadt's Battle with Luther* (Philadelphia: Fortress, 1978), 5-15. Also, see below, chap. 2, under "Developments in Hubmaier's Eucharistic Thought."

26. Pater, 290-294, 11.

27. Bromiley, 199-207; C. Lindberg, ed. & trans., "Karlstadt's Dialogue on the Lord's Supper, *MQR* 53 (Jan. 1979): 55; Barge, 178.

28. "Zwingli's Thought," a review of G. Locher's book, by C. W. Dugmore, *JEH* 41 (Apr. 1983): 291; Pater, 130-134.

29. Hertzsche, 32ff.; Bromiley, 212-216, 220-223.

30. Pater, 50-53; Bromiley, 236-237. Also, on Zwingli, see "Action or Use of the Lord's Supper" (a liturgy), in *Liturgies of the Western Church*, ed by B. Thompson (Cleveland: Collins, 1979), 153-154.

31. Bromiley, 187-193. The influence of Zwingli's tropistic interpretation on subsequent Mennonite teaching about the Lord's Supper is more pervasive than it was during the Reformation. It plays a significant but secondary role in the thought of two of our subjects, Pilgram Marpeck and Dirk Philips.

32. G. Hershberger, ed., *The Recovery of the Anabaptist Vision* (Scottdale, Pa.: Her-

ald Press, 1958), esp. 37. The most far-reaching interpretation of this view is J. H. Yoder, *Täufertum und Reformation in Gespräch* (Zurich: EVZ, 1968), esp. 3, with a summary.

33. C. J. Dyck, ed., *Legacy of Faith* (Newton, Kan.: Faith & Life, 1962), 79.

34. A comprehensive exposition on these changes may be found in Stayer, 84, note 2; also cf. J. Stayer, *Anabaptism and the Sword* (Lawrence, Kan.: Coronado Press, 1972); H. J. Goertz, ed., *Umstrittenes Täufertum* (Göttingen: Vandenhoeck und Ruprecht, 1975; W. Packull, *Mysticism and the Early South German–Austrian Anabaptist Movement* (Scottdale, Pa.: Herald Press, 1977); W. Klaassen, *Anabaptism: Neither Catholic nor Protestant* (Waterloo, Ont.: Conrad, 1973).

35. Goertz in *Die Täufer*, 12, 76, limits its commonalities to the rejection of infant baptism, the assertion of adult baptism, radical social dissent, and anticlericalism.

36. Even where this claim includes the influence of sacramentarianism, as in H. S. Bender, "Communion," *ME*, 1:651-656, it does not cover the diversity in early Anabaptist eucharistic thought. Recent research in the field of Swiss Brethren origins suggests, as noted above, that Karlstadt is the source of several tenets of the teaching concerning the breaking of bread as held by Zwingli and the Grebel circle. This theory is examined in more detail in the concluding chapter.

37. The formative influence of Hoffmann, Karlstadt, and Schwenckfeld on the figures of our study is evidence for this claim. See below, esp. chap. 4, "Dirk Philips."

38. For Menno Simons this was his initial point of dissent from the old church. *Menno Simons Writings* (Elkhart, Ind.: J. Funk, 1871) 40ff.

39. J. F. G. Göters, ed., *Studien zur Geschichte und Theologie der Reformation* (Neukirchen: Neukirchener, 1969), 259; W. Packull, "The Common Man" (unpublished ms., 1993), 4ff.

40. Yoder, 202.

41. Göters, 270.

42. Marpeck never tires of emphasizing that the Lord's Supper happens when believers meet in faith and love. Only then are they ready to be made one with each other and Christ: *Marpeck*, 263-268.

43. H. Relton, *A Study in Christology* (London: SPCK, 1917), 9, 37; J. McIntyre, *The Shape of Christology* (London: SCM, 1966), 91ff.

44. Bromiley, 212ff.; P. Walpot, ed., "Das grosse Artikelbuch," in R. Friedmann, ed., *Glaubenszeugnisse Oberdeutscher Taufgesinnter*, vol. 1 (Gütersloh: Gerd Mohn, 1967), 126-134, 154ff., et passim.

45. The difference between Luther's view and Schwenckfeld's is the most striking illustration of this fact.

46. *Schriften*, 104.

47. *Marpeck*, 76ff.

48. The latter Christology, for example, brings the two natures of Christ into full play in Marpeck's Lord's Supper. But the motif of the humanity of Christ (*menschheit Christi*) recedes in Marpeck. On the contrary, in Dirk it emerges at the end of his corpus as a corrective to the influence of another Christology.

49. Even Dirk, whose thought includes more emphasis on the individual communion of the believer with Christ than Marpeck and Hubmaier, retains the church's power of the keys and a strict biblicism as a counterpoint to it.

50. Marpeck develops this most explicitly in his teaching of co-witness, but it is present in all three theologians.

51. *Dirk*, 483.

52. *Schriften*, 301; *Marpeck*, 78ff. Though they make the same claim, their Christology and eucharistic doctrine are entirely different.

53. Aloys Grillmeier in *Christ in Christian Tradition* (Atlanta: John Knox, 1975), 545, describes the goal of the Council of Chalcedon as a solution to the problem of "how the confession of the one Christ may be reconciled with belief in the true God and true man," "perfect in Godhead, perfect in manhood." Though Hubmaier, Marpeck, and Dirk all subscribed to this confession, its functional role in their theology did not maintain the

balance. They all asserted the permanence of his humanity, yet that humanity had an uncertain role in Christ's present work in the world.

54. For a helpful discussion of the Gospel as a whole, but especially the history of the interpretation of John 6, see R. Brown, *The Gospel of John (i-xii)* (Garden City: Doubleday, 1966), 272ff.

Chapter 2: Balthasar Hubmaier

1. T. Bergsten, *Balthasar Hubmaier: Seine Stellung zu Reformation und Täufertum 1521-1528* (Kassel: J. G. Oncken, 1961), 456.
2. G. Westin and T. Bergsten, eds., *Balthasar Hubmaier Schriften* (Gütersloh: Gerd Mohn, 1962), 57. References are to this original text, hereafter called *Schriften*.
3. D. Steinmetz, *Reformers in the Wings* (Grand Rapids: Baker, 1971), 207.
4. C. Windhorst, "Wort und Geist," *MGB* 31, N.F. 16 (1974): 8.
5. Bergsten, 70-75.
6. Steinmetz, 199-200
7. W. Moore, "Catholic Teacher and Anabaptist Pupil: The Relationship Between John Eck and Balthasar Hubmaier," *ARG* 72 (1981): 79-93.
8. Bergsten, 76-90.
9. Bergsten, 96-103
10. *Schriften*, 73.
11. Steinmetz, 205; G. W. Bromiley, *Zwingli and Bullinger*, vol. 24 of Library of Christian Classics, ed. by G. Bromiley (Philadelphia: Westminster, 1958), 183-184.
12. *Schriften*, 110, 112, 383, 385, et passim.
13. R. Amour, *Anabaptist Baptism* (Scottdale, Pa.: Herald Press, 1966), 56.
14. "A Most Christian Letter," in H. Obermann, ed., *Forerunners of the Reformation: The Shape of Late Mediaeval Thought*, trans. by P. Nyhus (New York: Holt, Rinehart, and Winston, 1966), 268-277, esp. 274-275.
15. "On the Lord's Supper," in Bromiley, 187-192.
16. C. Pater, *Karlstadt as the Father of the Baptist Movements* (Toronto: University of Toronto, 1984), 101.
17. K.-H. zur Mühlen, "Zur Rezeption der augustinischen Sakramentsformel . . . in der Theologie Luthers," in *ZTK* 70 (1973): 51.
18. C. Windhorst, *Täuferisches Taufverständnis*, vol. 16 of Studies in Mediaeval and Reformation Thought (Leiden, E. J. Brill, 1976), 102.
19. *Schriften*, 352; H. Wayne Pipkin and John H. Yoder, eds., *Balthasar Hubmaier: Theologian of Anabaptism*, Classics of the Radical Reformation, vol. 5 (Scottdale, Pa.: Herald Press, 1989), 391. This is the translation cited, compared with the original, and amended where shown. Hereafter it is called *Hubmaier*.
20. *Schriften*, 346.
21. *Schriften*, 112, 114. Hubmaier nowhere spends time arguing this position but makes it a working assumption throughout his writings. He is indebted to the Abelardian moral-influence theory of the atonement and stands against the Anselmian satisfaction theory, which was pivotal for Luther's theology and part of the *Vorverständnis* of his sacramental teaching. 26.
22. *Schriften*, 104, 317-318; *Hubmaier*, 76.
23. *Schriften*, 393.
24. *Schriften*, 303.
25. *Schriften*, 103.
26. *Schriften*, 121-122.
27. *Schriften*, 181.
28. *Schriften*, 384.
29. *Zwingli*, 2:664-803.
30. *Zwingli*, 2:786.
31. *Zwingli*, 2:786.

32. *Zwingli*, 2:786-787.

33. *Zwingli*, 2:789.

34. R. J. Sider, *Andreas Bodenstein von Karlstadt: The Development of His Thought, 1517-1525* (Leiden: E. J. Brill, 1974), 5; Pater, 56-58, 134, 158.

35. Bromiley, 35.

36. But in 1525, when each of the three reformers had institutionalized a new liturgical practice, Grebel's position was maintained, Zwingli allowed for either, but Hubmaier allowed only for the minister's role. L. von Muralt and W. Schmid, eds., *Quellen zur Geschichte der Täufer in der Schweitz*, vol. 1 (Zürich: S. Hirzel Verlag, 1952), 15-16; B. Thompson, ed., *Liturgies of the Western Church* (Cleveland: Collins, 1962), 153-154.

37. *Zwingli*, 2:733, 736, 746.

38. G. Locher, *Zwingli's Thought: New Perspectives* (Leiden: E. J. Brill, 1981), 21.

39. G. Dix, *The Shape of the Liturgy* (London: Dacre, 1975), 630. Dix offers a succinct analysis of the notion of transubstantiation and Zwingli's attempt to give another answer to the age-old question of the nature of Christ's presence: Dix, 631-633.

40. Thompson, 153-154.

41. W. Roeter, *Des Heiligen Augustinus Schriften als liturgische Quellen* (Munich: Max Hüber, 1930), 134, 165.

42. K. Bornkamm and G. Ebeling, eds., *Martin Luther, ausgewählte Schriften* (Frankfurt/Main: Insel, 1982), 2:63-64.

43. Bromiley, 188.

44. Bromiley, 237.

45. *Schriften*, 72-74.

46. *Schriften*, 102.

47. *Schriften*, 103.

48. *Schriften*, 101.

49. *Schriften*, 102; Erich Hertzsche, ed., *Karlstadts Schriften aus den Jahren 1523-1525* (Halle: Max Niemeyer, 1957), 1:13, 20.

50. *Schriften*, 103.

51. *Schriften*, 103, 300.

52. Bornkamm and Ebeling, 55-58, 71. This emphasis is also found in Luther's description of the Lord's Supper but placed within different pneumatological assumptions than in Hubmaier.

53. A historical point of reference is illuminating here. The traditional wisdom on the subject held that *Deus non allegatus sacramentis* (God is not confined to the sacraments). Hubmaier takes this claim that God is not confined to the sacraments beyond the traditional intentions to insist that God cannot work through them.

54. *Schriften*, p. 121.

55. *Schriften*, 103; *Hubmaier*, 75; *Schriften*, 358, gives another formulation of the same thought.

56. *Schriften*, 104; *Hubmaier*, 76. Hubmaier's most radical sacramental claim for the Holy Supper, in which the thing signified is no longer Christ but the community, is not applied in the case of baptism. To illustrate, in an extended treatment of the triad, Spirit, word, and sacrament as it applies to baptism, Hubmaier again relates the Spirit entirely to the word which is at work in the inner person. But in this case, the outer act testifies to the inwardly given gift. This is the first reality signified by baptism. The second and inseparable part of this event is that believers pledge themselves by asking for the sign of baptism to begin the Christian life in the church (*Schriften*, 121-122).

This comparison of baptism and the Lord's Supper highlights the fact that two ceremonies are not parallel in the character of their outward and inward nature. The "inward essence" of the Supper is the church's covenant of love; the "inward essence" of baptism is the Spirit and the Spirit's work of imparting forgiveness. The inward essence of baptism precedes and is distinguished from the outer. It is the receiving of life, "with the fire of the divine word through the Holy Spirit" (*Schriften*, 104, 121). In contrast to baptism, the Lord's Supper is not preceded by a specific, inward act of the Spirit. The breaking of bread builds on the pledge made by the believer to live as a member of the body of Christ.

57. *Schriften,* 104; also see 301 for the elaboration of this theme.

58. *Schriften,* 122.

59. *Schriften,* 103.

60. *Schriften,* 193, 201, 203.

61. *Schriften,* 212.

62. Bromiley, 187ff.; *Schriften,* 118ff.

63. From the brevity of Hubmaier's reference to past debate on the nature of the Eucharist, we cannot determine the extent to which he is aware of examinations in previous centuries of the questions to which he turns. J. Pelikan summarizes the debate over the Lord's Supper from the eleventh to the sixteenth centuries: *The Christian Tradition,* vol. 3: *The Growth of Medieval Theology* (Chicago: University of Chicago, 1978), 184-214; vol. 4: *Reformation of Church and Dogma* (1984), 52-68.

64. *Schriften,* 212.

65. *Schriften,* 291.

66. *Schriften,* 293.

67. *Schriften,* 293.

68. In his analysis, Hubmaier could be described in words Bromiley, 37, uses of Zwingli: "Zwingli's theology has clarity and consistency which are not always apparent in the more diffuse if more profound writings of Luther. Indeed, the common impression made by Zwingli's dogmatic works is that he has brought to the task a more powerful intellectual understanding than spiritual inwardness and insight. In spite of his obvious stylistic weaknesses, he always presses home his arguments with great acuteness and dialectical skill; yet with all the logic of his presentation he often fails to carry complete conviction because even his constant appeals to Scripture suggest a lack of perception of the deeper bearing of the passages cited. It is not that Zwingli does not penetrate to the ultimate themes of Scripture. Nor is it that he is without a genuineley personal apprehension. But in his handling of individual passages he relies far too much upon logical subtlety rather than a basic spiritual apprehension."

69. *Schriften,* 296.

70. *Schriften,* 297.

71. *Schriften,* 297-298.

72. *Schriften,* 299.

73. *Schriften,* 300, 103.

74. *Schriften,* 300; *Hubmaier,* 333.

75. *Schriften,* 293.

76. *Schriften,* 293.

77. *Schriften,* 303-304.

78. Bromiley, 188ff.

79. *Schriften,* 103.

80. J. Calvin, *The Institutes of the Christian Religion,* ed. by J. McNeill, trans. by F. Battles (Philadelphia: Westminster Press, 1960), 2:1277-1278; Bornkamm and Ebeling, 52-68.

81. *Schriften,* 301; *Hubmaier,* 333-334.

82. *Schriften,* 301.

83. Roeter, 121, 129, 134.

84. C. Windhorst, "Das Gedächtnis des Leidens Christi und Pflichtzeichen brüderlicher Liebe," in H.-J. Goertz, ed., *Umstrittenes Täufertum 1525-1975* (Göttingen: Vandenhoeck und Ruprecht, 1975), 127, 130.

85. The relevent question is whether Hubmaier had simply not heard of Hoen's interpretation before he reconstructed his eucharistic thought or whether part of his initial reconstruction was the rejection of that approach. Hubmaier visited and worked with Zwingli during the time when the latter appropriated Hoen's tropism, but Hubmaier made no reference to that tropism. Obermann, 253; Bergsten, 110, 113.

86. Would Hubmaier not have found it difficult, perhaps even pointless, to participate in the Marburg Colloquy? He had already placed himself outside the frame of reference shared by its participants. See M. Lehman, ed., *Luther's Works* (Philadelphia: Fortress, 1980), esp. 38:5-15, 88.

87. *Schriften*, 300.

88. *Schriften*, 298.

89. *Schriften*, 297, 293.

90. *Schriften*, 298.

91. *Schriften*, 162, 300.

92. *Schriften*, 302.

93. Windhorst, "Das Gedächtnis," 123.

94. C. Mayer, *Die Zeichen in der geistlichen Entwicklung und in der Theologie des jungen Augustinus* (Würzburg: Augustinus, 1969), 29ff., 311, 330. Yet among other things, Augustine's Christology distinguishes his view from that of his sixteenth-century followers, for example, "Weil das Göttliche sich inkarniert hat sind Sakramente möglich" (Mayer, 311). Nevertheless, Zwingli cites Ambrose and Jerome as well as Augustine in defense of his "spiritualist" position (Bromiley, 231).

95. Windhorst, *Taufverständnis*, 200-213.

96. *Zwingli*, 2:718, 760.

97. Though their Christologies are quite different, Marpeck makes the same move as Hubmaier does in relating the incarnation to the church, and by extension, to the Supper; cf., *Marpeck*, 81, 85, 89, et passim. A. Beachy, *The Concept of Grace in the Radical Reformation* (Nieuwkoop: B. de Graaf, 1977), 94, sees the church in Dirk Philips' writing as a "quasi physical extension of the incarnation."

98. *Schriften*, 171.

99. *Schriften*, 370; *Hubmaier*, 414.

100. *Schriften*, 350.

101. *Schriften*, 371.

102. *Schriften*, 370.

103. R. Bauchlam in *Knowing God Incarnate* (Bramcote: Grove, 1983), 5-6, describes the type of Hubmaier's position as it has appeared in current theological debate. It is worth quoting at length: "This view, that for authentic Christianity the living Christ has a necessary and active role in the present has been challenged by some recent writers, notably, among British theologians, by G. W. H. Lampe, in *God as Spirit* and by A. T. Hanson in *The Image of the Invisible*. They claim that what Christians have meant when they have talked about the living presence of Christ can be adequately re-expressed today without reference to any personal activity of Jesus himself since his earthly history. For Lampe, it is better to talk about the presence and activity of God the Spirit who was in Jesus, while Hanson would say that we know God the Logos in the form or image of Jesus Christ. God has given revelation of himself in the life of Jesus of Nazareth, so that Christians now know God through the history of Jesus, but do not now know Jesus himself as a living person. Where this view falls short of traditional Christian belief is in holding that God's revelation of himself to us is not Jesus himself, but the earthly history of Jesus. Revelation took place in Jesus' life, death, and (for Hanson) resurrection, but then Jesus himself has no further role to play."

104. *Schriften*, 358-359.

105. *Schriften*, 318; *Hubmaier*, 355.

106. *Schriften*, 121.

107. *Schriften*, 111, 121-123, 194, et passim.

108. The one possible exception to this has already been mentioned: *Schriften*, 103. There is no causal relationship between word and ceremony in the case of the Supper. Compare the role of the word in baptism: *Schriften*, 127, 159, 370.

109. Regarding the role of the Trinity in baptism according to Marpeck, see *Marpeck* 84, 121, 139, 188, 338.

110. *Schriften*, 113, 159.

111. *Schriften,* 127.
112. *Schriften,* 355, 361-362.
113. *Schriften,* 355-356.
114. *Schriften,* 356-365.
115. *Schriften,* 355.
116. *Schriften,* 362.
117. Bergsten, 96.
118. S. Peachey and P. Peachey, "Answer of Some Who Are Called (Ana) Baptists
. . .," *MQR* 45 (1971): 10ff.; "Congregational Order," in J. Yoder, ed., *The Legacy of Michael Sattler* (Scottdale, Pa.: Herald Press, 1973), 44-45; "Gemeinsame Ordnung der Glieder Christ," in H. Fast, ed., *Der linke Flügel der Reformation,* vol. 4 of Klassiker des Protestantismus (Bremen: Carl Schünemann, 1962), 130-137.
119. Muralt and Schmidt, 13-21.
120. *Schriften,* 356.
121. *Schriften,* 356. The choice of reading remains his; what matters is that the death of the Lord be proclaimed, that people see the boundless goodness of Christ, and that the church be built up in love. The suggested lections say much about the tone the service will have. Hubmaier recommends that either the eucharistic passages in 1 Corinthians 10 or 11, the farewell discourses of John 13-17, or the penitential passages in Matthew 3, Luke 3, and Ecclesiastes 2 be used. The inclusion of the Johannine discourses is noteworthy. It provides a devotional, vertical dimension to the eucharistic gathering in addition to the ethical, horizontal emphasis of the penitential readings.
122. *Schriften,* 356. The congregants are cautioned against superficial chatter or speculation about the hiddenness of God or the last things. They are to concentrate on doctrine, faith, and love. The one who is given a revelation should teach it to the congregation. In its following of 1 Corinthians 14, *Nachtmahl* is on common ground with the other three Anabaptist orders of worship referred to above. It is probable that even prior to the formation of Anabaptist congregations, their assemblies were guided by this rule. The astonishing thing about Hubmaier's acceptance of this pattern is that he brings its charismatic freedom together with liturgical order.
123. *Schriften,* 356-357. This reading is not a bare recitation of the text but one shaped for the purposes of this liturgy. He omits verse 30, concerning the sickness of believers, and conflates verse 31 with the first line of verse 32. It is impossible to judge whether this form of the text was the result of a conscious process of editing or the result of citation from memory. An explanatory reference to the title of the presider is necessary here. Generally the term *Priester* is used in *Nachtmahl,* but at the fraction he is called *Bischoff* (Schriften, 362). By 1527 both terms are anachronistic in Hubmaier's frame of reference. Likely these titles were retained by the author to claim full validity for his Lord's Supper.
124. *Schriften,* 357.
125. *Schriften,* 358. The same claim is made by Dirk; see A. Kolb, trans., *Enchiridion* (Aylmer, Ont.: Pathway, 1978), 78-79.
126. *Schriften,* 358, 362; cf. 293 et passim.
127. *Schriften,* 375. Those who are to be excommunicated are called "sacrament breakers" (*sakramentsbrichig*) because they have broken the promise.
128. *Schriften,* 358-359; *Hubmaier,* 399.
129. *Schriften,* 361.
130. *Schriften,* 361-362; *Hubmaier,* 403-404. An earlier translation with commentary was made by W. McGlothlin, "An Anabaptist Liturgy of the Lord's Supper," *BRE* (Jan.) 1906:92.
131. Two interpretations of the manner of distribution are possible here. The more obvious one is that the narrative words are uttered once before the distribution. But the instructions are ". . . brichts, vnnd beut es den Beysitzenden in ire hennd vnd sagt. . . ." It is as if the words of institution are spoken to each communicant. It could also be that the words and the invitation are repeated not to one individual, but to a number of people as

the presider moves through the congregation. This was to be the common pattern in later Mennonite practice; cf. B. Eby, *Kurzgefasste Kirchengeschichte und Glaubenslehre* (Scottdale: Mennonitische Verlagshandlung, n.d. reprint of 1841 ed.), 203.

132. After the first statement of blessing, "Hiemit seyd got beuolhen," a seemingly unrelated call is given to praise God. This might be a variant of the response, "Thanks be to God," given by the people in some liturgies after the presider's words of parting. Then follow the closing words of the Mass: "Steend auft vnd geend hin in dem frid Christi Jesu." Is this last pronouncement an incorrect recapitulation of the first line of Paul's great blessing in the name of the triune God (2 Cor. 13:13)? Instead of the "grace of our Lord Jesus Christ," which he uses twice earlier in *Nachtmahl*, Hubmaier's text reads, the "grace of God be with us all." Whatever its source, the closing rite lacks the economy of language and straightforwardness of the other prayers in the service. This rather cumbersome conclusion to an otherwise refined and literate order of service resists easy explanation. Perhaps the upheaval in liturgical practice meant that among the reformers, there was not yet a standard form of dismissal.

133. *Schriften*, 364.

134. *Schriften*, 354.

135. *Schriften*, 358.

136. *Schriften*, 357-358; *Hubmaier*, 397.

137. *Schriften*, 104.

138. An echo of Paul's ecclesiology comes through: "Always carrying in the body the death of Jesus, so that the life of Jesus may also be made visible in our bodies. For while we live, we are always being given up to death for Jesus' sake, so that the life of Jesus may be made visible in our mortal flesh" (2 Cor. 4:10-11).

139. *Schriften*, 358.

140. *Schriften*, 104.

141. Windhorst, *Taufverständnis*, 211-212.

142. *Schriften*, 210.

143. The spoken parts of the service, that is, the prayers and instructions, in contrast to the accompanying commentary, are succinct and compact. This is particularly the case with the invitations to communion. Both invitations are parallel in structure and differ in content only to the extent that references appropriate to bread and wine are included (*Schriften*, 62, 363). Since such precision and brevity are not characteristic of Hubmaier's writing style, one is tempted to explain this dissonance by proposing that, like the confession of sin, the communion prayers and invitations might have been taken over from other liturgical sources. Though the difference between text and commentary consists not only of style but also of terminology, one striking example argues against assigning various parts of the service to different sources. It is the memorial phrase, "a living memorial of his suffering," or variations thereof. It appears in the commentary (*Schriften*, 358), the pledge (362), and the instructions for the bread (362). This suggests that the difference lies with the author. When he write theologically, he is expansive; when he writes liturgically, he is concise. This is not to say that no borrowing took place, but that throughout there is evidence of Hubmaier's thought. The pledge of love, though not as compact as other liturgical statements contained in *Nachtmahl*, so fully expresses the author's views that it was likely his composition. This probability is reinforced by the structural and substantive parallel between the questions in the pledge of love and those in the *Form zu Taufen* (*Schriften*, 349-350). The three orders—for baptism, communion, and the ban—betray a hand skilled in matters liturgical. They have an inner affinity of style and substance. Windhorst notes that the statement in the baptismal formulary on discipline, directly antecedent to the pledge of love, is without parallel in liturgical texts (*Taufverständnis*, 137). Lastly, any evaluation of Hubmaier's creativity needs to bear in mind that liturgy, especially that of the Lord's Supper, was the focus of Hubmaier's reform interests both in his Catholic years in Waldshut and at the Second Zurich Disputation.

144. *Schriften*, 364; *Hubmaier*, 406.

145. *Schriften*, 293.
146. *Schriften*, 358, 362; *Hubmaier*, 398, 404.
147. *Schriften*, 293.
148. *Schriften*, 368.
149. *Schriften*, 369.
150. *Schriften*, 369.
151. *Schriften*, 368.
152. *Schriften*, 370.
153. *Schriften*, 300.
154. Bromiley, 199, 211. *Marpeck*, 76-89, 422-423, relates the image of the flesh to the revelation of Christ's humanity. For Dirk's view, see *Kolb*, 69-71, 100-102.
155. R. Armour, *Anabaptism Baptism* (Scottdale, Pa.: Herald Press, 1966), 137.
156. C. Windhorst, "Balthasar Hubmaier," in H.-J. Goertz, ed., *Radikale Reformatoren* (Munich: C. H. Beck, 1978), 132.
157. *Schriften*, 43.

Chapter 3: Pilgram Marpeck

1. Manfred Krebs and Hans George Rott, eds., *Quellen zur Geschichte der Täufer*, vol. 7: *Elsass*, part 1 (Gütersloh: Gerd Mohn, 1959), 352. Hereafter this source is called *Elsass*.
2. Stephen Boyd has argued for the probable influence on Marpeck by the radical preacher Jakob Strauss, starting in 1522. Boyd follows Marpeck to Rattenberg, where the influence of Stephen Castenbauer and Leonhart Schiemer is documented. Their theology has a Lutheran spirit but is characterized by the ethics and mysticism of the *Theologia Deutsch*. Stephen Boyd, "Pilgram Marpeck and the Justice of Christ" (Ph.D. diss., Harvard University, 1984), 46ff., 56ff., 83ff.
3. William Klassen and Walter Klaassen, eds., *The Writings of Pilgram Marpeck*, The Classics of the Radical Reformation, vol. 2 (Scottdale, Pa.: Herald Press, 1978), 333-334. Hereafter this translation is called *Marpeck*.
4. Boyd, 226-238.
5. Neal Blough, *Christologie anabaptiste: Pilgram Marpeck et l'humanité du Christ* (Geneva: Labour et Fides, 1982), 33.
6. *Marpeck*, 211-221.
7. Gregory Dix, *The Shape of the Liturgy* (London: Daccre, 1975), 630.
8. *Inner* and *outer* are elastic terms. In this discussion, *inner* means simply the immaterial reality of God, and *outer* means the material manifestations of that reality without specifying the relationship between the two. This relationship will be spelled out as the investigation proceeds.
9. This claim had a revolutionary effect in preparing the way for reform. In its most radical form, such existential faith made outward means of grace redundant. See Steven Ozment, *The Age of Reform* (New Haven: Yale University Press, 1980), 115ff. Boyd, 2-4, 109-114, is able to identify Leonhart Schiemer and Hans Schlaffer as sources of mystical notions in Marpeck.
10. C. Windhorst, *Täuferisches Taufverständnis*, vol. 16 of Studies in Mediaeval and Reformation Thought (Leiden: E. J. Brill, 1976), 195. Dutch sacramentarianism is commonly identified as the mediator of this evolution in Augustinian theology to the Reformation, especially to Reformed and Anabaptist circles. See George Williams, *The Radical Reformation* (Philadelphia: Westminster, 1962), 27-37; Cornelius Krahn, *Dutch Anabaptism* Scottdale, Pa.: Herald Press, 1981), 44-56. The Dutch sacramentarian, Cornelius Hoen, put forth a revolutionary exegesis of the words of institution. Interpreting them tropistically, Hoen argued, "This signifies my body" (Oberman, H., ed., *Forerunners of the Reformation*, trans. by P. Nyhus [New York: Holt, Rinehart and Winston, 1966], 267). By means of this insight, Zwingli was able to complete the recasting of his theology of the Lord's Supper.

11. Dix, 631.

12. Klaus Deppermann, *Melchior Hoffmann* (Göttingen: Vandenhoeck & Ruprecht, 1979), 196ff. This lack of Melchiorite influence on Marpeck is arguable also from the internal evidence. The Christology of *BEK* and *VMN* is of a decidedly different composition than Hoffmann's. In fact, Hoffmann's Christology was the inspiration for that of Caspar Schwenckfeld, Marpeck's great rival. See Deppermann, 186-191.

13. P. Althaus, *The Theology of Martin Luther* (Philadelphia: Fortress, 1966), 376, 398.

14. Blough, 65-72. Blough establishes the affinity between Marpeck and Luther and argues for Luther's influence on Marpeck's Christology and his view of the ceremonies.

15. Among Marpeck's conversations with Bucer and the Strassburg city council, the most substantive was his presentation of a confession of faith and Bucer's submission of a commentary of the same length (*Elsass*, 351-410). The points of contention were the nature of faith, baptism, and the church. Marpeck contended against Bucer that baptism was indispensable to faith and that the church of believers was a visible body.

16. These treatises were rediscovered in the 1950s and first attributed to Marpeck's spiritualist opponents. William Klassen in *Covenant and Community* (Grand Rapids: Eerdmanns, 1968), 36-45, first argued the case that Marpeck was their author. Subsequent studies of these documents have confirmed his judgment. See, for example, Blough, 43-65. However, Blough questions Klassen's claim that the *KU* was written against Schwenckfeld.

17. *Marpeck*, 44, 52, 54

18. *Marpeck*, 45.

19. *Marpeck*, 60-64. *Marpeck*, 378-381, returns to this same theme in the Letter to Helene von Streicher.

20. *Marpeck*, 63. This anchor in the incarnation is in place in all Marpeck's writings under consideration. See *Marpeck*, 85, 228; J. Loserth, ed., *Pilgram Marbecks Antwort auf Kaspar Schwenckfelds Beurteilung des Buches der Bundesbezeugung von 1542*, Quellen und Forschungen zur Geschichte der oberdeutschen Taufgesinnten im 16. Jahrhundert (Wien: Carl Fromm, 1929), 112-113, 298, 558, 576.

21. *Marpeck*, 60, 65.

22. *Marpeck*, 76, 99.

23. *Marpeck*, 76, 82.

24. *Marpeck*, 76, 72, also calling ceremonies human "works of faith."

25. *Marpeck*, 79.

26. *Marpeck*, 80; also see Loserth, 561, 563, 565, for the same use of the term *parable.*

27. *Marpeck*, 84.

28. Frank Wray, "The *Vermanung* of 1542 and Rothmann's *Bekenntnisse*," *ARG* 47 (1956): 242-251. Two-thirds of *VMN* is Bernhard Rothmann's *Bekenntnis von beiden Sakramenten* of 1533, found in Robert Stupperich, ed., *Die Schriften Bernhard Rothmanns* (Münster: Aschendorfsche Verlagsbuchhandlung, 1970), 138-195.

29. It is not difficult to see what made *BEK* attractive to Marpeck. The only comparable-length treatment of the Lord's Supper in early northern Anabaptism is Hendrik Rol's, *Die Slotel van dat Secreet des Nachtmals,* pastoral rather than theological in tone and overtly spiritualistic. See *BRN* 5:44-123.

30. Copies of two sixteenth-century editions were rediscovered in the twentieth century. One was found in the Würtembergische Landesbibliothek and is the basis for a modern printing in Christian Neff, ed., *Gedenkschrift zum 400 Jährigen Jubiläum der Mennoniten oder Taufgesinnten* (Ludwigshafen: Konferenz der Süddeutschen Mennoniten, 1925), 185-282. The other copy was found in the British Museum and is the basis for the translation into English found in *Marpeck.* The outstanding virtue of the *Marpeck* edition is that it identifies with italics all the text added by Marpeck. This characteristic makes it the most helpful reference text. As we proceed, it will be systematically checked

against both the Neff and Stupperich editions.

31. *Marpeck,* 95-196, on the Trinity and ceremonies; 209-210, on baptism as participation in Christ's nonresistance, with explicit criticism of the Münsterites; 223-241, on baptism and the old and new covenants; 245-253, on infants, reason, and sin in relation to baptism.

32. *Marpeck,* 194, 249, 256, et passim.

33. See above in chapter 1, "Emerging Eucharistic Thoughts at the End of the Middle Ages," 26-29.

34. *Marpeck,* 163-164.

35. Klassen, 36-43, esp. 43.

36. Blough, 193-198. Other scholars in the field support this position: for example, Williams, 274, 465, 792; and Torsten Bergsten, "Pilgram Marbeck und seine Auseinandersetzung mit Caspar Schwenckfeld," *Kyrkohistorisk Arsshrift* 38 (1957-58): 112, 117, 130, 131 (offprint).

37. *Corpus Schwenckfeldianorum* (*CS*), ed. by E. E. Schultz Johnson (Leipzig: Breitkopf & Haertel, 1927), 8:169-214.

38. Loserth, 433.

39. *CS*, 8:179.

40. Loserth, 103 et passim.

41. This is most clearly set forth in "Vom Stillstandt beim Nachtmahl," in *CS,* vol. 4, ed. by C. D. Hartranft (Leipzig: Breitkopf & Haertel, 1914), 634-642.

42. Loserth, 61-584.

43. Klassen, 47.

44. *CV* and *KU* were first attributed to Bünderlin. On the basis of the continuity they exhibit with the purposes and novel theological constructs of *VMN* and *VWG*, present research supports Klassen's proposition that Marpeck wrote them (Klassen, 36-43, esp. 43). *CV* and *KU* are two early antispiritualist writings which exhibit a strong inner affinity with Marpeck's mature writings. *CV* introduces the incarnation as the basis of the church and its outward life; *KU* has a clear concept of the trinitarianism which is the genius both of *VMN* and *VWG*. The two early documents supply assumptions and arguments which reappear and are developed in the later two treatises. The commonality of authors is unmistakable. Whether there is more than one of them in each case is diffcult to judge. To unravel the authorship puzzle of *VMN* exceeds the bounds of this study. Briefly, the problem is the following: Wray has shown unmistakably that the source of *VMN* is Rothmann's *BEK* (see note 28, above). *VMN* has five signatories and the beginning of a eucharistic section with a completely different tone and orientation than that of the baptismal document under discussion. More than one author and more than one pattern of thinking must be present in them.

45. Scharnschlager was the acknowledged co-worker of Marpeck from 1527 to 1534 and again in the 1540s. Various assessments are offered of his theological and pastoral roles in the life of South German Anabaptism and of his relationship to Marpeck. All the assessments, however, share the following conclusion: "Any attempts to analyze differences between Marpeck and Scharnschlager is, however, futile, because in their writings we have what Horst Quiring first called a type of *Gemeindetheologie*" (G. Hein and W. Klassen, "Leupold Scharnschlager," *ME*, 4:446). A codex in which a handwritten copy of *VWG* is contained described it as the writing project of a collective of *elltisten Brüder* with no specific reference to Marpeck (Loserth, 49-50).

Kiewit takes this as adequate substantiation for the claim that Marpeck's writings are really a *Gemeindetheologie.* On the basis of stylistic differences between the two parts of *VWG*, he designates Marpeck as the author of the first part and Scharnschlager of the second: Jan J. Kiwiet, *Pilgram Marbeck* (Kassel: J. G. Oneken, 1957), 75. But then he adds immediately that the writings under scrutiny are not the work of an individual mind but the mirroring of the South German Anabaptist community. He comes to the conclusion that "Marpeck war ja nicht ein Theologe; er hat nicht privatim eine Art theologisches System aufstellen wollen, sondern gibt nur die Gedanken der oberdeutschen Taüfer wieder" (Kiwiet, 83).

46. Hans Guderian, *Die Täufer in Augsburg* (Pfaffenhofen: W. Ludwig, 1984), 98-100.

47. The introduction of novel terminology and a final retrenchment behind spiritualistic lines serve only to distinguish the last part of the VWG from its main body. The obvious suggestion is plausible, that it was finished by another member of the community, perhaps by Scharnschlager. But it suggests that the body of VWG as a whole is the work of an individual. When Marpeck died, another hand, not the master of the first author's thought, undertook to defend this position. The unknown scribe was willing to sacrifice Catholic substance in order not to be accused of sacrificing radical Protestant principle. His attempt to provide a final justification of what had been written in VMN represents neither Marpeck nor either version of the text we now identify with him. Examples of this are many. The different understanding of the term *humanity of Christ* stands in violation of Marpeck's usage. The sudden acknowledgment of a cleavage between the eucharistic passages in John and those in the rest of the New Testament, contradicts Marpeck's working assumption in all his writings.

48. Whether or not this hypothesis concerning authorship is true, two facts stand. First, Marpeck's writings articulate a theology of the Lord's Supper which unifies faith, element, and grace into a reality which is a communion with the body and blood of Christ. This teaching is sometimes obscure, unfinished in defense of the claims it advances, and occasionally contradictory in its inability to get beyond the retention of two eucharistic views to establish itself. But the line of its development is unmistakable. It transcends the contradictory eucharistic doctrines which emerged in the sixteenth century. Second, the closing pages of VWG are a capitulation to spiritualism, to the claim that faith and Spirit have no external reality and that the incarnation has no prolongation in the life of the church.

49. CV, *Marpeck*, 52, 65; KU, *Marpeck*, 76-81, 85, 88, 99, 103; VMN, *Marpeck*, 194, 215, 285, 292; VWG, Loserth, 452, 456, 467, 528-530, 559, 561, 568.

50. CV, *Marpeck*, 50; KU, *Marpeck*, 76-81, 83, 99; VMN, *Marpeck*, 194-196, 22-229; VWG, Loserth, 134-135, 482-488, 559.

51. KU, *Marpeck*, 88; VMN, *Marpeck*, 166, 186, 230, 249; VWG, Loserth, 109, 112, 124, 171, 455, 466, 567-568.

52. The incarnation as the basis and pattern of God's revelation is the decisive concept of KU (*Marpeck*, esp. 76-87). The threefold working of God is presented as the basis for sacraments and of the relationship between inner and outer in VMN (*Marpeck*, esp. 195-196, 226-229) as well as the chapters on the Eucharist in VWG (Loserth, 427-578). The sequence of revelation from Father to Son to Spirit, with many quotations of and allusions to John, is the subject of Marpeck's discussion of the old and new covenants in "Vom Glauben der alten Väter" (Loserth, 317-408).

53. Raymond Brown gives a helpful summary of them in *The Gospel of John (i-xii)*, Anchor Bible (Garden City: Doubleday, 1966), xxi-xl.

54. *Marpeck*, 76ff.

55. Loserth, 485, 535, et passim; *Marpeck*, 226-227.

56. *Marpeck*, 195; Loserth, 365, 381, 473, et passim.

57. *Marpeck*, 62, 76-77. At Schwenckfeld's accusation that he separates the two natures of Christ, Marpeck articulates his orthodox belief concerning the one person and two natures of Christ (Loserth, 496-502, 553-559).

58. This stands in contrast to the work of Hubmaier and Zwingli, whose sacramental views were examined in the previous chapter. Schwenckfeld was later to take advantage of Marpeck's theological rather than biblical thought patterns. He invalidated Marpeck's claims concerning the Eucharist because they were not taken from the text of Scripture (cf. Loserth, 441).

59. *Marpeck*, 195.

60. Loserth, 180-182, 186-187.

61. Loserth, 534ff., 561ff.

62. Loserth, 294, 302, 508.

63. *Marpeck*, 264; Loserth, 442-443.

64. *Marpeck*, 194; Loserth, 465-466.

65. *Marpeck*, 195, reasserts the humanity of Christ in its externality as the basis of the Lord's Supper; Loserth, 485-489.

66. Compare John 14 and 15, especially 14:6, 11, 20; 15:26. Both in John and in Marpeck, the references to the Holy Spirit are the culmination of the divine scheme of self-disclosure. While Marpeck's view of the relationship between Father and Son is clearly inspired by these texts, it is not in literal adherence to them. In John, for example the Father works in the Son; in Marpeck, the Father as Spirit works simultaneously with the Son. Historically speaking, during Jesus' time on earth, the Spirit is identified with the Father. After that, in the age of the church, the Spirit is identified with the Son. Marpeck follows the Johannine account in observing this distinction, crucial for the nature of ceremonies.

67. With this formulation of the parallel working of Son and Spirit, we can distinguish Marpeck's view of the church as the humanity of Christ and his view of the ceremonies from the views of Hubmaier.

68. *Marpeck*, 225.

69. *Marpeck*, 228.

70. *Marpeck*, 229, 231. This argument is referred to in the eucharistic section of VWG. It comes out most explicitly in the exegesis of the institutional narrative where he makes the remarkable claim that the Last Supper was no true Lord's Supper. Therefore, Christ was not yet glorified, since the Spirit was not yet working.

71. *Marpeck*, 232.

72. Loserth, 109, 508, 514.

73. *Marpeck*, 85.

74. *Marpeck*, 77.

75. Marpeck repeatedly makes this point in his christological wrangles with Schwenckfeld (Loserth, 496, 535, 553).

76. *Marpeck*, 81.

77. *Marpeck*, 86.

78. *Marpeck*, 226-237.

79. Blough, 65-71.

80. Deppermann, 190.

81. The train of thought presented by VWG in Loserth, 131-135, typifies the dynamic relationship between trinitarian and christological emphases. There is a strange description (131) of the Son as the third person of the Trinity. This strengthens the sense given in many of the fragments in this document that the character and role of the Son and Spirit are fluid and often interchangeable.

82. *CS*, 8:211.

83. Both of them place at the center the practice of the Christian life rather than dogma or ritual. They are agreed that its beginning lies in an existential relationship of faith in God through Christ. Nothing can substitute for that. Despite the spectacular *Stillstand* or suspension of sacraments which Schwenckfeld proposed in 1526, he remained open to the role of the ceremonies as signs in a Zwinglian fashion. In fact, Schwenckfeld's rationale for the suspension was that the sacraments had been too abused in a faithless manner for them to help the true believer to Christ.

84. Deppermann, 189, notes this act in relation to the progression of Schwenckfeld's argument.

85. Loserth, 471; Neff, 262.

86. Loserth, 472. Marpeck's text in VWG has "im h. geist warhaftig," and Loserth observes in a footnote that Schwenckfeld's original is also "im h. geist warhaftig."

87. Loserth, 472; see also 508, 558.

88. The germ of this idea originates in *CV, Marpeck*, 62-63.

89. Loserth, 474.

90. Loserth, 475.

91. Loserth, 476. The earlier distinction is repeated, however, on 477 et passim.

92. Loserth, 477.

93. Loserth, 478. This is the complete opposite of Marpeck's view, focused in his theory of the two covenants, both historically and theologically.

94. Loserth, 481.

95. This idea is present in the *KU*, where Marpeck is concerned about "despising the humanity of Christ" (*Marpeck*, 76-77, 85-86).

96. Loserth, 482.

97. Loserth, 483-484.

98. Loserth, 485.

99. Loserth, 486, 498.

100. Loserth, 559-578.

101. Loserth, 500.

102. Bergsten, 123, 125.

103. Loserth, 501, 505, et passim.

104. Loserth, 500, 501, 508.

105. Loserth, 502-507. On these pages Marpeck presents an apology for his christological views, claiming to answer questions left unaddressed by Schwenckfeld. The bulk of his argument concerns the localization of Christ in his physical being in heaven. One claim is particularly interesting because it involves his view of the relationship between Son and Spirit. Jesus could not have promised another Comforter if, in fact, that Comforter would be himself as they knew him. Throughout his writings, Marpeck conflates the Son in his spiritual being with the Spirit. So, the Spirit is the spiritual Christ. Marpeck's argument can be turned against him here. If the spiritual Christ and the Spirit are one, the sender and sent are one, something he discounts as impossible.

106. Loserth, 502.

107. Though Schwenckfeld formally repudiated Christ's creatureliness in the time of his incarnation, he continued to speak of a transformation; compare Marpeck's quotations of Schwenckfeld's *Von der leiblichen Stell* (Loserth, 498, 504).

108. Loserth, 507.

109. Loserth, 508. Marpeck moves from a theological to a biblical apologetic for his position. The disappearance of Jesus on the Emmaus road (Luke 24) and Paul's longing to die in order to be with Christ (Phil. 1)—these are two among many citations Marpeck employs to prove that in his human nature Christ is in heaven. Then he goes on to examine the spiritual body promised at the resurrection: it is still a human nature with all its characteristics. It will still not be able to be at more than one place at a time (Loserth, 509-515).

110. Loserth, 515.

111. Loserth, 516.

112. Bergsten, 123-125.

113. Bergsten, 123-135, takes this parallelism to suggest Marpeck as the author or, if not the sole author, certainly the guiding intellect behind both documents. See also Bergsten, 64, 133.

114. Both men use language which suggests this as their norm. Aloys Grillmeier discusses Chalcedon in *Christ in Christian Tradition* (Atlanta: John Knox, 1975), 544-554, esp. 553, and emphasizes the attempt to preserve the integrity of both Christ's nature and its consequences. Althaus, 376, points out that consubstantiation was Luther's attempt to use "the real presence . . . in exact analogy to Christology."

115. *Marpeck*, 47-49.

116. *Marpeck*, 88.

117. Neff, 207.

118. See note 51 for this chapter, above.

119. Loserth, 109. *Mitlaufend* is translated as "concomitantly" by Rollin Armour, *Anabaptist Baptism* (Scottdale: Herald Press, 1966), 125.

120. *Marpeck*, 94; Loserth, 82-83, reiterated on 102-103, 569-570.

121. *Marpeck*, 85. Cf. *VMN*, *Marpeck*, 195, 226; *VWG*, Loserth, 134, 535-537.

122. This basic conviction is sacrificed in the conclusion of *VWG*.

123. *Marpeck*, 99.

124. *Marpeck*, 88.

125. *Marpeck*, 169, 170.

126. *Marpeck*, 171-172.

127. In his notion of co-witness, Marpeck extends the vouching function to another level beyond the confession of the believer. A ceremony can vouch for the authenticity of faith held by the confessing individual. More is said on this development below.

128. *Marpeck*, 194.

129. *Marpeck*, 194.

130. Loserth, 127-178.

131. *CS*, 8:183-185. Schwenckfeld makes the curious accusation against Marpeck of patripassianism. He probably arrives at this judgment from the following equation: what the Father does inwardly, the Son does outwardly. This is not what is usually meant by patripassianism, but the logical extreme of Marpeck's position, one he does not follow, is that the Father must suffer inwardly if the Son is suffering outwardly.

132. Loserth, 127.

133. Loserth, 133, 134.

134. Loserth, 134-135. This argument recedes in *VWG II*, and the church as the unglorified body of Christ loses status. The debate focuses more and more on Christ's two natures as defined in classsical categories relating essentially to the person of Christ and not to the church.

135. Loserth, 135 and 154. This language comes into its own in the chapters dealing directly with the Lord's Supper. See Loserth, 427-493, et passim.

136. Loserth, 136-138.

137. Loserth, 179-188. Marpeck's direct response to Schwenckfeld was interrupted for a time in 1544. But the challenge the two movements posed to each other went on without a break.

138. Loserth, 181. This passage evokes the thought patterns of *KU*.

139. Loserth, 182.

140. Loserth, 186.

141. *CS*, 8:186.

142. *Marpeck*, 44, 52, 54, et passim.

143. This is the position accepted by Marpeck at the conclusion of *VWG*.

144. Guderian, 58ff.

145. See chap. 1, "Eucharist and Christology in the Reformation." Rothmann identifies its sources as Zwingli, Oecalampadius, Franck, and Bullinger (*Marpeck*, 278, 288).

146. Loserth, 559ff.

147. Neff, 255-256; *Marpeck*, 264.

148. Neff, 255; *Marpeck*, 264.

149. *Marpeck*, 265.

150. *Marpeck*, 265-267.

151. *Marpeck*, 266.

152. Neff, 257. The translation in *Marpeck* weakens the wording and meaning of both the Dutch (Stupperich, 178) and German (Neff, 257) by translating, "Become one with the body of Christ" (*Marpeck*, p. 267). The point is, rather, that when the church communes with Christ in faith and love, it becomes his body. Just before this, the translation has the effect of blunting what takes place in the Eucharist: "This eating and drinking is a sign of their participation in his body and blood and represents a lasting bond of love" (*Marpeck*, 266). Stupperich, 178, says, "The bread and cup of the Lord shall be eaten and drunk to the Lord's memory and to a participation of his body and blood and a constant bond of love." Neff, 256-257, says, "The bread and cup of the Lord shall be eaten and drunk by the true believers to the Lord's memory and to a participation of his body and blood and a constant bond of love." The force of the text suggests that commu-

nion in the bread and cup is participation in Christ's body and blood and is a bond of love. This view is undergirded by a comment later in the document in which unbelievers do not have true communion because they (rather than the elements) have not been consecrated (*Marpeck*, 274). The breaking of bread, then, is not the representation of an event but an event itself in which believers are transformed. This transformation is the gift of unity with Christ and with each other.

153. Stupperich, 178; Neff, 257; *Marpeck*, 267. Either Marpeck could not find a German work parallel to the Dutch or he thought the difference to be of no consequence for his position. The distinction suggests that the original author was intent to avoid an identity between the corporeal and sacramental body of Christ and the church.

154. W. Roeter, *Des Heiligen Augustinus Schriften als liturgische Quellen* (Munich: Max Hüber, 1930), 129, 134, 165.

155. *Marpeck*, 267-269.

156. *Marpeck*, 270.

157. *Marpeck*, 270.

158. Neff, 207; *Marpeck*, 195.

159. Neff, 254ff.; *Marpeck*, 263ff.

160. *Marpeck*, 273-274.

161. *Marpeck*, 274-275.

162. *Marpeck*, 278. Marpeck distances himself from authorities Rothmann cites. Especially in the case of Franck, this act of distancing is done in relation to his eucharistic theology. See *Marpeck*, 29.

163. *Marpeck*, 286-290. There is a strange turn in the text at this point. As it turns out, the figurative reading here advocated focuses not on the Zwinglian dictum that *est* means *significat* but the Karlstadtian claim that the body of which Christ spoke was his own as he sat at the table.

164. *Marpeck*, 291.

165. Bergsten, 133. He argues that the lack of unity and consistency in *VMN* and *VWG* is in part due to their having been composed by a circle of leaders of which Marpeck was the most prominent individual. For another view, see "The Question of Authorship," Bergsten, 127-128.

166. *CS*, 8:207; Loserth, 428, 430-431.

167. Loserth, 429.

168. *Loserth*, 435.

169. *Loserth*, 438.

170. *Loserth*, 440.

171. *CS*, 8:208-209. Marpeck works from Schwenckfeld's earlier assumption that the Lord's Supper is to be suspended. But in *JDM*, Schwenckfeld allows for ceremonies like the Lord's Supper as strictly human acts of response. He commends "a bodily gathering of believers to remember and imitate the love of Christ" but insists that the essential Supper is a spiritual feeding on Christ. Marpeck goes on to refute a contention Schwenckfeld has not made. He answers that to suspend the ceremonies is to say that "the Spirit of Christ's baptism" ceased working in the generation of the apostles. The Spirit gives life to the holy signs; when they are abrogated, the Spirit is also abrogated (Loserth, 433-434). Marpeck sees Schwenckfeld's concession to ceremonies as merely tactical because he isolates them from any contact with the Spirit.

172. Loserth, 442.

173. Loserth, 442, 443. The Johannine teaching on love is the basis for this thought pattern. The following are examples: "And so love comes to us through the recognition of God or of love." "It is just such love and the Holy Spirit which make life and make it lifegiving."

174. Loserth, 444.

175. Loserth, 444.

176. Loserth, 445.

177. Loserth, 446; reiterated in almost identical words on 447 and 448. This confes-

sion is the central assertion of Balthasar Hubmaier's eucharistic doctrine (*Schriften*, 104). In Marpeck's teaching on the subject, it is only one of a cluster of defining assertions.

178. *CS*, 8:211; Loserth, 447.

179. Loserth, 448. Later on the same page, he quotes a similar confession from *VMN*.

180. Loserth, 451-452.

181. Loserth, 452-453.

182. Loserth, 453.

183. Loserth, 454.

184. Loserth, 457. This passage is not unambiguous in its meaning. Poetical and metaphorical language appears throughout the treatise and leaves the reader uncertain as to how it is to be taken. Is this an unmediated spiritual communion with Christ in the Zwinglian sense? No. In the next paragraph, the author's intention becomes unmistakably clear. Though nothing happens to the elements, "their spiritual use, sense, and the understanding of faith prove to be a true communion or participation in the body and blood of Christ that through it he is truly present and so the outer and inner are a single Lord's Supper even though bread and wine remain themselves, namely, mere creatures and are not in themselves the Supper." This communion with Christ is with his whole humanity, spirit, soul, and body. This, Marpeck concludes, is the sense of Paul's words in 1 Corinthians 10.

185. Loserth, 457. The Spirit is repeatedly referred to as the *erinnerer*, the recaller. This is curious in the present line of thought, concerned with the presence of Christ, because it conjures up the Lord's Supper as a memorial. In addition, the previous argument is disjointed. It begins with memorial language, communion as a figure or sign of edification or judgment. Perhaps Marpeck is attempting to integrate terminology Schwenckfeld has pointed out as coming from *VMN*. But the point of comparison changes completely when he moves to his example. The original contention is that the Supper is a sign of a trusting or untrusting heart. In the example, the disciples see the breaking of bread only as a sign because it can become more than that only after Christ has shed his blood. Only after the resurrection-ascension-giving of the Spirit, in the life of the church, is the Eucharist a reality.

186. *Marpeck*, 437-463, esp. 431. This fits with his assertion in the letter concerning "The Lowliness of Christ." In it Marpeck contends that the merits of the new covenant came into effect only after Christ had died and descended into hell.

187. Loserth, 459.

188. Loserth, 462.

189. Loserth, 463.

190. Loserth, 464-465.

191. Loserth, 466.

192. Loserth, 467.

193. *CS*, 8:212.

194. *CS*, 8:212.

195. Loserth, 560. This claim does not tally with Marpeck's earlier assertion that there was no Lord's Supper at the Last Supper. He draws this deduction directly from his trinitarian assumptions about how the Son and Spirit are present in history. This seems to be a foreign concept used for apologetic purposes but not integrated with the train of thought.

196. Loserth, 563.

197. Loserth, 563.

198. Loserth, 483-484.

199. Loserth, 483-484.

200. Loserth, 578.

201. Familiar terms are used differently; alien ones abruptly appear. The spirit of the text changes. For instance, Marpeck adopts Schwenckfeldian, spiritualistic language and its presuppostions in his own argument. Christ is presented as speaking in two forms

(*zwayerlay gestalt*), essentially through his word and body, figuratively through the elements. This is repeated in Loserth, 563 and 565, where bread and wine are described as a parable and memorial in contrast to the essence of the Eucharist. The essence is witnessed to by the parable. *Essence* or *reality* (*wesen*) is distinct from its sign. The whole point of Marpeck's dynamic trinitarianism is the opposite. In fragment C the terms *reform, reformation,* and *sacrament* enter the discussion. Their repeated use within one page makes them an obvious intrusion (Loserth, 569-570). For the first time, the gospel is described as rich in grace (*gnadenreich evangelion*), and the Trinity is called *dreyfaltigkeit* rather than *trinitet* for only the second time in the treatise (Loserth, 571; cf. 550).

202. Loserth, 467.

203. *Marpeck,* 79.

204. *Marpeck,* 80.

205. *Marpeck,* 202-221, esp. 215 and 219.

206. Hans-Jürgen Goertz, *Die Täufer* (Munich: C. H. Beck, 1980), 77-95. Goertz, 92, sees the sacramental theology of the Swiss Brethren, Menno Simons and Marpeck, over against other Anabaptists and later Mennonites, as attempts to find a way between sacramentalism and spiritualism. By means of his middle way, where inner and outer are interdependent, "kann Marpeck die Taufe aus dem Bannkreis des zwinglianischen Spiritualismus endgültig heraus führen."

207. Y. Brillioth, *Eucharistic Faith and Practice, Evangelical and Catholic* (London: SPCK, 1934), 286-287, makes a similar judgment about the eucharistic theology of sacramental churches: "Transubstantiation, as expounded by Thomas Aquinas, is certainly not a materialistic doctrine; nevertheless, it made terms with a popular piety which was partly pagan in character, and it opened the way to a materialistic idea and use of the sacrament. But it is a more serious criticism of the doctrine of transubstantiation that it stated the problem of the eucharist in a wrong way, focusing attention to an altogether exaggerated extent on two points, the sacredness of the elements and the gift given in communion to the individual. The result has been that other aspects of the sacrament have been to an alarming extent left out of sight; and that alike in the Roman, Lutheran, and Anglican churches it has remained almost impossible to state the problem otherwise than as a Yes or No to the question whether the real presence in the elements is true.

"The problem has been stated in a wrong way; and it is very necessary today to raise the matter on to a higher level, and learn to see how much there is in the mystery of the sacrament which this way of approach leaves out of sight. It is not that the doctrine of the real presence in the elements says too much, but that it says too little. It does indeed guard the objectivity of the Divine operation in the sacrament, and bar the way to the subjectivism which makes all depend on the faith of the recipient; for it saves the connection of the sacrament with the Incarnation. The sacrament has a material basis because the Son of God became man, and the Divine redemption extends to the physical life of man as well as to his mental and spiritual life. The trouble is that the emphasis on the real presence in the elements shows a dangerous tendency to occupy almost the whole field of view. The result is, first, a materializing of that which is spiritual, when the consecration is fixed at a definite time-moment, and the presence localized as 'on' the altar; for the Saviour was locally present in Galilee and at Calvary, but the heavenly reality of that which is given in the sacrament is beyond time and place. Secondly, the other two modes of apprehending the mystery, the personal presence of Christ as Priest and the presence in his mystical Body, are in danger of being left out of sight."

208. Loserth, 438.

209. Boyd, 183. Also see 204, 206, 207.

210. The transformation which takes place in the sacramental encounter with Christ is thus moral and historical in character. Marpeck's usual fomulation, especially in *VMN,* is to set these two claims beside each other without collapsing them into a single event. But by their deliberate proximity, they explain one another.

211. Kiwiet, 84.

212. *VMN, Marpeck,* 195ff.; *VWG,* Loserth, 381, 385, 496, 508, 510-514.

213. Boyd, 274.

214. The term *transubstantiation* is still used at a few points in *VWG*, but there its meaning is already being assimilated to the new definition of Christ's two natures to which Marpeck turned (Loserth, esp. 381).

215. Typical illustrations of this may be found in chapters 72-79 of *VWG*. Christological motifs arise within Marpeck's defense of his ecclesiology and his theology of the covenants. In the references to inner and outer baptism, the new covenant of the incarnation, the beginning of salvation with the ascension, familiar language is used, but it remains undeveloped. In each case the train of thought is biblicistic, sometimes in direct references to Scripture or indirectly by referring the reader to Marpeck's concordance, the *Testamenterleuterung*. The argument is carried forward by piling assertions on top of one another and illuminating them by the inclusion of examples from Jesus' ministry. For Marpeck, the synoptic Gospels are the dominant reference point for Jesus' life and teaching, and the Pauline corpus and Hebrews are the basis for theological assertions about Jesus. Except for the chapter on the patriarchs, references to the Gospel of John are incidental, and the spirit of that Gospel is not invoked.

216. Loserth, 450ff.

217. Loserth, 404.

218. Blough, 132.

219. *Marpeck*, 79.

220. Boyd, 183. The theme is developed in "Concerning the Lowliness of Christ," *Marpeck*, 430-434.

221. *Marpeck*, 195.

222. *Marpeck*, 274.

223. *Marpeck*, 195.

224. Loserth, 500-517, 534-559.

Chapter 4: Dirk Philips

1. In sixteenth-century Netherlands, people were publicly addressed only by their Christian name. The second name was not a surname, only a patronym.

2. J. Ten Doornkaat Koolman, *Dirk Philips* (Haarlem: H. D. Tjeenk Willink, 1964), 1.

3. Koolman, 2.

4. William Keeney, "The Writings of Dirk Philips," *MQR* 23 (Oct. 1958): 304.

5. N. van der Zijpp, "Dirk Philips," *ME*, 2:65.

6. Koolmann, 116-118, emphasizes that the exact time when Dirk began his ministry in Danzig is not recorded.

7. Menno Simons, *Menno Simons Writings* (Elkhart: J. Funk, 1871), 1:40-52.

8. Christoph Bornhäuser, *Leben und Lehre Menno Simons* (Neukirchen-Vluyn: Neukirchener Verlag, 1973), 96-100; J. A. Brandsma, *Menno Simons von Witmarsum* (Kassel: J. G. Oncken, 1962), 15-16, 54-57; Cornelius Krahn, *Menno Simons* (Newton: Faith & Life, 1982), 139-142.

9. For *AML*, see *BRN* 10:111-134. *Dirk* hereafter identifies *Enchiridion*, translated by A. B. Kolb (Aylmer: Pathway, 1978). Kolb presents in English the *Enchiridion* (*ENC*), the dominant collection of writings in *BRN* 10, including all of Dirk's eucharistic writings. Quotations in the text of our study are from the Kolb translation, compared with the original, and altered where noted. Several Dutch editions of the *ENC* were issued between 1578 and 1627. The first German edition was published in 1802. The Kolb translation into English was first published in 1910. Available after this study was completed: *Cornelius J. Dyck, William E. Keeney, and Alvin J. Beachy, eds. The Writings of Dirk Philips, 1504-1568* (Scottdale, Pa.: Herald Press, 1992).

10. Van der Zijpp, 65.

11. *BRN* 10:4.

12. George Williams, *The Radical Reformation* (Philadelphia: Westminster Press,

1962), 28; Cornelius Krahn, *Dutch Anabaptism* (Scottdale, Pa.: Herald Press, 1981), 40, 72.

13. Both Alvin Beachy in *The Concept of Grace in the Radical Reformation* (Nieuwkoop: B. de Graaf, 1977), 103ff., and William Keeney in *The Development of Dutch Anabaptist Thought and Practice, 1539-1564* (Nieuwkoop: B. de Graaf, 1968), 102ff., note this peculiar Christology but fail to identify the unique consequences Dirk and Menno draw from it for their eucharistic doctrine.

14. S. Voolstra, *Het woord is vlees geworden* (Kampen: J. H. Kok, 1982), 137ff., 11ff.; Klaus Depperman, *Melchior Hoffmann* (Göttingen: Vandenhoeck und Ruprecht, 1979), 200-201.

15. H. J. Schoeps, *Vom himmlischen Fleisch Christi* (Tübingen: J. C. B. Mohr, 1951), 38, 43-44, traces the origin and survival of this teaching from the second to the sixteenth century.

16. Melchior Hoffmann, *Das XII Capitel des propheten Danielis ausgelegt . . .* (Stockholm: Königliche Druckerei, 1526), m iv verso, n ii recto. Both Schoeps, 45, and Deppermann, 113, draw attention to Hoffmann's sharp rejection of the tradition corporeal presence in the Supper and yet his affirmation of a spiritual presence.

17. Voolstra, 13ff.

18. Voolstra, 109.

19. *Dirk*, 70, 77, 85. In *MNG* Dirk applies his christological assumptions directly to the Lord's Supper. He does not make use of the two natures of Christ but focuses exclusively on the nature of his flesh (Dirk, 109). No prominence is given to the role of the Holy Spirit in relation to the Son there or in *KENN*.

20. *BRN* 10:135-153; *Dirk*, 95-115.

21. *BRN* 10:155-178; *Dirk*, 117-143.

22. *BRN* 10:25-26. Keeney, "Writings," 299, argues that this document is an expanded version of a 1545 writing.

23. *BRN* 10:138. *Dirk*, 97, unexplainably translates *wesentlijck* as *existing* rather than *essential*.

24. *Dirk*, 97. Elsewhere Dirk says, "The word of God and the flesh of Christ are one and the same" (*Dirk*, 100).

25. *Dirk*, 136.

26. Hoffmann's focus stands in pointed contrast to that of Dirk. After quoting and commenting on all the institutional narratives in Daniel, he concludes, "Who eats the bread, eats the body of the Lord, and who drinks the cup, drinks the blood of the Lord." Later in his text, Hoffmann returns to this language. There it is unmistakably clear that this sacramental realism is stronger than Dirk's and closer to the tenor of the early Lutheran reformation. This is not surprising because the Daniel commentary dates from 1526. Here is a quotation from that section: "For the bread which you take in faith and in the power of the word that is the body of Christ and that drink is his blood but that which remains is not a sacrament" (Hoffmann, *Das XII Capitel*, m i recto). He goes on to argue that, therefore, the use of a monstrance has no meaning. Concern about the moment and duration of change in the elements is a preoccupation which has completely receded by the time of Dirk's writing. The historical context of Dirk's thinking is a generation removed from that of Hoffmann and results in the dominance of quite different eucharistic motifs in each of them.

27. *Dirk*, 98.

28. *Dirk*, 99.

29. *Dirk*, 100.

30. *Dirk*, 100.

31. *Dirk*, 111.

32. *Dirk*, 113.

33. *Dirk*, 114.

34. *Dirk*, 112.

35. *Dirk*, 114.

36. *Dirk*, 125-127; also 12, where it is part of his confessional statement. This stands in sharp contrast with the Christology of Marpeck, in which Christ the human being is the medium of redemption (*Marpeck*, esp. 76-82). The divinization of the born-again believers is also a dimension of Marpeck's thought, but there it is derived from Christ's incarnation in our flesh (*Marpeck*, 99, 430). A noteworthy exception to Dirk's focus on Christ's divinity is his contemplation of his suffering and mortality (*Dirk*, 132-134).

37. *Dirk*, 130.
38. *Dirk*, 134.
39. *Dirk*, 135.
40. *BRN* 10:69-111; *Dirk*, 18-66.
41. *BRN* 10:393-408; *Dirk*, 463-486.
42. *BRN* 10:445-459; *Dirk*, 444-460.
43. *BRN* 10:481-506; *Dirk*, 463-486.
44. *BRN* 10:29.
45. *Dirk*, 483-400.
46. *Dirk*, 79.
47. *BRN* 10:101; *Dirk*, 55.
48. *Dirk*, 55-57.
49. *Dirk*, 57.
50. *Dirk*, 57.
51. *Dirk*, 58.
52. *Dirk*, 57.
53. *Dirk*, 479-453.
54. *BRN* 10:452-454; *Dirk*, 452-454. Kolb suddenly changes his translation of *teecken* from *sign* to *token* (*Dirk*, 452), but he also translates *waerteecken* as *token* (454). This inconsistency obscures the significance of the concept of *sign* in Dirk's conceptual framework. It is worth noting that both these notions are used by Rothmann in a similar context and manner except that he, contrary to Dirk, allows them to be signs of grace; see R. Stupperich, ed., *Die Schriften Bernard Rothmanns* (Münster: Aschendorffsche Verlagsbuchhandlung, 1970), 151-155.

55. *Dirk*, 454, 475.
56. *Dirk*, 475, 479.
57. *Dirk*, 479, 480, 483.
58. *Dirk*, 479, 453.
59. *Dirk*, 480.
60. *Dirk*, 483-484.
61. *Dirk*, 365, 374.
62. *Dirk*, 483, 199ff. In the latter passage, sacraments are said to embody the life of the church.

63. *Dirk*, 69-71.
64. *Marpeck*, 76.
65. *Dirk*, 67.
66. *Dirk*, 87.
67. *Dirk*, 87.
68. *Dirk*, 88.
69. *Dirk*, 68.
70. *Dirk*, 69, 84.
71. *Dirk*, 453-454.
72. *Die Slotel* in *BRN* 5 (1909): 86.

73. J. Calvin, *The Institutes of the Christian Religion*, ed. by J. McNeill, trans. by F. Battles (Philadelphia: Westminster Press, 1960), 2:1360.

74. *Dirk*, 79. Dirk's elaboration is reminiscent of Augustine's dictum, "Believe, and thou hast already eaten." This equation of eating and believing has clearly been appropriated from Sacramentarianism, probably through the mediation of Karlstadt.

The nature of Karlstadt's relationship to Dutch Sacramentarianism and Zwinglianism is a complex and disputed subject. K. Vos, "Kleine bijdragen over de Doopersche beweging in Nederland tot het optreden van Menno Simons," *DB* 54 (1917): 90ff., argues that the flow of influence is from Sacramentarianism to Karlstadt to Zwingli and the Swiss Anabaptists. In his exhaustive analysis of Karlstadt's role in the radical reformation, Pater follows a similar path. Two of his claims are directly relevent to our study. First, Karlstadt has a formative influence on Hoffmann. Karlstadt mediated his own revisionist understanding of the early Luther to Hoffmann, including a eucharistic doctrine; see C. Pater, *Karlstadt as the Father of the Baptist Movement* (Toronto: University of Toronto, 1984), 173-249, esp. 209ff. and 238ff. Second, according to Pater, both Karlstadt and Hoffmann retained a belief in the real presence of Christ, spiritually, in the Supper. Pater (239) concludes his point: "Hoffmann does not aim for genuine concomitancy; thus there is tactical juxtaposition, not true parallelism." Such is the case with Dirk, as will be presented below.

This understanding of the Eucharist originated prior to Zwingli and developed along a parallel but different track. A final point should be noted in this connection. Though there was a mutual influence between them, Karlstadt never accepted Hoffmann's celestial flesh Christology. Pater (245) acknowledges this but does not include it as a factor in distinguishing the views of the two men. We will elaborate on the significance of the heavenly flesh assumptions for the Lord's Supper, below.

75. Pater, 453-454.

76. Pater, 453-454.

77. Pater, 140ff.

78. Pater, 141.

79. Pater, 142.

80. Pater, 109. Keeney, *Dutch Anabaptist Thought*, 98, goes so far as to say that as Christ was transformed into a man by the Holy Spirit, so "man may now become God."

81. *BRN* 10:112; *Dirk*, 68.

82. *Dirk*, 69.

83. *BRN* 10:113; *Dirk*, 169.

84. *Dirk*, 70.

85. Compare esp. Dirk's devotional commentary on verses in John (*Dirk*, 140-143, 447).

86. Two comparative comments are in order here. One concerns Karlstadt, who gave currency to the tenet that Christ could not be in two places at once. Dirk agrees with that but works with it differently than Karlstadt does. The latter uses it to negate the presence of Christ at the breaking of bread, the former to assert the true mode of his presence. Absent from Dirk's schematization of the matter is reliance on the word as the means by which Christ comes to the believer. The second comment concerns Luther's belief about the communication of idioms. He employed this notion to counter Karlstadt's localization of the human nature of Christ in heaven: Christ is ubiquitous in both his natures. In effect, this is a divinizing of Christ's human nature so that it can be present in the sacrament.

87. *Dirk*, 86.

88. Though this conflation of the roles of Son and Spirit is less prominent in Dirk and Hubmaier than in Marpeck, all three of them turn to it in order to eliminate certain claims which threaten the spiritual character of their communion.

89. *Dirk*, 86.

90. *Dirk*, 71.

91. *Dirk*, 72.

92. *Dirk*, 72.

93. *Dirk*, 57.

94. Elsewhere the agent of grace changes, and it is the Son himself who "fulfills in us the signification of the sacraments" (*Dirk*, 58).

95. *Dirk*, 79; cf. 90, 74.

96. *Dirk*, 67. The only passage where Dirk talks about eating the elements is where he is giving liturgical instructions. Their function is to correct noncommunicating attendance just as, in the same text, Dirk's insistence that preaching accompany the Supper is to correct a service of sacrament without verbal proclamation.

97. *Dirk*, 72.

98. *Dirk*, 73-74.

99. *Dirk*, 69, 71; see 261, on exegesis.

100. *Dirk*, 283-285.

101. *Dirk*, 68-69.

102. *Dirk*, 78-79, 90. Such a concomitancy is mentioned also in relation to baptism, meaning that outer baptism by the church reminds us that Christ baptizes from within.

103. *Dirk*, 72. The prominence of Judas as the foil for the true believer, the counterexample of what is not a true participation in the Lord's Supper, parallels Hoffmann's use of him in his commentary on Daniel (Hoffmann, *Das XII Capitel*, m iv recto, m iv verso.

104. *Dirk*, 73.

105. *Dirk*, 74.

106. *Dirk*, 67ff., 77ff.

107. *Dirk*, 483.

108. *Dirk*, 223ff., 365ff.

109. Hans-Jürgen Goertz, *Die Täufer* (Munich: C. H. Beck, 1980), 40-48; Voolstra, 158.

110. *Dirk*, 69, 70, 71, 74-77.

111. Menno Simons, *Menno Simons Writings*, 2:1-17, esp. 14; 2:143-176, esp. 114; Kolb, 14.

112. *Dirk*, 113.

113. *Dirk*, 84.

114. *Dirk*, 82.

115. *Dirk*, 89.

116. *Dirk*, 394-399.

117. Cf. Hubmaier, *Schriften*, 355-356.

118. Jan Wessel, *De Leerstellige Strijd* (Assen: Van Gorcum, 1945), 249, 250-251, 265, 267; W. J. Kühler, *Geschiedenis der Nederlandsche Doopsgezinden in de Zestiende Eeuw* (Haarlem: H. D. Tjeenk Willink, 1932), 283ff., 346ff.

119. Keeney, *Dutch Anabaptist Thought*, 102-104; Beachy, *The Concept of Grace*, 110-112.

120. Schoeps, 25-26.

121. *Dirk*, 98.

122. This is claimed in *MNG* and *AML*. Only in the latter is it explained.

123. Dirk's Christology stands in sharp contrast to Schwenckfeld's at this point. Though Hoffmann is the inspiration for both of their views, Dirk emphatically retains Christ's human nature with its physical limitations. By contrast, Schwenckfeld's mature Christology speaks of Christ's human nature as no longer having limitations. It can, therefore, be part of Christ's presence in communion with the believer.

124. *Schriften*, 104, 284, et passim; P. Walpot, "Das grosse Artikelbuch," in *Glaubenszeugnisse oberdeutscher Taufgesinnter*, ed. by R. Friedmann (Gütersloh: Gerd Mohn, 1967), 1:126-134, 154ff., et passim.

Chapter 5: Conclusion

1. H. MackIntosh, *The Doctrine of the Person of Jesus Christ* (New York: Charles Scribner's Sons, 1912), 240-242.

2. H. de Ries, "De Derde Predikatie," in J. Gerrits, *Vijf Stichelelijke Predikaten* (Amsterdam: Gerrit van Goedesbergh, 1650), 37ff.

3. H. de Ries, 53-54.

4. H. de Ries, 54-57.

5. L. Clock, "Formulier Etlichen Christlichen Gebäthe," in T. T. van Sittert, *Christliche Glaubensbekentnus* (Amsterdam: Johan Pashorium, 1664), 60ff.

6. J. Coffman, ed., *Confession of Faith and Minister's Manual* (Scottdale: Mennonite, 1890), 21-22.

7. *Glaubensbekenntnis . . . der Hochdeutsche[n] . . . Mennoniten-gemeinden* (Odessa: Franzow and Nitsche, 1853), 19-21.

8. C. Ris, *Die Glaubenslehre der Mennoniten oder Taufgesinnten nach deren öffentlichen Glaubensbekenntnissen* (Berne: Mennonite Book Concern, 1906), 41-43.

9. Coffman, 43-44.

10. *Kurze und Einfältige Unterweisung* (Elbing: Agathon Wernich, 1837), 33-34.

11. D. H. Epp, *Kurze Erklärungen und Erläuterungen zum Kathechismus* (Rosthern: Dietrich Epp, 1941), 162-167.

12. C. H. Wedel, *Meditationen* (n.p.: n.p., 1910), 236, 234-243.

13. V. Dahlem, *Allgemeines und Vollständges Formularbuch* (Neuwied: J. T. Haupt, 1807), 34; B. Eby, *Kurzgefasste Kirchengeschichte und Glaubenslehre* (Scottdale: Mennonitische Verlagshandlung, n.d.), 197.

14. H. & D. Janzen, eds., *Minister's Manual* (Newton: Faith & Life, 1982), 40, also 29-41.

15. *ML*, 1 (1913): 6.

16. *ML*, 1:6-9.

17. *ME*, 1:651-655; 3:394; 5:170-172.

18. J. C. Wenger, *Introduction to Theology* (Scottdale, Pa.: Herald Press, 1954).

19. Wenger, 68-70, 150ff.

20. Wenger, 272.

21. Wenger, 303ff.

22. Wenger, 216ff.

23. Wenger, 240-242.

24. G. Kaufman, *Systematic Theology: A Historicist Perspective* (Charles Scribner's Sons, 1968).

25. Kaufman, 96.

26. Kaufman, 209, 180, 190.

27. Kaufman, 235-242.

28. Kaufman, 428-432, 492.

29. Kaufman, 445-446.

30. Kaufman, 491.

31. Kaufman, 491.

32. Kaufman, 492.

33. Kaufman, 492-494.

34. Robert Friedmann, *The Theology of Anabaptism* (Scottdale, Pa.: Herald Press, 1973). Friedmann studied Anabaptists and Mennonites, wrote about them, and was a member of the Eighth Street Mennonite congregation of Goshen, Indiana.

35. Friedmann, 18-20.

36. Friedmann, 49-57.

37. Friedmann, 116, 81, 117.

38. Friedmann, 134-140.

39. Thomas N. Finger, *Christian Theology: An Eschatological Approach* (Scottdale, Pa.: Herald Press, 1985-89), 2:333n. Volume 1 supplies initial christological background, though the author reserves that subject principally for volume 2, where he also treats the sacraments. Finger kindly let me consult volume 2 in typescript, but these references have been adjusted to the published volumes.

40. Finger, 2:331-350.

41. Finger, 2:334-342.

42. Finger, 2:228-233.

43. Finger, 2:338-342.

44. Finger, 2:341.

45. Finger, 2:341-342.

46. Aloys Grillmeier, *Christ in Christian Tradition* (Atlanta: John Knox, 1975), 541-545. "Chalcedon sought to discover the solution to just one disputed question: now the confession of the 'one Christ' may be reconciled with the belief in the 'true God and true man,' 'perfect in Godhead, perfect in manhood' " (J. Loserth, ed., *Pilgram Marbecks Antwort auf Kaspar Schwenkfelds Beurteilung des Buches der Bundesbezeugung von 1542*, Quellen und Forschungen zur Geschichte der oberdeutschen Taufgesinnten im 16. Jahrhundert [Wien: Carl Fromme, 1929], 508).

47. *Dirk*, 483.

48. *Baptism, Eucharist, and Ministry (BEM)*, Faith and Order #111 (Geneva: World Council of Churches, 1982). Since its appearance, commentaries on this document have appeared from around the world, such as these: M. Thurian, ed., *Ecumenical Perspectives on Baptism, Eucharist, and Ministry*, Faith and Order Paper #116 (Geneva: World Council of Churches, 1983); M. Thurian and G. Wainwright, eds., *Baptism and Eucharist: Ecumenical Convergence in Celebration*, Faith and Order Paper #117 (Grand Rapids: Eerdmans, 1983); C. Hinz, "Aspekte zum Gespräch um das Abendmahl," *ZdZ* 36 (Mar. 1982): 66-73; John Rempel, "Baptism, Eucharist, and Ministry," in *WOR* (Sept.) 1983:451-454.

49. Friedmann, 27ff.

50. It is significant that Marpeck's writings disappeared for over 200 years. When they were discovered in the 1920s, they were immediately published and drawn to the attention of the theological world. Dirk's writings have always been in print. This accounts for the greater affinity of Mennonite treatments of the subject, in the seventeenth to nineteenth centuries, with Dirk's theology of the Lord's Supper.

51. Among the few contemporary attempts to do this is the work of Hans-Jürgen Goertz, *Die Täufer* (Munich: C. H. Beck, 1980), 77-97; and W. F. Goltermann, "Een Consens over de doop," in *De Geest in net Geding* (n.p.: H. D. Tjeenck Willink, 1978), 73-85.

52. Typical examples are *Andachten, Gebete, und Lieder vor und nach dem Abendmahl* (Elbing: F. T. Harman, 1823); R. Rahusen, *Predigten und Reden* (Bremen: G. L. Foerster, 1784).

53. H. S. Bender, "The Anabaptist Vision," in Guy F. Hershberger, ed., *The Recovery of the Anabaptist Vision* (Scottdale, Pa.: Herald Press, 1957), 19-56.

54. In his encyclical, *Mysterium Fidei* (Huntington: Our Sunday Visitor, 1965), Pope Paul VI articulated the official Roman Catholic position concerning alternative interpretations of the real presence. He allowed for transignification and transfiguration as meaningful concepts but not as substitutes for transubstantiation. The subsequent Catholic-Protestant dialogue on the Eucharist must be seen in light of this encyclical.

55. *BEM*, I:13.

56. *BEM*, D:21.

57. *BEM*, D:20, 26.

Bibliography

"Abendmahl." In *Realenzylopaedie für Theologie und Kirche*. Vol 3. Göttingen: Vandenhoeck und Ruprecht, 1964.

Althaus, Paul. *The Theology of Martin Luther*. Philadelphia: Fortress Press, 1966.

Andachten, Gebete, und Lieder vor und nach dem heiligen Abendmahl. Elbing: F. T. Harman, 1823.

Armour, Rollin. *Anabaptist Baptism*. Scottdale: Herald Press, 1966.

Baillie, D. *The Theology of the Sacraments*. London: Faber and Faber, 1957.

Baptism, Eucharist, and Ministry. Faith and Order #111. Geneva: World Council of Churches, 1982.

Bauckham, Richard. *Knowing God Incarnate*. Bramcote: Grove, 1983.

Beachy, Alvin. *The Concept of Grace in the Radical Reformation*. Nieuwkoop: B. de Graaf, 1977.

Bergsten, Torsten. *Balthasar Hubmaier: Seine Stellung zu Reformation und Täufertum 1521-1528*. Kassel: J. G. Oncken, 1961.

——————. "Pilgram Marbeck und seine Auseinandersetung mit Caspar Schwenckfeld." *Kyrkohistorisk Arsshrift* 38 (1957-58), 39-135 (offprint).

Bibliotheca Reformatoria Neerlandica. Ed. by Samuel Cramer. Vols. 5 (1909) and 10 (1914). 's Gravenhage: Martinus Nijhoff.

Blough, Neal. *Christologie anabaptiste: Pilgram Marpeck et l'humanité du Christ*. Geneva: Labour and Fides, 1982.

Bornhäuser, Christoph. *Leben und Lehre Menno Simons*. Neukirchen-Vluyn: Neukirchener Verlag, 1973.

Bornkamm, K., and G. Elseling, eds. *Martin Luther ausgewählte Schriften*. Vol. 2. Frankfurt/Main: Insel, 1982.

Boyd, Stephen. "Pilgram Marpeck and the Justice of Christ" (Ph.D. diss., Harvard University, 1984).

Brandsma, J. A. *Menno Simons von Witmarsum*. Kassel: J. G. Oncken, 1962.

Brecht, M. "Herkunft und Eigenart der Taufauschauung der Züricher Täufer." *Archiv für Reformationsgeschichte* 64 (1973): 147-153.

Brilioth, Y. *Eucharistic Faith and Practice, Evangelical and Catholic.* London: SPCK, 1934.

Bromiley, G. W., ed. *Zwingli and Bullinger.* Philadelphia: Westminster, 1958.

Brown, R. *The Gospel of John (i-xii).* Anchor Bible. Garden City: Doubleday, 1966.

Calvin, John. *The Institutes of the Christian Religion.* Vol. 2. Ed. by J. T. McNeill. Trans. by F. Battles. Library of Christian Classics. Philadelphia: Westminster Press, 1960.

Clock, L. "Formulier etlichen Christlichen Gebäthe." In T. T. van Sittert, *Christliche Glaubensbekentnus.* Amsterdam: Johan Pashorium, 1664.

Coffman, J., ed. *Confession of Faith and Minister's Manual.* Scottdale, Pa.: Mennonite Publishing House, 1890.

Corpus Schwenkfeldianorum. Vol. 4 (1914), ed. by C. D. Hartranft. Vol. 8 (1927), ed. by E. E. Schultz Johnson. Leipzig: Breitkopft Härtel.

Dahlem, V. *Allgemeines und Vollständges Formularbuch.* Neuwied: J. T. Haupt, 1807.

Damerau, R. *Die Abendmahlslehre des Nominalismus ins besondere die des Gabriel Biel.* Giessen: W. Schmitz, 1963.

Depperman, Klaus. *Melchior Hoffmann.* Göttingen: Vandenhoeck und Ruprecht, 1979.

Dirk Philips. *See* Philips, Dirk.

Dix, Gregory. *The Shape of the Liturgy.* London: Daccre, 1975.

Dugmore, C. W., "Zwingli's Thought." *Journal of Ecclesiastical History* (Apr.) 1983:291.

Dyck, C. J., ed. *Legacy of Faith.* Newton: Faith & Life Press, 1962.

Eby, B. *Kurzgefasste Kirchengeschichte und Glaubenslehre der Taufgesinnten Christen oder Mennoniten.* Scottdale: Mennonitische Verlagshandlung, 1841 (reprinted).

Egli, E., and G. Finster, eds. *Huldreich Zwinglis sämtliche Werke.* Corpus Reformatorum, vols. 88ff. Leipzig: M. Heinsius Nachfolger, 1904ff.

Epp, D. H. *Kurze Erklärungen und Erläuterungen zum Kathechismus.* Rosthern: Dietrich Epp, 1941.

Finger, Thomas N. *Christian Theology: An Eschatological Approach.* Vol. 1, Nashville: Thomas Nelson, 1985. 2 vols., Scottdale, Pa.: Herald Press, 1987-89.

Friedmann, Robert. "Lord's Supper." In *The Mennonite Encyclopedia,* ed. by C. Krahn et al., 3:395. Scottdale, Pa.: Herald Press, 1957.

_____, *The Theology of Anabaptism*. Scottdale, Pa.: Herald Press, 1973.

Gansfort, Wessel. *Wessel Gansfort, Life and Writings*. Trans. by J. W. Scudder. New York: G. T. Putnam's Sons, 1917.

"Gemeinsame Ordnung der Glieder Christi." In *Der linke Flügel der Reformation*, ed. by H. Fast. Klassiker des Protestantismus, vol. 4. Bremen: Carl Schünemann Verlag, 1962.

Glaubensbekenntnis . . . der Hochdeutsche[n] . . . Mennonitengemeinden. Odessa: Franzow and Nitsche, 1853.

Goertz, Hans-Jürgen. *Pfaffenhass und gross Geschrei*. Munich: C. H. Beck, 1987.

_____, *Die Täufer*. Munich: C. H. Beck, 1980.

_____, ed. *Umstrittenes Täufertum: Neue Forschungen*. Göttingen: Vandenhoeck und Ruprecht, 1975.

Göters, J. F. G., ed. *Studien zur Geschichte und Theologie der Reformation*. Neukirchen: Neukirchener Verlag, 1969.

Goltermann, W. F. "Een Consens over de doop." In *De Geest in net Geding*, 73-85. N.p.: H. D. Tjeenck Willink, 1978.

Grillmeier, Aloys. *Christ in Christian Tradition*. Atlanta: John Knox, 1975.

Guderian, Hans. *Die Täufer in Augsburg*. Pfaffenhofen: W. Ludwig, 1984.

Hein, G., and W. Klassen. "Leupold Scharnschlager." In *The Mennonite Encyclopedia*, ed. by C. Krahn et al., 4:443-446. Scottdale, Pa.: Herald Press, 1959.

Hershberger, Guy F., ed. *The Recovery of the Anabaptist Vision*. Scottdale, Pa.: Herald Press, 1957.

Hertzsche, Erich, ed. *Karlstadts Schriften aus den Jahren 1523-1525*. Vol. 1. Halle: Max Niemeyer, 1957.

Hinz, C. "Aspekte zum Gespräch um das Abendmahl." *Zeichen der Zeit* 36 (Mar. 1982): 66-73.

Hoffmann, Melchior. *Das XII Capitel des propheten Danielis ausgelegt*. . . . Stockholm: Königliche Druckerei, 1526.

Hubmaier, Balthasar. *Balthasar Hubmaier Schriften*. Ed. by G. Westin and T. Bergsten, Quellen und Forschungen zur Reformationsgeschichte, 29; Quellen zur Geschichte der Täufer, 9. Gütersloh: Gerd Mohn, 1962.

_____. *Balthasar Hubmaier, Theologian of Anabaptism*. Ed. by H. W. Pipkin and J. H. Yoder. Classics of the Radical Reformation, vol. 5. Scottdale, Pa.: Herald Press, 1989.

Janzen, H. & D., eds. *Minister's Manual.* Newton: Faith & Life, 1982.

Jungmann, J. *The Early Liturgy.* Notre Dame: University of Notre Dame, 1959.

Kaufman, Gordon. *Systematic Theology: A Historicist Perspective.* New York: Charles Scribner's Sons, 1968.

Keeney, William. *The Development of Dutch Anabaptist Thought and Practice, 1539-1564.* Nieuwkoop: B. de Graaf, 1968.

_____. "The Writings of Dirk Philips." *Mennonite Quarterly Review* 23 (Oct. 1958): 304.

Kiwiet, Jan J. *Pilgram Marbeck, ein Führer der Täuferbewegung der Reformationszeit.* Kassel: J.G. Oncken, 1957.

Klaassen, Walter. *Anabaptism: Neither Catholic nor Protestant.* Waterloo: Conrad Press, 1973.

Klassen, William, *Covenant and Community.* Grand Rapids: Eerdmanns, 1968.

Köhler, W. *Zwingli und Luther.* Vol. 1. New York: Johnson Reprint, 1971.

Koolman, J. Ten Doornkaat. *Dirk Philips.* Haarlem: H. D. Tjeenk Willink, 1964.

Krahn, Cornelius. "Communion." In *The Mennonite Encyclopedia,* ed. by C. Krahn et al., 1:651-656. Scottdale, Pa.: Herald Press, 1955.

_____. *Dutch Anabaptism.* Scottdale, Pa.: Herald Press, 1981.

_____. *Menno Simons.* Newton: Faith & Life, 1982.

Kühler, W. J. *Geschiedenis der Nederlandsche Doopsgezinden in de Zestiende Eeuw.* Harlaam: H. D. Tjeenk Willink, 1932.

Kurze und Einfältige Unterweisung. Elbing: Agathon Wernich, 1837.

Locher, G. *Zwingli's Thought: New Perspectives.* Leiden: E. J. Brill, 1981.

Lortz, J. *Die Reformation in Deutschland.* Vol. 1. Quoted in S. Ozment, ed., *The Reformation in Mediaeval Perspective,* Chicago: Quadrangle, 1974.

Luther, Martin. *Luther's Works.* Ed. by M. Lehman. Vol. 38. Philadelphia: Fortress, 1980.

McCue, J., "The Doctrine of Transubstantiation from Berengar to Trent: The Point of Issue." *Harvard Theological Review* 61 (1968): 385-430.

McDonnell, K. *Jesus Christ, the Church and the Eucharist.* Princeton, N.J.: Princeton University Press, 1964.

McGlothin, W. J. "An Anabaptist Liturgy of the Lord's Supper." *Baptist Review and Expositor* (Jan.) 1906:92.

MackIntosh, H. *The Doctrine of the Person of Jesus Christ.* New York: Charles Scribner's Sons, 1912.

McIntyre, J., *The Shape of Christology.* London: SCM, 1966.

Marpeck, Pilgram. *Pilgram Marbecks Antwort auf Kaspar Schwenkfelds Beurteilung des Buches der Bundesbezeugung von 1542.* Ed. by J. Loserth. Quellen und Forschungen zur Geschichte der oberdeutschen Taufgesinnten im 16. Jahrhundert. Vienna: Carl Fromme, 1929.

_____. *Quellen zur Geschichte der Täufer.* Ed. by Manfred Krebs and Hans Geroge Rott. Vol. 7: *Elsass,* part 1. Gütersloh: Gerd Mohn, 1959.

_____. *The Writings of Pilgram Marpeck.* Ed. by William Klassen and Walter Klaassen. Classics of the Radical Reformation, vol. 2. Scottdale, Pa.: Herald Press, 1978.

Mayer, C. P. *Die Zeichen in der Geistigen Entwicklung und in der Theologie des Jungen Augustinus.* Würzburg: Augustinus, 1969.

Moore, W. "Catholic Teacher and Anabaptist Pupil: The Relationship Between John Eck and Balthasar Hubmaier." *Archiv für Reformationgeschichte* 72 (1981): 79-83.

Mühlen, K.-H. zur. "Zur Rezeption der Augustinischen Sakramentsformel . . . in der Theologie Luthers." *Zeitschrift für Theologie und Kirche* 70 (1983).

Muralt, L. von, and W. Schmidt, eds. *Quellen zur Geschichte der Täufer in der Schweitz.* Vol. 1. Zürich: S. Hinzel Verlag, 1952.

Neff, C., ed. *Gedenkschrift zum 400 Jährigen Jubiläum der Mennoniten oder Taufgesinnten.* Ludwigshafen: Konferenz der Süddeutschen Mennoniten, 1925.

_____, "Abendmahl." In *Mennonitische Lexikon.* Frankfurt: n.p., 1913.

Oberman, H., ed. *Forerunners of the Reformation.* Trans. by P. Nyhus. New York: Holt, Rinehart and Winston, 1966.

_____. *The Harvest of Medieval Theology.* Grand Rapids: Eerdmans, 1967.

Ozment, Steven. *The Age of Reform.* New Haven: Yale, 1980.

Packull, W. *The Common Man.* (Unpublished manuscript.)

_____. *Mysticism and the Early South German-Austrian Anabaptist Movement.* Scottdale, Pa.: Herald Press, 1977.

Pater, C. *Karlstadt as the Father of the Baptist Movement.* Toronto: University of Toronto, 1984.

Peachey, S., and P. Peachey. "Answer of Some Who Are Called (Ana) Baptists. . . ." *MQR* 45 (1971): 5-32.

Pelikan, J. *The Christian Tradition.* Vol. 3: *The Growth of Medieval Theology* (1978); vol. 4: *Reformation of Church and Dogma* (1984). Chicago: University of Chicago Press.

Pesch, O. *Die Theologie der Rechtfertigung bei Martin Luther und Thomas von Aquin.* Mainz: Matthias Grünewald Verlag, 1967.

Philips, Dirk. See *Bibliotheca Reformatoria Neerlandica* 10 (1914).

——————————. *Enchiridion.* Trans. by A. B. Kolb. Aylmer: Pathway Publishing Corporation, 1978.

——————————. *The Writings of Dirk Philips, 1504-1568.* Ed. by C. J. Dyck, W. E. Keeney, and A. J. Beachy. Classics of the Radical Reformation, vol. 6. Scottdale, Pa.: Herald Press, 1992.

Rahusen, R. *Predigten und Reden.* Bremen: G. L. Förster, 1784.

Relton, H. *A Study in Christology.* London: SPCK, 1917.

Rempel, John. "Baptism, Eucharist, and Ministry." *Worship* (Sept.) 1983:451-454.

——————————. "Communion." In *The Mennonite Encyclopedia,* ed. by C. J. Dyck et al., 5:170-172. Scottdale, Pa.: Herald Press, 1990.

Ries, H. de. "De Derde Predikatie." In J. Gerrits, *Vijf Stichelelijche Predikaten.* Amsterdam: Gerrit van Goedesbergh, 1650.

Ris, C. *Die Glaubenslehre der Mennoniten oder Taufgesinnten nach deren öffenflichen Glaubensbekenntnissen.* Berne: Mennonite Book Concern, 1904.

Rol, Hendrick. *Die Slotel van dat Secreet des Nachtmals.* In *Bibliotheca Reformatoria Neerlandica* 5 (1909).

Röter, W. *Des Heiligen Augustinus Schriften als liturgische Quellen.* Munich: Max Hüber, 1930.

Schoeps, H. J. *Vom himmlischen Fleisch Christ.* Tübingen: J. C. B. Mohr, 1951.

Schwenckfeld, Caspar von. See *Corpus Schwenckfeldianorum*

Sider, R. *Andreas Bodenstein von Karlstadt: The Development of His Thought, 1517-1525.* Leiden: E. J. Brill, 1974.

Simons, Menno. *The Complete Works of Menno Simon (sic).* Elkhart, Ind.: John F. Funk and Brother, 1871.

——————————. *The Complete Writings of Menno Simons.* Trans. by Leonard Verduin. Ed. by J. C. Wenger. Scottdale, Pa.: Herald Press, 1956, 1984.

Stayer, J. *Anabaptist and the Sword.* Lawrence: Coronado, 1972.

—————————— et al. "From Monogenesis to Polygenesis: The Historical Discussion About Anabaptist Origins." *Mennonite Quarterly Review* 49 (1975): 83-121.

Steinmetz, D. *Reformers in the Wings.* Grand Rapids: Baker Book House, 1971.

Stupperich, R., ed. *Die Schriften Bernard Rothmanns.* Münster: Aschendorffsche Verlagsbuchhandlung, 1970.

Thompson, B., ed. *Liturgies of the Western Church.* Cleveland: Collins, 1962.

Voolstra, S. *Het woord is vlees geworden.* Kampen: J. H. Kok, 1982.

Vos, K. "Kleine bijdragen over de Doopersche beweging in Nederland tot het optreden van Menno Simons." *Doopsgezinde Bijdragen* 54, 5 (1917): 90.

Walpot, P. "Das grosse Artikelbuch." In *Glaubenszeugnisse Oberdeutscher Taufgesinnter*, ed. by R. Friedmann. Vol. 1. Gütersloh: Gerd Mohn, 1967.

Wedel, C. H. *Meditationen.* N.p.: n.p., 1910.

Wenger, J. C. *Introduction to Theology.* Scottdale, Pa.: Herald Press, 1954.

Wessel, Jan. *De Leerstellige Strijd.* Assen: Van Gorcum, 1945.

Williams, G. *The Radical Reformation.* Philadelphia: Westminster, 1962.

Windhorst, C. "Balthasar Hubmaier." In *Radikale Reformatoren*, ed. by Hans-Jürgen Goertz. Munich: C. H. Beck, 1978.

——————————. "Das Gedächtnis des Leidens Christi und Pflichtzeichen brüderlicher Liebe." In *Umstrittenes Taüfertum 1525-1975*, ed. by Hans-Jürgen Goertz. Göttingen: Vandenhoeck und Ruprecht, 1975.

——————————. *Täuferisches Taufverständnis.* Studies in Mediaeval and Reformation Thought, vol. 16. Leiden: E. J. Brill, 1976.

——————————. "Wort und Geist." *Mennonitische Geschichtsblätter* 31, N.F. 16 (1974).

Wray, Frank. "The *Vermanung* of 1542 and Rothmann's *Bekenntnisse*." *Archiv für Reformationgeschichte* 47 (1956): 242-251.

Yoder, J. H., ed. *The Legacy of Michael Sattler.* Scottdale, Pa.: Herald Press, 1973.

——————————. *Täufertum und Reformation in Gespräch.* Basler Studien zur Historischen und Systematischen Theologie, vol. 13. Zurich: EVZ, 1968.

Zijpp, N. van der. "Dirk Philips." In *The Mennonite Encyclopedia*, ed. by C. Krahn et al., 2:65-66. Scottdale, Pa.: Herald Press, 1956.

Index

The Author

John Rempel is the minister at Manhattan Mennonite Fellowship in New York City. He also represents the Mennonite Central Committee at the United Nations. Rempel was born in Kitchener, Ontario, in 1944 to Henry and Katharina Rempel. After attending Conrad Grebel College at the University of Waterloo (Ont.) and Associated Mennonite Biblical Seminaries (Elkhart, Ind.), he spent a year in a voluntary service unit in Sarasota, Florida. During 1971-73, he studied theology in East and West Berlin with a World Council of Churches scholarship.

For 1973-89 Rempel served at Conrad Grebel College as the chaplain and as a lecturer in religious studies, and for much of that time as dean of students. He spent a sabbatical year in the Philippines with Mennonite Central Committee, teaching theology at Ateneo de Davao, a Jesuit university. In 1987 with the dissertation now adapted for this book, he completed doctor of theology studies at St. Michael's College, Toronto School of Theology.

Since his undergraduate years, Rempel's thinking and writing have been informed by attempts to hold together worship and justice, piety and activism. Most of his popular and scholarly writings pursue these themes. During 1983-92, he served on the worship committee for the joint Mennonite and Church of the Brethren hymnal project. He has been a retreat leader and member of the theological concerns commission in the Mennonite Conference of Eastern Canada.

Rempel has also devoted himself to ecumenical involvements, including several years as the chairperson of the University of Waterloo chaplains and on the Faith and Order Commission of the Canadian Council of Churches. In his pastoral as well as academic work, Rempel has sought to make a place for Mennonite tradition as well as for incorporating into Mennonite worship sacramental, liturgical, and doctrinal learnings from the wider Christian church. Among his writings are *Forever Summer, Forever Sunday* (with Paul Tiessen) and *Planning Worship*.

As a minister in New York City, John Rempel has ample opportunity to apply years of pastoral and academic learning in a cosmopolitan, secular setting and to correlate contemporary urban missions with historical and systematic theology.